The Transatlantic Economy 2010

Annual Survey of Jobs, Trade and Investment between the United States and Europe

Daniel S. Hamilton and Joseph P. Quinlan
Center for Transatlantic Relations
Johns Hopkins University
Paul H. Nitze School of Advanced International Studies

Hamilton, Daniel S., and Quinlan, Joseph P., *The Transatlantic Economy 2010: Annual Survey of Jobs, Trade and Investment between the United States and Europe*
Washington, DC: Center for Transatlantic Relations, 2010.

Center for Transatlantic Relations
American Consortium on EU Studies
EU Center of Excellence Washington, DC
The Paul H. Nitze School of Advanced International Studies
The Johns Hopkins University
1717 Massachusetts Ave., NW, Suite 525
Washington, DC 20036
Tel: (202) 663-5880
Fax (202) 663-5879
Email: transatlantic@jhu.edu
http://transatlantic.sais-jhu.edu
ISBN 978-0-9841341-3-7

Table of Contents

Preface and Acknowledgements

This annual survey offers the most up-to-date picture of the deep and intricate economic relationship binding European nations to America's 50 states. This year we have added two new features. The first compares U.S.-European economic ties with those of the U.S. and Europe with rapidly developing markets in the wake of the global financial crisis. The second feature tries to make the reality of a deeply interconnected transatlantic economy real by looking at its impact on jobs, trade and investment in local communities. We point to a number of "transatlantic motors"—city-regions whose jobs and future prosperity are deeply linked to a vibrant transatlantic links.

This annual survey supplements other publications in which we use both geographic and sectoral lenses to examine the deep integration of the transatlantic economy, and the role of the U.S. and Europe in the global economy, with particular focus on how globalization affects American and European consumers, workers, companies, and governments.

We would like to thank Jessica Martin, Grant M. Long, Nikolay Filchev, Nikolas Foster, Gretchen Losee, Andrew Vasylyuk, and Peggy Irvine for their assistance in producing this study.

We are grateful for generous support of our annual survey from Daimler AG; the American Chamber of Commerce to the European Union and its member companies Caterpillar, Hewlett-Packard, Hill & Knowlton, and Symantec; and the European-American Business Council and its member companies, Amgen, Dell, Kodak, and Telefonica. We also would like to welcome as a sponsor the European Council of American Chambers of Commerce (ECACC).

The views expressed here are our own, and do not necessarily represent those of any sponsor or institution. Other views and data sources have been cited, and are appreciated.

Daniel S. Hamilton
Joseph P. Quinlan

The Transatlantic Economy 2010
Executive Summary

- Despite the recession, the United States and Europe remain each other's most important foreign commercial markets. No other commercial artery in the world is as integrated and fused as the transatlantic economy. We estimate that the transatlantic economy continues to generate close to $4.28 trillion in total commercial sales a year and employs up to 14 million workers in mutually "onshored" jobs on both sides of the Atlantic.

The Rocky Road to Recovery

- The United States and most of Europe emerged from recession over the second half of 2009. The outlook is for a fragile recovery. The real estate sector remains the Achilles Heel for many nations, and the jobs outlook remains precarious.
- Public sector deficits and the ability to service these deficits remain key concerns. Greece's federal budget deficit as a percent of GDP was 12.7% in 2009; Ireland's 11.7%, Spain's was 10% the UK's 9.9% and Portugal's 9.3%. The U.S. deficit was 10% in FY 2009 and is expected to decline only modestly, to 9.2%, in FY 2010.
- The IMF expects output in the euro area to rise just 1% in 2010, as compared to a 3.9% decline in 2009. The U.S. is expected to expand by 2.7% in 2010, vs. a 2.5% drop in 2009.
- After surging over the 2002-2007 period, U.S. foreign affiliate income earned in Europe peaked in the first half of 2008 before declining sharply thereafter. U.S. affiliate income fell 25% in the first nine months of 2009 from the same period a year earlier. We estimate that affiliate income totaled $137 billion for all of 2009, down 23% from the peak in 2007.
- U.S. affiliate income in the UK was down 38% in the first nine months of 2009 versus the same period in 2008, and dropped nearly 260% in Sweden, 104% in Greece, 101% in Portugal, 60% in Spain, 50% in France, and 47% in Germany. Hungary, Austria, and Ireland were the only countries in which U.S. affiliate income rose—17%, 10%, and less than 1% respectively.
- Between 2002 and 2007, European affiliate earnings in the U.S. surged three-fold from $26.7 billion in 2002 to $72 billion in 2007. In 2008, however, most European affiliates saw their U.S. earnings decelerate sharply. The downturn was extended in 2009, with total European affiliates dropping 22% in the January-September period 2009 versus a year earlier. Affiliate earnings of French companies fell 30%, Dutch by 20% and British by 12%.
- German companies were a great exception: affiliate earnings in the U.S. rose nearly 230%.
- Manufacturers on both sides of the Atlantic are rethinking their businesses in the wake of the recession, leading to some important shifts in the transatlantic industrial base. During 2009, U.S. capacity to produce motor vehicles and chemicals fell 4.4% and 1.7%, respec-

tively, the largest declines since 1949. Capacity declines were also recorded in textiles (7%), printing (over 6%), furniture (more than 5%), and plastics and rubber products (3%). Production capacity grew for semiconductors (10.4%), communications equipment (almost 8%), computers (almost 6%), electricity (more than 2%), and oil and gas (.5%).

- In the eurozone and in central Europe only a few industries can expect strong growth in 2010. Motor vehicle production is set to grow by 8% in the eurozone and 8.4% in central Europe. Industrial production of computers and electronics in central Europe is slated to grow by 14.5% in 2010 and by 18.3% in 2011; a slower but still significant turnaround is also expected for this sector in the eurozone over the next two years.
- U.S. city-regions account for 18 of the top 20 metro areas in the world in terms of labor productivity, with only Luxembourg and Brussels breaking into the top 20. Although European regions had been catching up with their American counterparts in the 1970s and 1980s, this process stalled in the 1990s and U.S. metro regions remain ahead of the game.

Transatlantic Trade

- U.S. exports to Europe in the first three quarters of 2009 fell nearly 20%, and U.S. imports fell 24%, from the same period in 2008.
- U.S. exports to the UK dropped 18%; to France 9.5%, and to Germany 20% through September 2009 from the same period in 2008.
- Although in overall terms the U.S. now trades more with Asia, Europe retains critical importance as an export market for a vast number of American cities and metropolitan regions. The city of Philadelphia, for instance, exports more to the UK alone than to all of Asia. The UK is also the most important export market in the world for goods from the Washington, DC metropolitan region. And the second-largest global export market for goods from the New York metropolitan area? Switzerland.
- U.S. cities ranging from Bloomington, Indiana and Savannah, Georgia to Lawton, Oklahoma, Little Rock, Arkansas or Richmond, Virginia export more to the EU than to any other world region or economic entity.
- The New York city area leads all U.S. metropolitan regions in merchandise exports to Europe, and is the top metro area exporter to the UK, France, Germany and Switzerland. Seattle, Washington is the #2 U.S. metro exporter to Europe, followed by Houston, Texas; Los Angeles; Boston; Philadelphia; Chicago; San Jose, California; and Cincinnati, Ohio.
- Europe accounts for over half of the global exports of such U.S. cities as Salt Lake City, Utah (61.7%), Worchester, Massachusetts (57.6%), Bloomington, Indiana (56.3%), Norwich-New London, Connecticut (55.6%), and Greenville, South Carolina (51.9%).
- Top U.S. metro regions exporting to France in 2008 were, in order, New York, Seattle, Los Angeles, Houston, Boston, Detroit, Cincinnati, Hartford, and Indianapolis.
- Top U.S. metro exporters to Germany were New York, Boston, San Jose-Sunnyvale-Santa Clara, Los Angeles, Chicago, Seattle, Hartford, Greenville, South Carolina, and Tuscaloosa, Alabama.

- Top U.S. metro exporters to the United Kingdom were New York, Philadelphia, Los Angeles, Houston, Seattle, Boston, Washington DC, Cincinnati, Providence, and Salt Lake City.

Transatlantic Investment: Still Driving the Transatlantic Economy

- Trade alone is a misleading benchmark of international commerce; mutual investment is the real backbone of the transatlantic economy. Together the U.S. and Europe accounted for only 27.1% of global exports and 34.6% of global imports in 2008. But together they accounted for 61.7% of the inward stock of foreign direct investment (FDI), and a whopping 74.9% of outward stock of FDI. Moreover, each partner has built up the great majority of that stock in the other economy. In short, mutual investment in the North Atlantic space is very large, dwarfs trade, and has become essential to U.S. and European jobs and prosperity.
- Europe's direct investment stocks in the U.S. in 2008 totaled a record $1.6 trillion, a 7.6% rise from 2007 and nearly double the level a decade earlier. Corporate Europe accounted for 71% of total foreign direct investment in the U.S. in 2008 ($2.3 trillion).
- Over the past decade, European firms invested roughly $1.2 trillion into the U.S., roughly double that of the 1990s. Europe accounted for roughly 76% of total U.S. investment inflows 1990-1999 and 73% from 2000-2009.
- FDI inflows from just the major European countries alone account for over half of total FDI into every region of the United States except the Rocky Mountains (41.6%) and the Far West (31.7%).
- Foreign direct investment to the U.S. from the UK fell 65% and from the Netherlands fell 48% in the January-September 2009 time frame versus a year earlier. Investment from France held relatively steady, at less than 1% less than the same period the previous year.
- German investment bucked the trend, growing by 96% in this period.
- The Southeast and Mideast account for one-third of all EU FDI in the United States. The Southeast's share was roughly 17% and the Mideast's share 16.6% in 2007. The share of the Great Lakes dropped significantly to 11.5%.
- Texas, California and New York are the top three destinations of European FDI. They account for nearly one-fourth of total European FDI in the U.S., just as they represent roughly one-fourth of the U.S. population.
- U.S. capital flows to Europe declined 44% in the first nine months of the year versus the prior year. Declines were reported in Germany, the Netherlands, Spain and a handful of other nations.
- FDI (most of it from Europe) was responsible for about 10% of the total economic output of New York City, and for creating one in twenty jobs in the New York City economy.
- FDI (most of it from the United States) is even more important to London, accounting for more than 25% of the London economy. London remains the #1 European metro

destination for U.S. FDI, and one in ten U.S. businesses investing in London come from the tri-state area surrounding New York City.

- After hitting a cyclical peak in 2007, transatlantic M&A deals fell steeply in 2009. U.S. M&A deals in the EU27 totaled just $32 billion in 2009, a 60% decline from 2008. EU27 M&A deals in the U.S. declined roughly 86% to $22.5 billion in 2009, well off the peak level of $200 billion in 2007.
- Worries over the strength of the U.S. economy, the sub-prime credit crunch, and the U.S. dollar converged in 2008 to produce sharp selling among European investors of U.S. securities. U.S. capital inflows from Europe fell nearly $100 billion in 2008 from 2007 but were back in positive territory through November of 2009. Including the U.K., inflows to the U.S. from the EU were down 67% in 2008 from the prior year but were up 36% in the first 11 months of 2009 versus the same period of 2008.
- After U.S. capital outflows to the EU soared in 2006 ($211 billion) and 2007 ($220 billion), U.S. investors in 2008 were net sellers, selling some $36 billion of European securities and nearly $3 billion in British securities. In the first 11 months of 2009, however, U.S. investors purchased $21 billion in British securities, but had yet to return as net buyers in the region through the first 11 months of 2009.
- U.S. foreign direct investment to Europe (including non-EU states like Switzerland, Norway, Russia and Turkey) dropped roughly 23% in 2008 and plunged by 44% in the first nine months of 2009 versus the same period a year earlier. U.S. FDI flows declined 124% to Spain, 65% to the United Kingdom, 43% to Germany, and 10% to Italy. U.S. FDI flows over this period declined by 68% to Brazil and by 49% to India.
- While the drop in US FDI flows to Europe are considerable, they pale in comparison to the 185% drop in U.S. FDI flows to China in the first three quarters of 2009 versus the same period in 2008. In fact, while U.S. FDI outflows to Europe declined during this period, they still totaled a positive $82.4 billion, whereas for the same period U.S. firms actually *disinvested* in China—there was a net reversal of U.S. FDI out of China of $6.3 billion.
- Even with these sharp cyclical declines mentioned above, U.S. investment flows to Europe continue to outweigh considerably U.S. investment elsewhere. U.S. investment in China in 2008 ($15.7 billion) was just 70% of total U.S. investment in Ireland. U.S. investment in the Netherlands was more than three times larger than U.S. investment in China in 2008. U.S. investment in France was double the amount U.S. firms invested in India ($2.6 billion).
- On a historic cost basis, the U.S. investment position in Europe was nearly four times larger than corporate America's investment position in all of Asia at the end of 2008. U.S. investment stakes in Spain ($70 billion) alone were greater than the combined U.S. investment position in China and India ($62 billion).
- Over the last decade, five out of the top ten overseas markets for U.S. direct investment were in Europe. The Netherlands ranked first, UK second, Ireland fourth, Switzerland fifth, and Germany seventh. France ranked eleventh, Belgium twelfth and Spain fifteenth. Nafta neighbors Canada and Mexico ranked third and sixth. Singapore ranked eighth, Japan ninth and Australia tenth.

- U.S. investment 2000-2009 in Ireland was three times U.S. investment in China. U.S. investment into the UK was nearly seven times larger than into China, and U.S. investment into the Netherlands was almost nine times greater than U.S. investment into China. U.S. firms invested more in the Netherlands over the last decade than they invested in South and Central America, the Middle East, and Africa combined.
- U.S. investment 2000-2009 in Brazil was roughly 70% of total U.S. investment in Spain. U.S. investment in Russia was half that into Italy. U.S. investment into India was less than U.S. investment into Norway.
- Similarly, the U.S. was the top recipient of extra-EU FDI outflows in 2008. Outflows to the U.S. totaled €121 billion, 34.8% of the extra-EU27 total, followed by Switzerland (9.8%), Russia (7.4%) and Singapore (4.4%). In terms of capital stock, the EU's investment stock in the United States rose by 43% between 2000 and 2008, with the U.S. accounting for roughly one-third of extra-EU27 FDI stock abroad.
- EU FDI in the U.S. in 2008 totaled €1.1 trillion, versus total combined investment of €66.5 billion in China and India. EU FDI in China totaled €47.2 billion in 2008, while EU FDI in India tallied just €19.3 billion.
- EU FDI outflows to the BRICs are focused primarily on Russia, and then Brazil, rather than China or India. EU FDI outflows to Russia in 2007 and 2008 totaled €42.8 billion, roughly three times EU FDI to Brazil, four times EU FDI to China and six times EU FDI to India. EU FDI outflows to Russia in 2007-2008, in turn, represented only about one-seventh the value of EU FDI outflows to the United States in this period.
- EU investment assets in the U.S. are nearly 33% of extra-EU27 investment stock. EU investment assets in Brazil were roughly one-tenth of those in the United States in 2008. EU investment assets in Russia were about 8% of those in the U.S. In China, the comparable figure was less than 5% of EU investment stock in the United States. India's total above was even smaller, coming in less than 1% of extra-EU27 investment stock in 2008. All told, EU investment assets in the BRICs are one-quarter of EU investment assets in the United States.
- Between 2001 and 2008 EU FDI outflows to the BRICS represented only 8.3% of global EU FDI outflows outside the EU27, and most of that was to Russia, not China and India. U.S. FDI outflows to the BRICS during this same period accounted for only 4.5% of global U.S. FDI outflows.
- The total output of U.S. foreign affiliates in Europe ($611 billion in 2007) and of European affiliates in the U.S. ($412 billion) is greater than the total gross domestic output of most nations. Combined transatlantic foreign affiliate output rose 7% in 2007 and 21% from the levels of 2000. Total output of transatlantic foreign affiliates is equivalent to the aggregate output of such nations as South Korea, the Netherlands, or Switzerland.
- Global output of U.S. affiliates was nearly $1.12 trillion in 2007; Europe accounted for roughly 55% of the total. The UK accounted for 28% of total U.S. affiliate output in Europe, Germany 14% and France 9%. Output was evenly split between services and manufacturing.

- U.S. affiliates in Ireland accounted for 21% of Ireland's total output in 2007, 6.7% of Switzerland's output, 6.2% of the UK's output, 5.2% of Belgium's output and 3.6% of Hungary's total output.
- U.S. foreign affiliate output in Belgium in 2007 ($23.7 billion) was some 6% larger than U.S. foreign affiliate output in China in 2007 ($22.4 billion) and more than three times as large as affiliate output in India ($7.32 billion).
- U.S. affiliate output in Poland jumped 29% in 2007, to $8.5 billion, after rising 12% in 2006, to $6.4 billion, exceeding U.S. output in more developed markets like Austria, Portugal, and Denmark.
- European affiliates accounted for nearly two-thirds of the $658 billion contributed by foreign affiliates to U.S. aggregate production in 2007. The U.S. output of British firms reached nearly $118 billion in 2007, or nearly 30% of the total. Output from German affiliates operating in the U.S. totaled $86 billion, up nearly 20% from a year earlier, while output from French affiliates rose nearly 5% to $61 billion in 2007.
- Aggregate U.S. foreign assets totaled over $13 trillion in 2007. 63% was in Europe. U.S. assets in the UK alone totaled $3.5 trillion in 2007, roughly one-quarter of the global total, and an amount greater than total combined U.S. assets in South America, Africa and the Middle East.
- U.S. assets in the Netherlands ($1.3 trillion) were the second largest in the world in 2007. America's asset base in Germany ($613 billion) was nearly double the U.S. asset base in South America. The U.S. asset base in Poland, Hungary, and the Czech Republic (roughly $65 billion) was twice the size of corporate America's assets in India.
- In 2007 European firms held roughly three-quarters of total foreign assets in the U.S.—some $9.1 trillion in U.S. assets, a figure that includes bank and non-bank affiliates. The UK was the largest holder of U.S. assets in 2007 ($2.2 trillion), followed closely behind by Swiss firms ($2 trillion), France and Germany.
- Foreign investment and affiliate sales increasingly drive transatlantic trade. A substantial share of transatlantic trade is conducted by companies trading among their own affiliates. Nearly 67% of U.S. imports from Germany and 60% from the EU consisted of this "related party trade" in 2008. Roughly 45% of total U.S. exports to the Netherlands and 31% of U.S. exports to the EU in 2008 was "related party trade."
- Europe accounted for 56% ($2.8 trillion) of total U.S. foreign affiliate sales in 2007, up 15% and well in excess of U.S. exports of $1.6 trillion. U.S. affiliate sales in Europe were roughly double comparable sales in the entire Asia/Pacific region. Affiliate sales in the United Kingdom ($672 billion) exceeded aggregate sales in Latin America. U.S. affiliate sales of $146 billion in China in 2007 were slightly below sales to Italy ($155 billion) and well below those in Germany ($357 billion) or France ($228 billion).
- Affiliate sales are also the primary means by which European firms deliver goods and services to consumers in the United States. In 2007 European affiliate sales in the U.S. ($1.8 trillion) were roughly three times larger than U.S. imports from Europe ($577 billion). German affiliate sales in the U.S. of $383 billion were nearly three times U.S. imports from Germany.

- The transatlantic economy enjoyed a profits boom between 2002 and 2007, but the tide turned in the second half of 2007 and into 2008. U.S. affiliates in Europe earned $173 billion in 2008, down slightly from 2007 but more than three times the cyclical lows of 2001.
- In the first nine months of 2009, U.S. affiliate income earned in Europe plummeted 25% from the same period a year earlier. A slight rebound is expected in 2010, but we do not expect affiliate profits to reach their pre-crisis levels until 2011 or 2012.
- That said, on a global basis, Europe remains the most profitable region of the world for U.S. multinationals, with Europe accounting for half of total global affiliate earnings in 2007 and 2008. U.S. affiliate income from Europe was more than double the total earnings from Latin America and Asia in 2008. Combined U.S. affiliate income from China and India in 2008 ($7.7 billion) was nearly 20% less than affiliate earnings in Germany ($9.4 billion). Affiliates earned nearly three times in Ireland in 2008 than they did in India and China combined.

Services: The Sleeping Giant of the Transatlantic Economy

- Sales of services of U.S. foreign affiliates in Europe soared in 2007 to a record $565 billion. U.S. affiliate sales of services were nearly 180% larger than U.S. service exports to Europe in 2007. The United Kingdom accounted for nearly 38% of U.S. foreign affiliate sales of services in 2007. On a global basis, Europe accounted for 55% of total U.S. affiliate sales of services in 2007.
- European affiliate sales of services in the U.S. totaled $419 billion in 2007; more than 2½ times U.S. service imports from Europe ($152 billion).
- Europe accounted for 43% of total U.S. service exports and for 44% of total U.S. service imports in 2008. Five out of the top ten export markets for U.S. services in 2007 (the last year of available data) were in Europe. The UK ranked Number 1, followed by Germany (4th), Ireland (6th), France (7th), and Switzerland (8th). Similarly, the same five nations that ranked in the top ten U.S. export markets also ranked among the top ten service providers to the U.S.
- The U.S. enjoyed a $52 billion trade surplus in services with Europe in 2008, compared with the U.S. $120 billion trade deficit in goods with Europe.
- New York and London rank as the "most connected" global cities in advanced producer services. 9 Asian and European cities ranked among the top 20 cities; Toronto was the only other North American city.

Transatlantic Jobs

- Despite stories about local U.S. and European companies decamping for cheap labor markets in Mexico or Asia, most foreigners working for U.S. companies outside the U.S. are Europeans, and most foreigners working for European companies outside the EU are American.

- Roughly 42% of the 10 million people employed by U.S. majority-owned affiliates in 2007 lived in Europe—most in the UK, Germany and France, and almost evenly split between manufacturing and services.
- U.S. affiliates employed just as many manufacturing workers in Europe (1.9 million) in 2007 as they did in 1990. Yet the geographic distribution has shifted within Europe towards lower cost locations like Ireland and Poland. Between 1990 and 2007 U.S. affiliate manufacturing employment fell roughly 32% in the United Kingdom and 18% in Germany, but soared 30% in Ireland.
- Even with the decline of manufacturing employment in Germany, the manufacturing workforce of U.S. affiliates in Germany alone totaled 372,000 workers in 2007, not far from the number of manufactured workers employed by U.S. affiliates in China (402,800).
- European majority-owned bank and nonbank foreign affiliates directly employed roughly 3.6 million U.S. workers in 2007. The top five employers were firms from the UK (949,300), Germany (653,900), France (516,000), the Netherlands (391,200) and Switzerland (396,900). European firms employed more than two-thirds of the 5.5 million U.S. workers on the payrolls of majority-owned bank and nonbank foreign affiliates in 2007.
- European affiliates directly employed the most U.S. workers in California (303,600), New York (271,300) and Texas (210,700).

The Transatlantic Knowledge Economy

- Research and development by U.S. foreign affiliates totaled $35 billion in 2007, 66% of which was invested in Europe. Four European countries alone—UK, Germany, France, and Sweden—accounted for roughly 45% of U.S. global R&D spending.
- Research and development by foreign affiliates in the U.S. totaled nearly $40 billion in 2007, up nearly 15% and accounting for roughly 15% of total R&D spending in the U.S. 78% emanated from world-class leaders from Europe in research-intensive sectors like energy, chemicals, telecommunications, and automobiles.
- British-owned affiliates were the largest foreign source of R&D in the U.S. in 2007 ($10.5 billion), up roughly 50% and accounting for 26% of total affiliate R&D in the U.S. Swiss-owned affiliates were second with a 15% share and German affiliates third with a 14% share ($5.6 billion).
- San Jose, California, the home of Silicon Valley, is the most competitive knowledge region in the world. Boston, Massachusetts ranks #2 and Hartford, Connecticut #3. Stockholm ranks #6, the top European city-region. The top twenty knowledge regions include 13 U.S. regions, 5 European regions, and 2 Japanese regions.
- Istanbul, Turkey, the OECD region with the highest percentage of foreign co-patenting, shared 94% of its foreign co-inventions with North America, and only slightly more than 5% with regions in Europe.
- California shared 64% of its foreign co-inventions with Europe and only 16% with other non-U.S. regions in North America.

- The Southeast of England and the Southern and Eastern region of Ireland each share about 50% of their foreign co-inventions with regions in North America, and only about 40% with regions in Europe. Lisbon, Portugal and the western Netherlands share about 40 percent of their foreign co-inventions with regions in North America.
- U.S. cities accounted for 14 of the top 20 metro areas in the world in terms of per capita R&D expenditure by business, with only the Swedish regions of Göteberg and Stockholm and four Japanese regions breaking into the top 20. Sweden's strong business R&D investments are also apparent in the strong showing of Sweden's regions within Europe's top 20 regions in this category, accompanied by five German regions.
- U.S. cities accounted for 19 of the top 20 metro areas in the world in terms of per capita recipients of government-channeled R&D expenditures. Beijing, China was the only non-U.S. city even breaking into the top 20, with European cities all far behind.

Chapter 1

The Rocky Road to Recovery: The Transatlantic Economy in 2010

The financial storm has passed but the near-term economic outlook for the transatlantic economy is anything but sunshine and blue skies. The Great Recession proved to be shorter and shallower than had been feared, but the aftershocks of the financial crisis of 2008-2009 will be felt well into 2010, resulting in sub-par economic growth for the transatlantic economy over the next twelve months.

That said, relative to last year's survey the economic backdrop has greatly improved, with the United States and most of Europe emerging from recession over the second half of 2009. The rebound was due in good part to aggressive monetary and fiscal policies on both sides of the Atlantic that were unprecedented in peacetime. Super-low interest rates helped to recapitalize the transatlantic banking sector, bringing with it more stability and confidence in the global capital markets, as well as a sharp rebound in the transatlantic equity markets. While consumer and business confidence remains rather frail, the mood among both groups is much improved from a year ago. Robust fiscal spending has helped promote growth, notably in the all-important automobile sector, where various "cash-for-clunker" deals helped generate more manufacturing production for both U.S. and European vehicle makers.

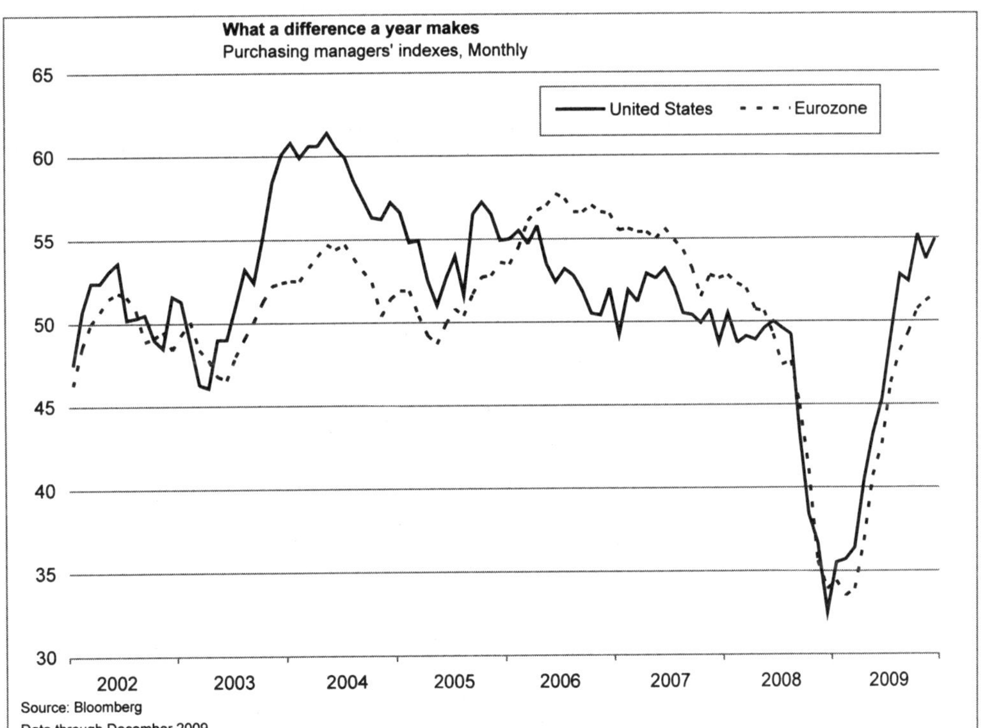

Financial Sector Write-downs & Credit Losses vs. Capital Raised*
(Regional aggregates, Billions of $)

Period	Worldwide		Americas		Europe		Asia	
	Loss	Raised	Loss	Raised	Loss	Raised	Loss	Raised
Prior	(4.9)	0.0	(4.3)	0.0	(0.3)	0.0	(0.3)	0.0
3Q07	(59.8)	15.8	(42.9)	3.1	(15.7)	12.8	(1.3)	0.0
4Q07	(223.2)	74.8	(128.3)	47.1	(83.4)	27.6	(11.5)	0.0
1Q08	(227.3)	91.2	(135.0)	64.5	(80.8)	22.8	(11.6)	3.9
2Q08	(179.0)	200.5	(112.4)	103.8	(62.8)	82.9	(3.8)	13.8
3Q08	(268.6)	109.9	(205.5)	44.1	(57.3)	56.7	(5.8)	9.1
4Q08	(397.5)	442.0	(243.1)	266.4	(150.0)	146.6	(4.4)	29.0
1Q09	(144.8)	251.4	(100.9)	122.0	(40.3)	109.7	(3.7)	19.7
2Q09	(151.7)	118.6	(103.1)	91.8	(48.5)	15.2	(0.1)	11.6
3Q09	(41.0)	69.8	(33.7)	16.1	(7.4)	33.4	(0.1)	20.3
4Q09	(36.7)	108.4	(34.6)	21.0	(2.1)	81.9	0.0	5.5
1Q10	0.0	10.7	0.0	0.0	0.0	0.0	0.0	10.7
Total	**(1,734.5)**	**1,493.1**	**(1,143.8)**	**779.9**	**(548.6)**	**589.6**	**(42.6)**	**123.6**

Sources: Bloomberg

Data through February 1, 2010

* Includes all banks, brokers, insurers and GSEs; Reflects amounts reported or announced for the respective calendar quarter

The real estate sector remains the Achilles Heel for many nations, with a badly bloated, debt-laden commercial real estate market in the United States expected to be a sizable drag on construction output again this year. In Europe, excess real estate capacity and the attendant jump in non-performing loans remain acute issues for Spain, Ireland and Portugal. Bank profits on both sides of the Atlantic have improved although the transatlantic capital markets remain fragile. Despite very low interest rates and substantial government assistance, the financial health of both the United States and Europe remain key concerns in 2010. Since the financial crisis began in 2008, European banks have written off over $550 billion in bad loans. That is a large figure, although by some estimate, European banks have only written off 40% of their bad loans. U.S. banks are thought to have written off 60% of their non-performing loans.

The fragile nature of the recovery and the deep economic bonds linking the two sides of the Atlantic have been underscored by jitters about Europe's wobbly periphery. Large government deficits in nations like Greece, Portugal, Ireland and Spain have rattled investor confidence in their ability to repay their substantial debt, engage in structural reform, reinvigorate growth and reduce high jobless rates without substantial outside assistance, which could drag down other European economies and reverberate across the Atlantic, threatening America's own fragile recovery.[1]

Relative to the eurozone ceiling of 3% of Gross Domestic Product (GDP), Greece's federal budget deficit as a percent of GDP was 12.7% in 2009. Ireland's budget deficit was not

[1] "Global Markets Shudder," *Wall Street Journal*, February 5, 2010; Ylan Q. Mui and Steven Mufson, "Market gains erased as fear grips investors," *The Washington Post*, February 5, 2010.

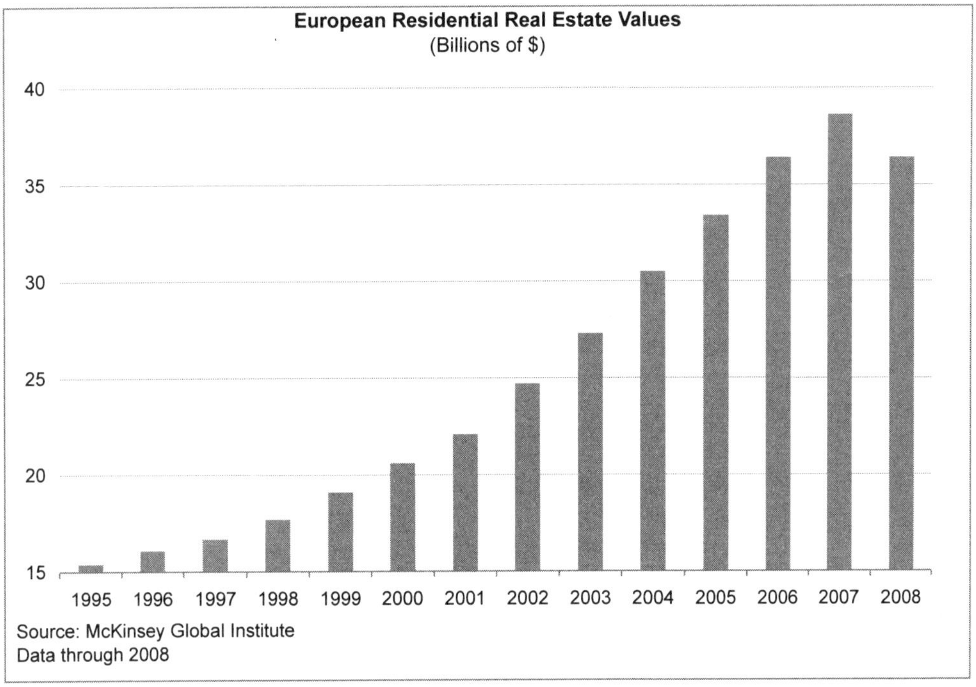

much better at 11.7% of GDP. Spain's deficit was 10% of GDP, while the United Kingdom's and Portugal's deficits were 9.9% and 9.3%, respectively. Italy's government is also highly leveraged and it too must cut spending and regain competitiveness.[2]

A number of European nations (Ireland, Portugal, Spain, the Czech Republic, and Romania) have pledged to reduce public sector expenditures over the near-term. This has appeased the credit markets to a degree, although the risk is that tightening measures in some of Europe's weaker states could come too soon and abort the nascent economic rebound.

This shaky situation also poses a real test for the 16-country eurozone. While the central core of the eurozone seems solid, it is an open question how the group as a whole will decide how to deal with those member states that are in deep financial trouble. Unlike the United States, where federal solutions are available to individual states that may find themselves in a fiscal crisis, the eurozone lacks appropriate burden-sharing mechanisms and lacks an effective central authority to enforce the currency union's own rules limiting deficits to 3% of GDP. How the eurozone decides to deal with this problem may determine much about the future of European economic and monetary coordination.[3]

Of course, public sector deficits and the ability to service those deficits are not only a European problem. The U.S. deficit was 10% in fiscal year 2009 and is expected to decline only modestly, to 9.2%, in fiscal year 2010.

---

[2] Nouriel Roubini and Arnab Das, "Medicine for Europe's sinking south," *Financial Times*, February 3, 2010.

[3] Floyd Norris, "Fraying at the Edges," *New York Times*, February 5, 2010, p. B1.

Unemployment remains a primary concern on both sides of the Atlantic. As Lawrence Summers, President Obama's principal economic adviser, has noted, what we are seeing is "a statistical recovery and a human recession."[4] In two years the U.S. economy shed 7.2 million jobs, pushing the jobless rate from 5% to 10%. The unemployment rate in the United States has peaked at around 10%, but is expected to decline slowly over the balance of this year. Since the early 1990s jobs have been slower to recover from recessions. After the 2001 downturn ended, for instance, job losses in the United States continued for nearly two years, in contrast to the deep downturn of 1981-1982, when jobs rebounded quickly.

Across many parts of Europe, meanwhile, unemployment rates are expected to rise in 2010 as temporary work programs come to an end and companies are forced to shed more workers. In November 2009, the euro area's unemployment rate rose to 10%, but is higher still in Spain (19.4%), Belgium (12.1%), Poland (11.9%), and Hungary (10.5%). The jobless rate in France was 10% in November. Germany limited the rise in its jobless ranks to just over 5%, compared with increases of more than 50% in the U.S. and the UK; its rate of unemployment of 8.2% was similar to levels a year earlier. Job losses have been mitigated by state-subsidized working schemes, labor contracts offering flexible working hours, and labor-management deals to forego or delay bonuses. These programs are slated to end, slanting unemployment to the upside.

In contrast to many European firms, U.S. firms were quick to pare their workforces in 2009, resulting in a 2.5% rise in productivity. However, productivity levels in Europe fell last year, with declining output and less labor-shedding practices resulting in less output per hour worked in many European companies.

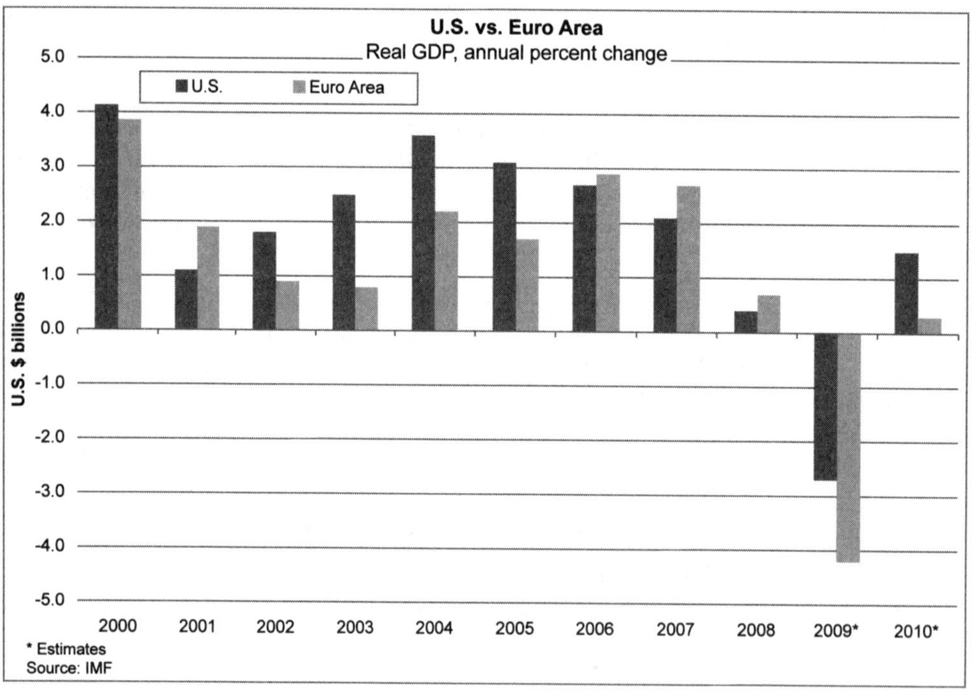

[4] Cited in Martin Wolf, "What the world must do to sustain its convalescence, *Financial Times*, February 3, 2010.

Burdened with high unemployment rates and mounting public sector debt, the eurozone's economic rebound is expected to be rather tepid this year; the IMF expects output in the euro area to rise just 1% this year. That is much improved from 2009, when output declined 3.9%. Germany's economy is projected to grow 2.1%, but other eurozone member states are likely to record weak or no growth. Poland and Switzerland are also expected to outperform the rest of Europe with growth rates in the 3-5% range in 2010.[5] The U.S. economy is expected to expand by 2.7% this year, following a 2.5% drop in output last year.

While the U.S. and European economies emerged from recession during the second half of 2009, industrial production has remained sluggish. Manufacturers on both sides of the Atlantic are rethinking their businesses in the wake of the recession, leading to some important shifts in the transatlantic industrial base. The U.S. manufacturing economy is not only shrinking, it is shifting from heavy sectors such as automobiles and basic chemicals to higher-tech products like ultra-fast computer chips. During 2009, America's capacity to produce motor vehicles and chemicals fell 4.1% and 1.7%, respectively, the largest declines since 1949. Capacity in U.S. textile mills in 2009 registered a decline of 7%, in printing a decline of over 6%, in furniture a decline of more than 5%, and in plastics and rubber products a decline of about 3%. Its capacity to produce semiconductors, in contrast, grew an estimated 10%, in communications equipment by almost 8%, in computers by almost 6%, in electricity more than 2%, and 1.3% in oil and gas.[6]

In the eurozone and in central Europe only a few industries can expect strong growth in 2010, including motor vehicles, which is set to grow by 8% in the eurozone and 8.4% in central Europe. Industrial production of computers and electronics in central Europe is slated to grow by 14.5% in 2010 and by 18.3% in 2011; a slower but still significant turnaround is also expected for this sector in the eurozone over the next two years.

U.S. Industrial Production Capacity, 2009

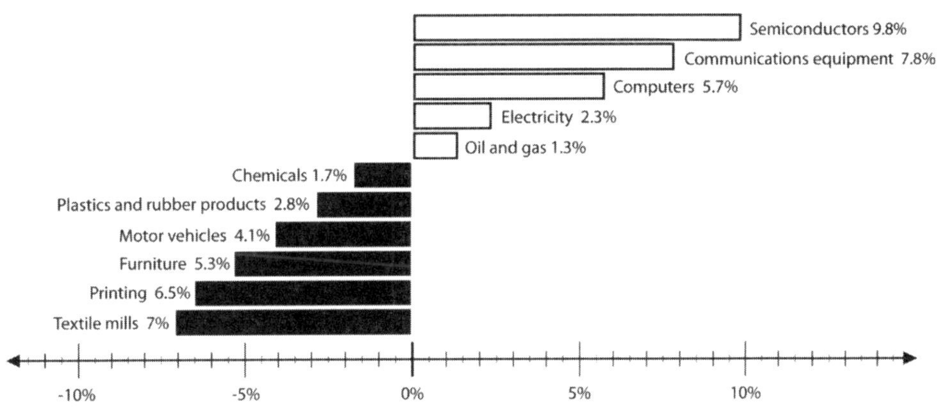

Source: Federal Reserve, "Industrial Capacity: Manufacturing, Mining and Utilities," http://www.federalreserve.gov/releases/g17/Current/table3_sup.htm; Mark Whitehouse, "Radical Shifts Take Hold in U.S. Manufacturing," Wall Street Journal, February 3, 2010, p. B1.

[5] Krzystof Bledowski, *MAPI European Industrial Outlook: 2009-2010* (Arlington, VA: Manufacturers Alliance, January 2010).

[6] Federal Reserve, "Industrial Capacity: Manufacturing, Mining and Utilities," http://www.federalreserve.gov/releases/g17/Current/table3_sup.htm; Mark Whitehouse, "Radical Shifts Take Hold in U.S. Manufacturing," *Wall Street Journal*, February 3, 2010, p. B1.

Industrial Production, Eurozone

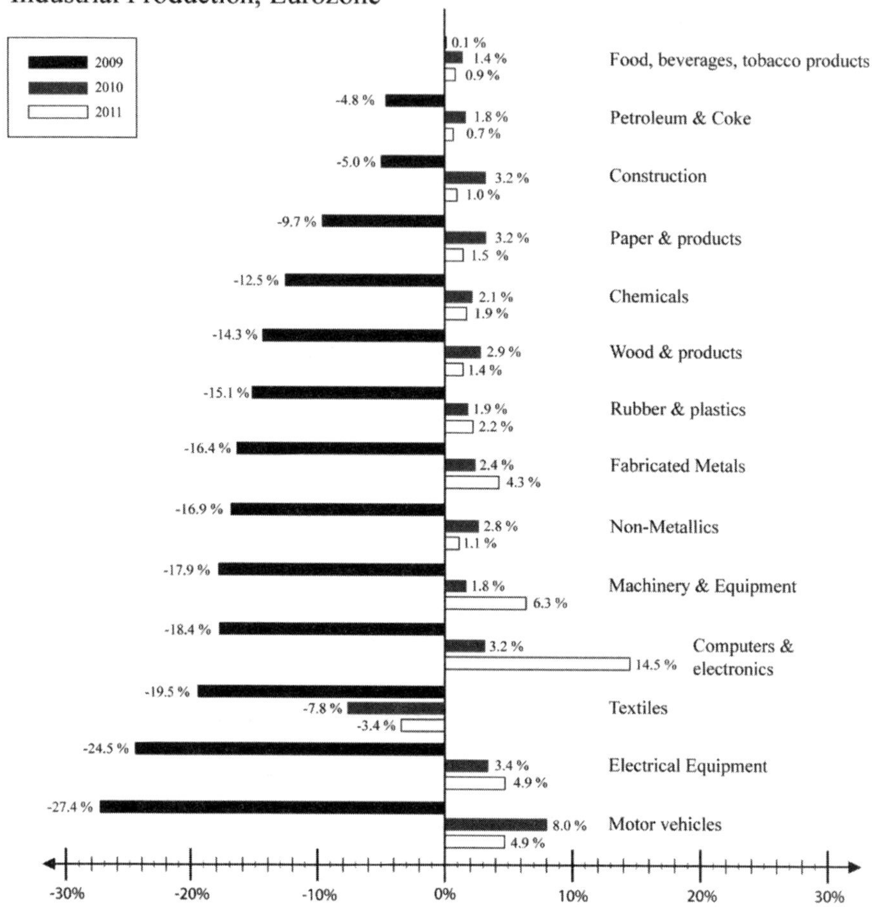

Source: Krzystof Bledowski, MAPI European Industrial Outlook: 2009-2010 (Arlington, VA: Manufacturers Alliance, January 2010).

The Fallout from the Great Recession of 2008-2009

By many measures 2009 was a very challenging year for all transatlantic stakeholders—consumers, workers, companies and countries. The collateral damage from the recession is evident from the following:

After surging over the 2002-2007 period, U.S. foreign affiliate income earned in Europe peaked in the first half of 2008 before declining sharply thereafter. U.S. affiliate income fell 25% in the first nine months of 2009 from the same period a year earlier. We estimate that affiliate income totaled $137 billion for all of 2009, down 23% from the peak in 2007.

U.S. affiliate income earned in the United Kingdom, among the most important markets in Europe for American companies, was down 38% in the first nine months of 2009 versus the same period in 2008. Meanwhile, affiliate income over the same period declined nearly 260% in Sweden, 104% in Greece, 101% in Portugal, 60% in Spain, 50% in France, and

Industrial Production, Central Europe[1]

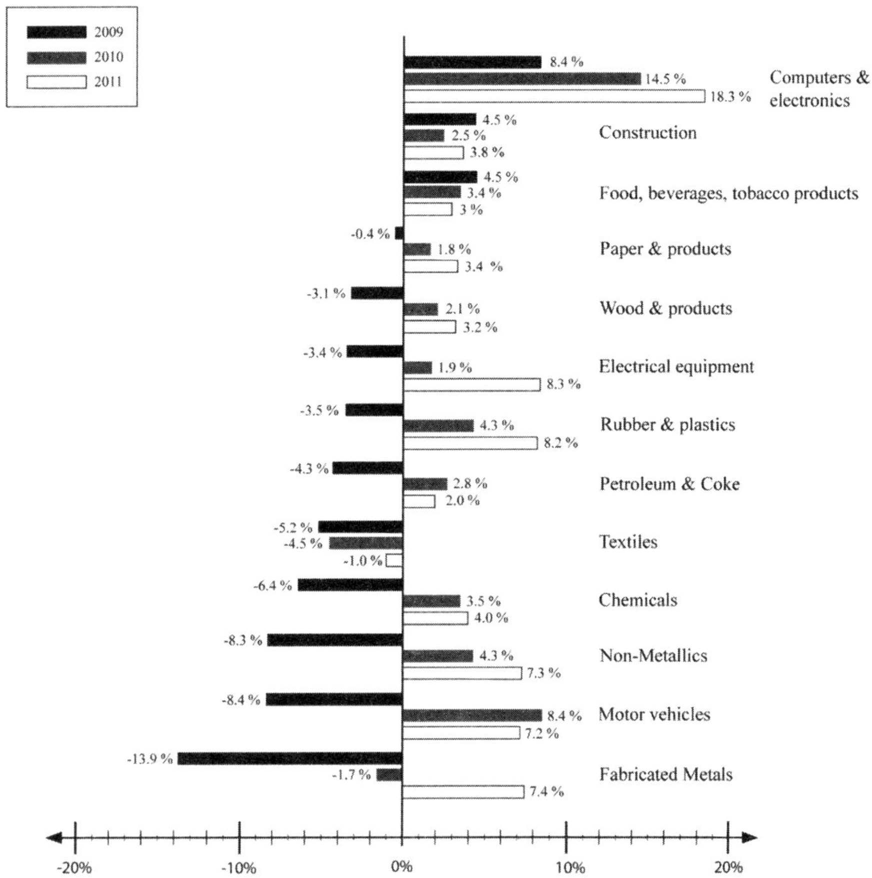

[1] Poland, the Czech Republic, and Hungary.

Source: Krzystof Bledowski, MAPI European Industrial Outlook: 2009-2010 (Arlington, VA: Manufacturers Alliance, January 2010).

47% in Germany. Hungary, Austria, and Ireland were the only countries in which U.S. affiliate income rose 17%, 10%, and less than 1% respectively.

Not surprisingly, the U.S. economic downturn has taken its toll on the earnings of European affiliates operating in the United States. Between 2002 and 2007, affiliate earnings rose more than three-fold, surging from $26.7 billion in 2002 to $72 billion in 2007. In 2008, however, European affiliates saw their U.S. earnings decelerate sharply. The downturn was extended in 2009, with total European affiliates dropping 22% in the January-September period 2009 versus a year ago. Affiliate earnings of French companies fell 30%. British and Dutch affiliates saw their U.S. earnings slip by roughly 12% and 20%, respectively, in the first nine months of 2009. Overall, German companies were a great exception: affiliate earnings of German companies in the U.S. rose nearly 230% in the period January-September 2009, compared with a year earlier. As the U.S. economy recovers in 2010, affiliate earnings for other European affiliates should also rebound.

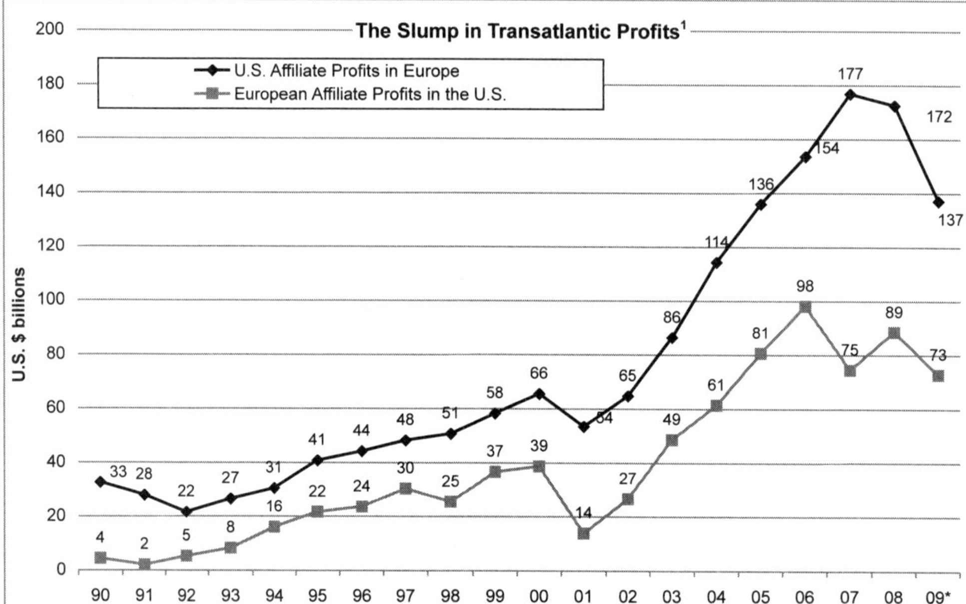

[1]Income of affiliates
Source: Bureau of Economic Analysis
Data through 3Q2009, Data annualized for full year estimate

Because earnings are a significant component of foreign direct investment, it is not surprising to report that as affiliate income declined on both sides of the Atlantic last year, so did transatlantic foreign direct investment flows. For instance, foreign direct investment from the Netherlands to the U.S. plunged 48% in the January-September time frame versus the same period a year earlier. Investment from the United Kingdom fell 65% over the same period. Investment from France held relatively steady, at less than 1% less than the same period the previous year. German investment bucked the trend, however, growing by 96% in this period.

U.S. investment flows to Europe also exhibited a decelerating trend in 2009. U.S. capital flows to Europe declined 44% in the first nine months of the year versus the prior year. Declines were reported in Germany, the Netherlands, Spain and a handful of other nations.

After hitting a cyclical peak in 2007, transatlantic merger and acquisition (M&A) deals fell rather steeply in 2009. For instance, U.S. M&A deals in the EU27 totaled just $32 billion in 2009, a 60% decline from the prior year. Meanwhile, EU27 M&A deals in the United States also declined in 2009, by roughly 86%. Total deals were valued at $22.5 billion in the year, well off the peak levels of 2007, when total M&A deals in the U.S. topped nearly $200 billion. Beyond the drop in deal-making: the rising cost of capital, weaker corporate earnings, and the cyclical downturn in the transatlantic economy. All three variables have converged both to end the five-year boom in transatlantic M&A.

Trends in transatlantic trade were similar to trends in transatlantic investment and foreign affiliate income. U.S. exports to Europe in the first three quarters of 2009, for example, fell by nearly 20% from the same period a year earlier, one of the steepest declines in years.

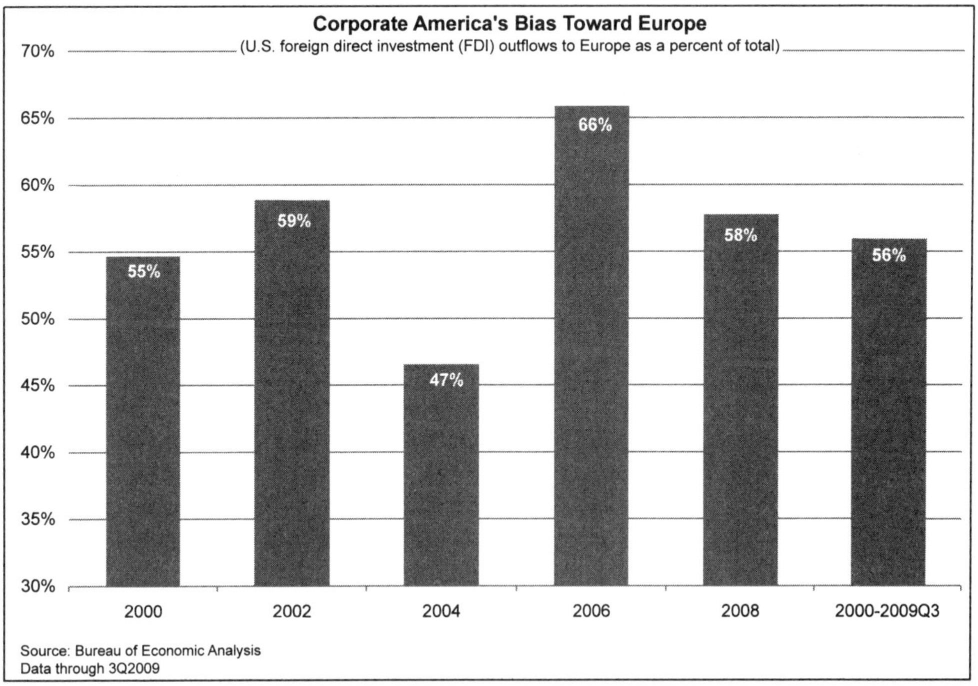

U.S. imports from Europe fell 24% in the first three quarters of 2009 versus the same period in 2008.

Despite the lower value of the dollar relative to the euro, U.S. exports to the United Kingdom dropped 18% through September 2009 from the same period in 2008. Exports of goods and services to France and Germany fell 9.5% and 20% respectively through the first three quarters of 2009 from the same period in 2008.

Trends in transatlantic capital flows reflect many of the variables just mentioned above. Europe remains a key provider of capital to the United States, although U.S. capital inflows from the European Union (excluding the global money center, the United Kingdom) have tailed off significantly since 2006. Worries over the strength of the U.S. economy, the sub-prime credit crunch, and the U.S. dollar converged in 2008 to produce sharp selling among European investors of U.S. securities. Indeed, U.S. capital inflows from Europe fell nearly $100 billion in 2008 from 2007 but were back in positive territory through November of 2009.

As a footnote, capital flow figures do not include capital from the United Kingdom, since a great deal of capital that flows from the United Kingdom originates elsewhere (Russia, the Middle East). Net inflows from the U.K. have fallen from a high of nearly $550 billion in 2007 to $328 at the end of 2008 and to $182 in the first 11 months of 2009. Including the U.K., inflows to the U.S. from the EU were down 67% in 2008 from the prior year but were up 36% in the first 11 months of 2009 versus the same period of 2008.

U.S. capital outflows to the EU have also declined over the past year. Indeed, after outflows to the EU soared in 2006 ($211 billion) and 2007 ($220 billion), they turned negative in

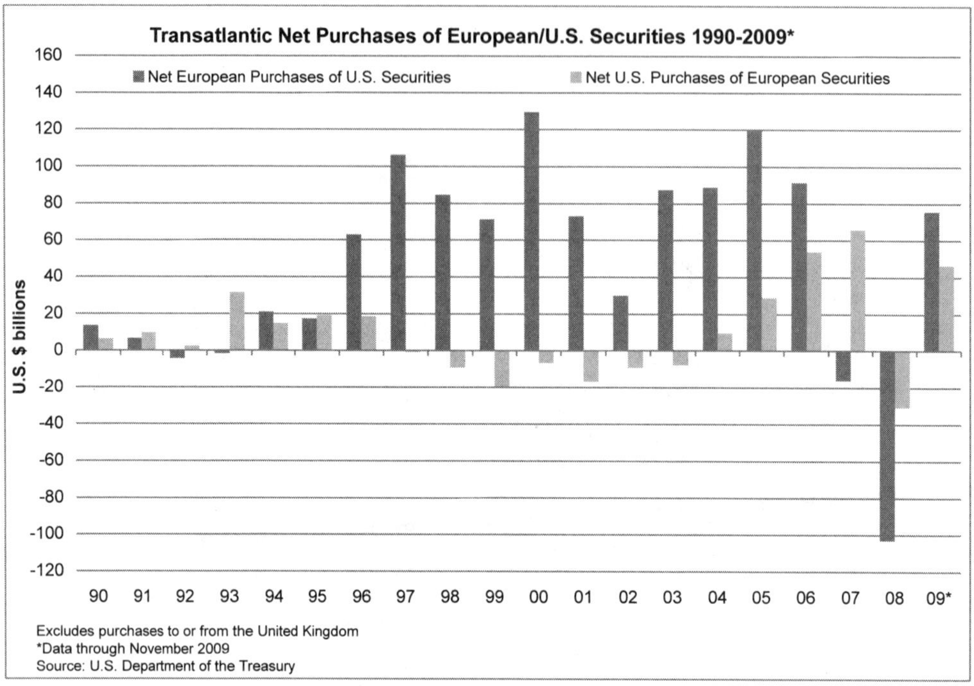

2008. U.S. investors were net sellers, in other words, ridding themselves of some $36 billion of European securities in 2008. Even U.S. purchases of U.K. securities, traditionally a market of choice, were negative in 2008, with U.S. investors selling nearly $3 billion in British securities. In the first 11 months of 2009, however, U.S. investors purchased $21 billion in British securities. Furthermore, U.S. investors were net sellers in most parts of Europe in 2008 except for Ireland, Luxembourg, Norway, and Switzerland and had yet to return as net buyers in the region through the first 11 months of 2009.

Even with the sharp cyclical declines mentioned above, on a secular basis, U.S. investment flows to Europe continue to be considerably outweigh U.S. investment elsewhere. For example, while U.S. foreign direct investment to China has increased sharply over the past few years, total U.S. investment in China in 2008 ($15.7 billion) was just 70% of total U.S. investment in Ireland in the same year. U.S. investment in the Netherlands was more than three times larger than U.S. investment in China in 2008. U.S. investment in France was double the amount U.S. firms invested in India ($2.6 billion).

On a historic cost basis, the U.S. investment position in Europe was nearly four times larger than corporate America's investment position in all of Asia at the end of 2008. U.S. investment stakes in Spain at the end of 2008, some $70 billion on a historic cost basis, were greater than the combined U.S. investment position in China and India ($62 billion).

The service economies of the United States and Europe have never been as intertwined as they are today, notably in such activities as financial services, telecommunications, utilities, insurance, advertising, computer services, and other related activities.

Foreign affiliate sales of services on both sides of the Atlantic have exploded over the past decade. In fact, affiliate sales of services have not only supplemented trade in services to become a viable second channel of delivery for U.S. and European multinationals, they have become the overwhelming mode of delivery in a rather short period of time.

Sales of services of U.S. foreign affiliates in Europe soared again in 2007, rising to a record $565 billion. U.S. affiliate sales of services were nearly 180% larger than U.S. service exports to Europe in 2007. The United Kingdom accounted for nearly 38% of U.S. foreign affiliate sales of services in 2007. On a global basis, Europe accounted for 55% of total U.S. affiliate sales of services last year.

Sales of services by U.S. affiliates of European firms have also soared over the past decade. As Europe's investment position in services has expanded in the U.S., so have Europe's foreign affiliate sales of services. In 2007, affiliate sales of services in the U.S. totaled $419 billion, nearly triple U.S. service imports from Europe in the same year ($152 billion). In total, sales of services in the U.S. by American affiliates of European companies accounted for 62% of all such sales by foreign-owned affiliates in 2007.

Transatlantic trade in services also remains substantial. Europe accounted for 43% of total U.S. services exports and for 44% of total U.S. services imports in 2008. Five out of the top ten export markets for U.S. services in 2007 (the last year of available data) were in Europe. The United Kingdom ranked Number 1, followed by Germany (4th), Ireland (6th), France (7th), and Switzerland (8th). Similarly, the same five nations that ranked in the top ten U.S. export markets also ranked among the top ten services providers to the U.S. The U.S. enjoyed a $52 billion trade surplus in services with Europe in 2008; however, that stands in sharp contrast to the U.S. $120 billion trade deficit in goods with Europe in the same year.

In sum, the United States and Europe remain each other's most important foreign commercial markets, a fact still not fully appreciated by opinion leaders on both sides of the transatlantic. Put simply, no other commercial artery in the world is as integrated and fused together as the transatlantic economy.

A Test of the Transatlantic Commitment to Globalization

The aftershocks of the transatlantic recession will no doubt test the resiliency of the transatlantic partnership, a partnership that has weathered many problems in the past. However, the deeper and more prolonged the economic pain lingers in 2010, the greater the risks of inward, insular policies on both sides of the Atlantic as governments are pressed to respond to aggrieved voters. The rate of unemployment in both the U.S. and Europe is poised to remain high in the near-term. The higher the jobless rate, the greater the pressure on policymakers to guard against outside forces and policies deemed detrimental to their domestic economies. While it is encouraging that both the U.S. and Europe have opted for aggressive fiscal and monetary measures to halt the slide in economic activity, this semblance of macroeconomic coordination could be undermined by diverging microeconomic policies that are protectionist and parochial in nature. Moreover, the massive fiscal stimuli unleashed in the U.S., Europe and elsewhere will have to be restrained at some point. But if spending is cut too soon, or in willy-nilly fashion, economies could fall back into recession. If, on the other hand, loose money policies are uncoordinated or continued for too long, they could deepen government deficits and stoke the kinds of speculative bubbles that burst so spectacularly in 2008.[7]

In addition, and more broadly speaking, the current recession will test and challenge the commitment of both the United States and Europe to globalization, or the process that has resulted in more cross-border trade and foreign direct investment, as well as greater global mobility of people, capital and ideas. As we have highlighted many times before, in many different forums and venues, both the United States and Europe have been big winners from globalization. A variety of forces—rapid technological diffusion, greater trade opportunities, lower barriers to investment, policy reforms at home—have generated greater flows of goods and services, people, capital and ideas between the U.S., Europe and the rest of the world. On the whole, these forces have fostered large gains for the transatlantic economy, including an expansion in trade, strong inflows and outflows of investment, greater technological diffusion, net portfolio inflows, net inflows of labor, downward pressure on inflation and interest rates, more jobs, higher incomes, and in general, higher rates of GDP growth.

On balance, the transatlantic economy has reaped handsome rewards from globalization, but that said, even before the current economic downturn, many important constituents in both the U.S. and Europe had begun to have second thoughts about globalization, unsure and increasingly unconvinced of the benefits of "the openness boom," as referred to by former EU Trade Commissioner Peter Mandelson. Our concern is that in the year ahead, globalization will become a scapegoat for what ails the transatlantic economy and an excuse for policies that are inimical to a more open and unfettered global trade and investment environment.

Since investment rather than trade largely drives commercial ties between the U.S. and Europe, calls in some political quarters to restrict investment flows could have a significantly negative impact on the world's wealthiest market—the transatlantic economy. Before rushing to limit such flows, pundits and policymakers would do well to recall the benefits of inward foreign direct investment—stable capital flows, higher-paying jobs than domestically-sourced jobs, greater inflows of research and development funding, greater capital investments and higher exports.

Beyond the immediate crisis looms an even more fundamental question: does the current recession mark the end of the consumer-friendly model of deepening integration, driven by easy credit and the financial integration of the transatlantic economy? The U.S. and European governments have all proposed sweeping and far-reaching financial regulatory reforms. Our concern is that ad hoc, uncoordinated measures could leave the transatlantic capital markets fragmented, less efficient, and less dynamic in generating future growth of the giant transatlantic services economy.

The mounting regulatory tide could result in a sweeping revamp of the U.S. financial system and the global monetary architecture of the past thirty years. A key result could be a more closed, rather than open, transatlantic services economy.

Since the end of the gold standard in 1971, and the subsequent shift towards floating exchange rates in 1973, capital flows between the United States and Europe have steadily increased, helping to bind the transatlantic economy together. The removal of capital controls, technological advances in communications and the creation of new financial instruments all converged to allow rising flows between the U.S. and Europe.

---

[7] See the special *Financial Times* overview section, "The World 2010," January 27, 2010.

That said, calls for the return of Bretton Woods is notably disconcerting since the desire to rewind the clock back to a bygone era could result in more stifled and constrained global capital flows and by extension, a far less dynamic partnership between the U.S. and Europe. After soaring over the past quarter century, global capital flows could easily become more restrictive and constrained in the years ahead, a prospect that throws sand in the wheels of globalization.

Just as the rise of globalization in the early 1980s was largely underwritten by ever-rising levels of cross border capital flows, more tightly controlled and regulated global finance could lead to the decline of globalization. If the pendulum of financial reform swings too far toward regulation, the global financial architecture of the future could be characterized by tighter rules and regulations regarding capital ratios, liquidity requirements, and risk management metrics. The pace of innovation in the financial sector could slow, impairing the earnings of financial institutions.

In addition to the above, the necessity for banks in the developed nations to reduce risk taking and rebuild their impaired capital base implies less cross-border lending, or lending at higher rates. Risk-averse banks, many of them bailed out by their own governments, are expected to focus their future lending on home markets at the expense of markets overseas. In addition, great financial regulation that restricts global capital flows is also likely to raise the cost of capital for companies wishing to conduct global mergers and acquisitions. Since access to foreign capital is important to global trade and foreign direct investment, the more rules and regulations put in place to contain the flow of global capital, the less capital available to lubricate the real global economy.

In the end, to what extent the global financial landscape will be recast in the next few years remain to be seen. Proposals vary. French President Nicolas Sarkozy favors the creation of a new Bretton Woods system. China has advocated a new world's reserve currency, one that would dethrone the U.S. dollar as the world's top currency. Some European leaders have joined with the Obama Administration to favor policies that would limit the size and activities of banks. As such efforts are debated and advanced, there is a risk that they are crafted in uncoordinated, national and fragmented ways that gum up global capital markets.

To paraphrase an old Chinese adage, "a crisis is a terrible thing to waste." With that as a backdrop, sustaining the primacy of the transatlantic economy requires more than large dollops of fiscal and monetary stimuli, but well thought out initiatives that address the structural problems of the transatlantic economy. Bolder thinking and action are required. Economic recessions are invitations for change, for new ideas. The present economic climate is ripe for change, and on this score, an ideal time for both the United States and Europe to jointly work on such large scale initiatives as global capital markets reform, energy sustainability and global climate change. All of these industries could generate new long-term avenues of growth and prosperity for the transatlantic economy.

Another source of new, secular growth: the transatlantic services economy, which we believe represents the sleeping giant of the transatlantic partnership. As we have discussed at length in other venues, services sector reforms in such industries as capital markets, airlines, health care, telecom services and many others would provide an enormous economic boost to the transatlantic economy and enhance the global competitiveness of both sides of the Atlantic.

In the end, the search for future growth between Europe and the United States should be focused on each other, in addition to satisfying demand from the rising middle classes of the

China as *Exportweltmeister*: A Cause for German Angst?

Media pundits have hailed the fact that China overtook Germany as the world's top exporter in 2009 as another sign of China's rise as a global economic force. Chinese exports of $1.20 trillion slightly exceeded the $1.17 trillion in German exports for the year. The transition will cause some angst in Germany, but four points are worth considering.

First, inordinate attention to shares and rankings ignores the far more significant fact that, in absolute terms, both global exports as a whole and German exports in particular have grown considerably over the past decade. 82 million Germans may not be exporting as much in the future as 1.2 billion Chinese, but they are still exporting quite a lot, and overall the pot itself is much bigger, because of the explosive demand generated by billions of new consumers who have entered the global economy over the past two decades. A growing global economy is not zero-sum; more exports from China does not mean less exports from Germany. And on a per-capita basis, Germany exports considerably more to the world than does China.

Second, even in light of China's export rise, Germany is expected to remain a premier global exporter well into the future, thanks in large part to the country's high-end, sophisticated export mix that is beyond China's current export capabilities. China is best known as a supplier of shoes, toys, furniture and other low-tech goods, while Germany exports machinery and other higher-value products. There are still no indigenous Chinese firms to compete with the likes of Siemens or SAP.

Third, German and other foreign-funded companies make up 85% of China's processing trade, which accounts for nearly 50% of China's exports. Products "Made in China" are not necessarily products "Made by China"—many German exports to China are comprised of intermediate goods shipped by German parent companies to their own affiliates in China.

Fourth, China's rising export capabilities have come more at the expense of other developing nations—South Korea, Taiwan, Thailand, Mexico, for instance—than at the expense of developed nations like Germany.

emerging markets. The latter, no doubt, represent a secular growth dynamic for both the U.S. and Europe, although within the transatlantic economy itself, there are plenty of untapped growth streams available, assuming forward-looking, enlightened policies from both parties. Moreover, it is important to remember that because the EU and the U.S. are the largest two single continental markets in the world, even relatively low growth in such huge markets can generate sizable opportunities to companies, even more than high growth in small markets. A GDP annual growth rate of only 2% in the EU, for instance, would create a new market the size of the entire country of Argentina.

The 2008-2009 recession should be seized upon as an opportunity to deepen transatlantic economic linkages. Today, despite all the chatter about the rise of China and others, trend lines and numerous metrics still point to a predominant role for the transatlantic economy.

Investment, not trade, drives the transatlantic commercial ties, and investment flows between Europe and North America dwarf those between any other continents. Despite the current downturn, this is likely to remain the case in the future.

G-20, G-2, Gee-Who?

During 2009 there was much talk of a new "G-2," but in our opinion this is unlikely to stand for the United States and China. Shifts in the global economic balance are very real. But a number of rapidly developing countries do not share the core principles or basic structures that underpin open rules-based international commerce. And even though the credibility of U.S. and European management of the global economy has been damaged, no plausible alternative is in sight.

We counsel caution about extrapolating economic statistics into predictions about economic—much less political—alignment between the U.S. and China. Of course the U.S. and Europe retain a keen interest in good economic relations with China; a trade war could tip the world back into recession. Tolerable economic relations, however, is hardly the stuff of "G2" dominion. It remains an open question whether China's economic rise will lead to domestic political liberalization and a responsible stakeholder role in the global economy. The U.S. and Europe each find themselves confronted with an array of difficulties when it comes to dealing with China's Leninist leadership, issues of human rights, religious and media freedom, cyberdefense and military security challenges such as involving Taiwan, North Korea and Iran, and problems of energy sustainability, currency rates and trade practices.

Moreover, China itself balks at the kind of leadership role that the term "G2" implies. China sees itself as a developing country with tens of millions living in poverty and GDP per capita less than $4,000. China's economy is as large as it is because it has more than a billion people, not because it has discovered the secret to economic prosperity. Its economy remains largely closed; it ranks 140 out of 179 countries in this year's Heritage Foundation/*Wall Street Journal* Index of Economic Freedom.[8] China's authoritarianism blocks investments and domestic reforms that could truly unleash the country's potential. As Zhou Hong, director of the Institute for European Studies at the Chinese Academy of Social Sciences puts it, "China is big. But it is poor. Its preoccupation will still be internal."[9]

There is no doubt that the concept of "Chimerica" has become the latest fashion for pundits everywhere. Nevertheless, what we call "Eurmerica"—bigger, more prosperous, more tightly linked, more aligned in terms of free markets and open societies—remains the largest and most influential economic entity in the world. As the accompanying exhibit highlights, by virtually any measurement, the economic clout of "Eurmerica" surpasses that of "Chimerica," "Chindia," and Asia itself.

The bottom line: despite the recession, the transatlantic economy remains very strong on a secular and structural basis. We estimate that the transatlantic economy continues to generate close to $4.28 trillion in total commercial sales a year and employs up to 14 million workers in mutually "onshored" jobs on both sides of the Atlantic. These workers enjoy

---

[8] Kim R. Holmes, "When China rules the world? Sorry, not likely," *The Washington Times*, February 4, 2010.

[9] Cited in David Pilling, "China will not be the world's deputy sheriff," *Financial Times*, January 28, 2010.

The Power Brokers of the Global Economy Compared

	Eurmerica	Asia	Chindia	Chimerica
GDP, PPP	43.6%	32.3%	16.2%	32.2%
GDP, Nominal	55.5%	24.5%	9.1%	30.8%
Market cap. (as of 1/4/2010)	$25.3 trillion	$14.7 trillion	$4.6 trillion	$17.2 trillion
Personal consumption exp.	60%	22%	6.3%	33.1%
M+A Sales	70%	13.9%	2.2%	34.3%
M+A Purchases	60%	21.4%	7.2%	16.2%
Inward FDI stock	61.7%	18.4%	3.4%	17.8%
Outward FDI stock	74.9%	15.1%	1.3%	20.4%
Inflows (2000-2008)	59.9%	17.7%	7.0%	22.0%
Outflows (2000-2008)	75.3%	13.4%	1.8%	18.3%
Exports* (Goods)	27.1%	28.4%	13.9%	23.3%
Imports* (Goods)	34.6%	25.8%	11.7%	26.7%
Military Spending	$825.50 67.3%	$204.50 16.7%	$88.4 7.2%	$612.2 50.0%
Top 100 Global Brands (2009)	89 brands valued at $1 tr.	9 brands valued at $110 bil.	None	51 brands (all American) at $726.4 bil.

* Total does not include Intra-EU27 + Norway & Switzerland trade

Sources: IMF, Bloomberg, UNCTAD, SIPRI, Interbrand, EIU
All data for 2008 otherwise noted

high wages and high labor and environmental standards. In addition, we continue to espouse the view that the transatlantic economy remains at the forefront of globalization—meaning that the commercial ties between the U.S. and Europe are deeper and thicker than between any other two continents, and that the policy challenges that stem from this deep integration affect the U.S. and Europe first. This is evident once again from this year's survey, which paints a picture of continuing prosperity for both parties.

In the end, the most recent data point to a transatlantic economy in flux and under a great deal of recessionary strain. In the near term, transatlantic economic prospects will closely mirror those of the global economy. That is not surprising given that the transatlantic economy is the largest economy in the world, and highly integrated and intertwined with the rest of the globe. In this context, the United States and Europe reaped major rewards as the transatlantic and global economy boomed over the past five years. The downside is that the current deceleration in global growth has not spared the transatlantic economy, and has already dampened transatlantic jobs, trade and investment.

Our outlook for 2010 is one of guarded optimism. The transatlantic economy is on the mend but its future health is not only dependent on the cyclical economic rebound underway. It also rests on more proactive, coordinated and forward-looking policy initiatives from policymakers and legislators. Just as we counsel caution about the notion of a China-America "G2," so do we hesitate to predict that the potential of "Eurmerica" will necessarily translate into continued Western leadership—for the scars of the financial crisis and economic recession cut deep, and it is also an open question whether the U.S. and Europe will stop spending significant political capital on such niggling transatlantic disputes as chlorine-washed chicken and state aid to industry and start investing in new forms of transatlantic collaboration that could enable them to be true pathfinders of the global economy, repositioning the West as it works to integrate others into effective mechanisms of global good governance.

Special Focus
The U.S. Dollar: America's Currency, Europe's Problem

In 1971, then U.S. Treasury Secretary John Connolly told his European counterparts: the dollar is our currency but your problem. Fast forward to today and Connolly's statement again rings true.

As the buck slumped in 2009, the euro became a favorite alternative to foreign investors and central banks. The holdings of euros among central banks rose to a record in the second quarter of last year, with the euro accounting for 27.8% of global currency reserves. Pleasing many in Europe, the euro's global stature has increased over the past year.

Less pleasing is the rising prospect of a strong euro derailing the continent's nascent economic recovery, should the dollar come under another bout of selling. The stronger the euro, the greater the pain for exporters and export-dependent countries. Yes, Europe's biggest companies are enjoying a rebound in exports to the emerging markets. However, the bulk of their global earnings are still tied to the one market where foreign investment ties are the deepest—the United States. Hence, a muscular euro relative to the greenback—which dilutes the earnings of U.S.-based European affiliates when profits are converted to euros—is notably detrimental to the bottom line of Corporate Europe.

All too mindful of the fragility of the eurozone's recovery, Jean-Claude Trichet, president of the European Central Bank, has become increasingly vocal about the dollar's slide. In mid-October, for instance, Mr. Trichet said the U.S. commitment to a strong dollar policy was "extremely important." That's true—but more for Europe than the United States.

The fact is the U.S. needs a weak dollar to generate export-led growth and to re-orient its economy away from rampant personal consumption. With the U.S. consumer saving more and spending less, dollar weakness over the medium-term is mandatory to global rebalancing. Washington policy makers know this and are not about to fiddle with success. Hence, "strong dollar" pledges ring hollow, especially when the Obama Administration has announced an ambitious new program to boost U.S. exports.

Besides, Trichet should direct more of his comments towards Asia, where various monetary authorities have intervened in the markets in recent months to support the dollar. Asian policymakers want to slow the pace of the dollar's decline in order to protect their export-dependent economies. In doing so, however, Asia is shifting the burden of the dollar's long-term slide and the brunt of global rebalancing onto Europe.

By various metrics, most of Asia's currencies are among the most undervalued in the world right now. In particular, with the Chinese yuan basically repegged to the U.S dollar, the slide in the dollar has coincided with a decline in the trade-weighted value of the yuan, making Chinese exports cheaper and imports more expense. The upshot: rising Chinese exports to Europe, which has triggered European anti-dumping investigations, among other things.

In the end, there remains a great deal of concern about the future path of the U.S. dollar. Although fears about the debt woes of southern European countries such as Greece prompted the euro to fall 9% against the dollar in January 2010, most investors expect the greenback to continue to weaken over the medium term, with America's precarious financial health the chief reason for concern. Hence, Europe's effort to talk up the U.S. dollar is likely to fail. Washington is comfortable with a weak currency as a means to promote exports, while Asia is not about to abandon its export-led growth model. That suggests that the burden of the dollar's adjustment will continue to weigh disproportionally on the euro and Europe.

Chapter 2

The Transatlantic Economy Today: The Eight Ties that Bind

Trade is the conventional yardstick by which opinion leaders and media commentators often measure and monitor economic interaction between countries. But trade alone is a misleading benchmark of international commerce. As we have highlighted in the past, it is foreign investment—the deepest form of global integration—that binds the transatlantic economy together, not trade. The latter, the cross-border movement of goods and services, is a shallow form of integration and often associated with the early phases or stages of bilateral commerce. In contrast, a relationship that rests on the foundation of foreign investment is one in which both parties are extensively embedded and entrenched in each other's economies. This is a relationship that creates more jobs, produces higher incomes, and generates greater wealth for both parties. The transatlantic economy epitomizes this type of economic integration. As such, American foreign affiliates in Europe are increasingly indistinguishable from local German, British, or Dutch firms, while European affiliates operating in the United States are barely distinguishable to U.S. consumers who enjoy European goods and services on a daily basis without much thought.

Moreover, these affiliates invest in local communities. European affiliates in the United States employ millions of American workers and are the largest source of onshored jobs in America. Similarly, U.S. corporate affiliates in Europe employ millions of European workers and are the largest source of onshored jobs in Britain, Ireland and across the continent.

There is no commercial artery in the world as large as the one binding the United States and Europe together. When one half of the transatlantic partnership suffers or goes into recession, like the United States in 2008, the other half suffers as well. The transatlantic economic recession has been deep and painful, and has yet to run its course. Of course, the reverse is also true: growth on one side of the Atlantic is good for the other. No two regions of the global economy are as economically fused as the two parties straddling the Atlantic, making the transatlantic economy the largest and wealthiest in the world.

That said, it has long been our contention that one of the most dangerous deficits affecting the transatlantic partnership is not one of trade, values, or military capabilities but rather a deficit in understanding among opinion leaders of the vital stakes Americans and Europeans have developed in the success of each other's respective economies.

Exports and imports have become the most common measurement of cross-border business between nations. Trade flows are relatively visible to most everyone. But is the unappreciated, invisible and little understood activities of foreign affiliates that represent the real backbone of the transatlantic economy. This is illustrated in the chart below. Taken together U.S. and European exports to the world accounted for only 27.1% of global exports in 2008; and combined U.S. and European imports accounted for 34.6% of global imports. But the U.S. and Europe together accounted for 61.7% of the inward stock of foreign direct investment (FDI), and a whopping 74.9% of outward stock of FDI. Moreover, each partner has built up the great majority of that stock in the other economy. In short, mutual

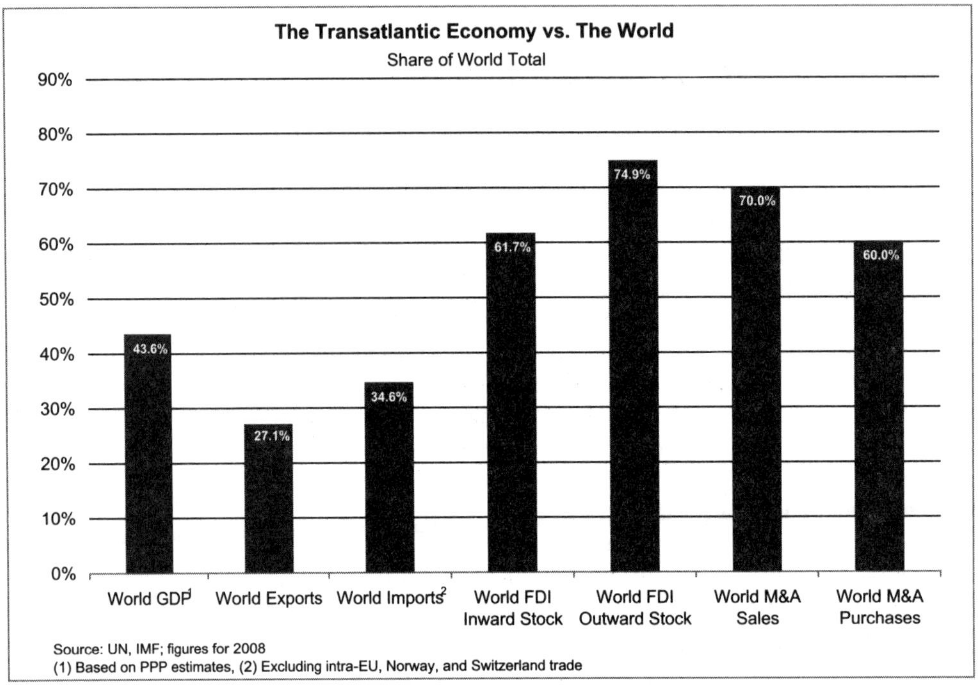

investment in the North Atlantic space is very large, dwarfs trade, and has become essential to U.S. and European jobs and prosperity.

The Ties that Bind—Quantifying the Transatlantic Economy

Foreign affiliates on both sides of the Atlantic have constructed a formidable commercial infrastructure over the past half century. Remarkably, notwithstanding all the stress and strain on the transatlantic partnership over the past decade, this infrastructure remains solid and dynamic. Even in the face of the transatlantic recession of 2008-2009, we expect the transatlantic foundation to remain firm.

Over the past few years we have suggested eight key indices that offer a clearer picture of the "deep integration" forces shaping the transatlantic economy. This chapter updates those indices with the latest available data. Each variable, in general, grew in size and importance from our last survey, although in the face of the transatlantic recession of 2008-2009, many of the variables discussed below are in a state of flux and have contracted in the face of the economic downturn of the past year. This is to be expected, and as the transatlantic economy rebounds in 2010, so will many of the metrics below.

1. Gross Product of Foreign Affiliates

In their own right, U.S. affiliates in Europe and European affiliates in the United States are among the largest economic forces in the world. For instance, the total output of U.S. foreign affiliates in Europe ($611 billion in 2007) and of European affiliates in the U.S. ($412

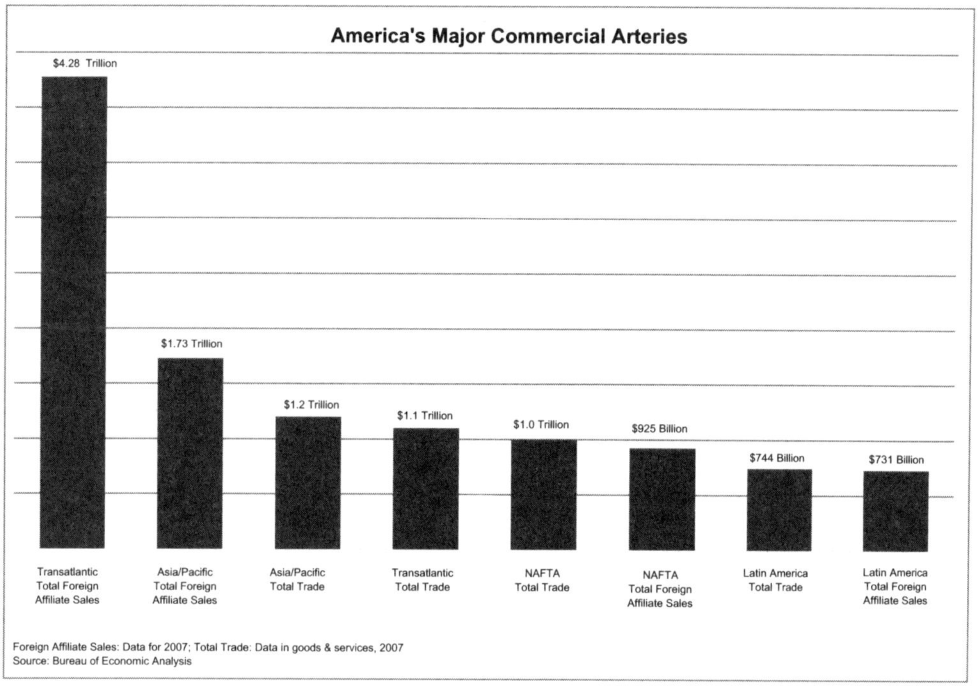

billion) is greater than the total gross domestic output of most nations. Combined, transatlantic foreign affiliate output rose 7% from the prior year and up 21% from the levels of 2000. The total output of transatlantic foreign affiliates is equivalent to the aggregate output of such nations as South Korea, the Netherlands, or Switzerland.

On a global basis, aggregate output of U.S. affiliates reached nearly $1.12 trillion in 2007, with Europe accounting for roughly 55% of the total. The latter figure was up slightly from the prior year. The United Kingdom, where U.S. investment ties are among the deepest, accounted for 28% of total affiliate output in Europe, followed by Germany (14%) and France (9%). These three nations accounted for more than half of total U.S. affiliate output in Europe in 2007. By sector, output was almost evenly split between services and manufacturing output.

The presence of U.S. affiliates in some European nations is particularly noteworthy. The gross output of American affiliates in Ireland, for instance, represented 21% of Ireland's total output in 2007, roughly unchanged from the prior year. This dynamic reflects, in part, the large U.S. investment base, notably among U.S. technology companies, in the "Celtic Tiger." It also underscores the point that the U.S. and Ireland are joined at the economic hip, a favorable pole position for Ireland when the U.S. economy is expanding. However, as the U.S. economy has slumped over the past two years, the knock-on effects have been painful for Ireland. U.S. affiliates in Ireland are in the process of trimming their workforce and deferring additional capital spending, trends that have added to Ireland's already weak economy. Such are the ties that bind the U.S. together with many European states like Ireland.

Elsewhere, U.S. affiliates accounted for 6.2% of the United Kingdom's aggregate output in 2007, 6.7% of Switzerland's, and 5.2% of Belgium's total output. Regarding the latter, it is interesting to note that U.S. foreign affiliate output in Belgium in 2007 ($23.7 billion) was some 6% larger than U.S. foreign affiliate output in China in 2007 ($22.4 billion) and more than three times as large as affiliate output in India ($7.32 billion). Reflecting the rising presence of U.S. affiliates in Hungary, U.S. affiliate output accounted for 3.6% of the host nation's GDP in 2007, up from 3% the prior year. U.S. affiliate output in Poland, meanwhile, jumped 29% in 2007, to $8.5 billion, after rising 12% in 2006, to $6.4 billion, exceeding U.S. output in more developed markets like Austria, Portugal, and Denmark.

In the United States, European affiliates are major economic producers in their own right, with British firms of notable importance. Their U.S. output reached nearly $118 billion in 2007, or nearly 30% of the total. Output from German affiliates operating in the U.S. totaled $86 billion, up nearly 20% from a year earlier, while output from French affiliates rose nearly 5% to $61 billion in 2007. Beyond European affiliates, only Corporate Japan has any real economic presence in the United States—Japanese affiliate output totaled $81.4 billion in 2007, well below output from British affiliates and to a lesser degree, output from German affiliates. Overall, foreign affiliates contributed nearly $658 billion to U.S. aggregate production in 2007, with European affiliates accounting for nearly two-thirds of the total.

2. Assets of Foreign Affiliates

America's global commercial presence has never been larger, with aggregate foreign assets of corporate America totaling over $13 trillion in 2007. That represents a rise of 17% from the prior year. The bulk of these assets—roughly 63%—were located in Europe, with the largest share, by far, in the United Kingdom. U.S. assets in the latter totaled $3.5 trillion in 2007, roughly one-quarter of the global total, and an amount greater than total combined U.S. assets in South America, Africa and the Middle East.

U.S. assets in the Netherlands ($1.3 trillion) were the second largest in the world in 2007 (after the United Kingdom). America's sizable asset base in the Netherlands reflects the host nation's strategic role as an export platform/distribution hub for U.S. firms doing busi-

Global Engagement: Foreign Affiliate Sales vs. Trade

$ billions, 2007	U.S. Foreign Affiliate Sales vs. Trade
Global Sales of U.S.-owned Affiliates[1] (G&S)	4,736.0
Total U.S. Exports (G&S)	1,643.2
U.S. Sales of Foreign-owned Affiliates[1]	3,013.3
Total U.S. Imports (G&S)	2,344.6
European Sales of U.S.-owned Affiliates[1]	2,488.8
U.S. Exports to Europe (G&S)	487.5
U.S. Sales of European-owned Affiliates[1]	1,785.8
U.S. Imports from Europe (G&S)	577.5

Source: Bureau of Economic Analysis

[1] Majority-owned nonbank affiliates

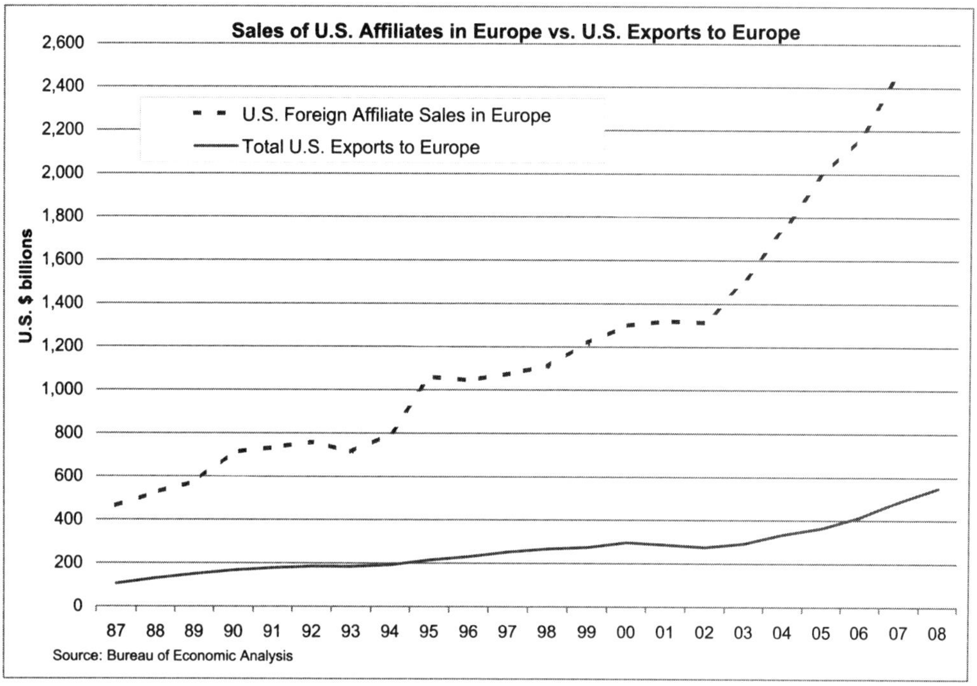

ness in the rest of the European Union. To this point, more than half of affiliate sales in the Netherlands are for export, namely within the EU. Meanwhile, America's asset base in Germany ($613 billion) was nearly double the base of South America in 2006. The collective asset base in Poland, Hungary, and the Czech Republic (roughly $65 billion) was twice the size of corporate America's assets in India.

As for foreign-owned assets in the United States, Europe's stakes are sizable and continue to expand. In 2007 European firms held some $9.1 trillion in U.S. assets, a figure that include bank and non-bank affiliates. That equates to roughly three-quarters of total foreign assets in the United States. The United Kingdom ranked first as the largest holder of U.S. assets in 2007 ($2.2 trillion), followed closely behind by Swiss firms ($2 trillion). France and Germany ranked third and fourth, respectively, in 2006.

3. Affiliate Employment

The common perspective is that when it comes to hiring workers overseas, the bulk of corporate America's overseas work forces toils in the developing nations. Reality is different. Most foreign workers on the payrolls of U.S. foreign affiliates are employed in the industrialized nations, notably Europe.

Out of a global overseas workforce of 10 million people employed by U.S. majority-owned affiliates in 2007, roughly 42% were located in Europe. The bulk of these workers were based in the United Kingdom, Germany and France. The European workforce of U.S. majority-owned foreign affiliates was almost evenly split between manufacturing and serv-

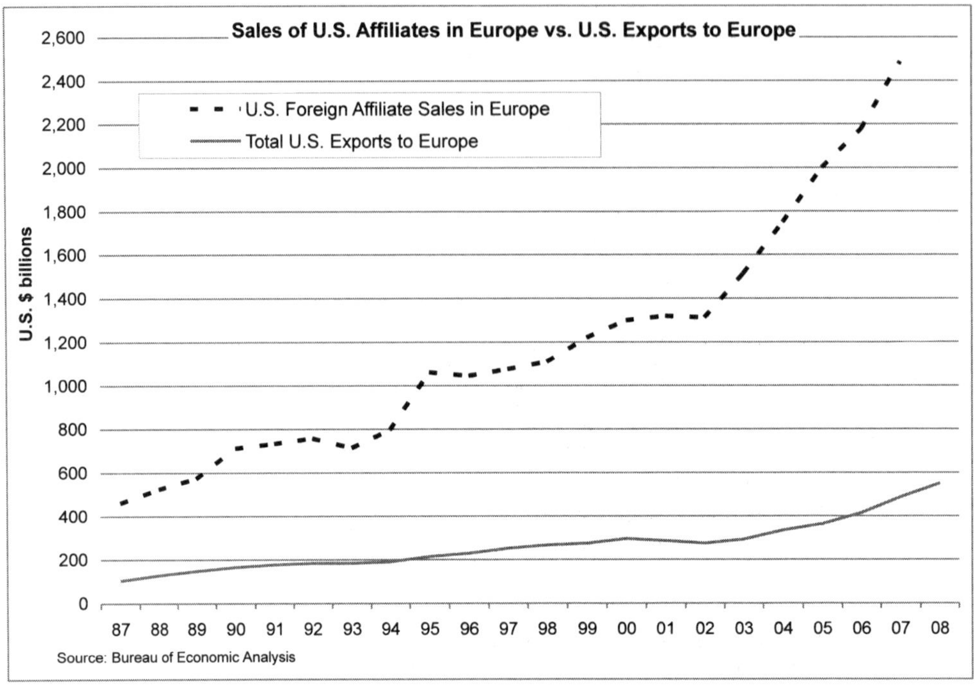

ice workers. That said, it is interesting to note that U.S. affiliates employed just as many manufacturing workers in Europe (1.9 million) in 2007 as they did in 1990. However, while the aggregate number has stayed the same, the geographic distribution of U.S. manufacturing employment in Europe has shifted over the past fifty years. In general, the shift has been towards lower cost locations like Ireland, at the expense of the United Kingdom and Germany. Between 1990 and 2007, for instance, U.S. affiliate manufacturing employment in the United Kingdom and Germany fell by roughly 32% and 18%, respectively. Meanwhile, manufacturing employment in Ireland soared 30% over the same period. However, even with the decline of manufacturing employment in Germany, the manufacturing workforce of U.S. affiliates in Germany alone totaled 372,000 workers in 2007, not far from the number of manufactured workers employed in China by U.S. affiliates (402,800).

The transportation equipment sector continued to be the largest source of manufactured employment in Europe; wholesale employment was among the largest sources of service-related employment, which includes employment in such areas as logistics, trade, insurance and other service-related activities.

When it comes to affiliate employment, trends in the United States are similar to those in Europe. In other words, despite stories on the continent about local European companies decamping for cheap labor markets in central Europe or Asia, most foreigners working for European companies outside the EU are American. European majority-owned bank and nonbank foreign affiliates directly employed roughly 3.6 million U.S. workers in 2007.[1] The

[1] These figures are for majority-owned bank and nonbank affiliates. All tables in chapter 4 show data for majority-owned nonbank affiliates only, except for UK and Switzerland, which show employment for majority-owned bank and nonbank affiliates.

The U.S. - European Employment Balance
Thousands of employees, 2007

Country	European Affiliates[1] of U.S. Companies	U.S. Affiliates[1] of European Companies	Employment Balance
Austria	39.6	13.3	-26.3
Belgium	127.4	140.5	+13.1
Denmark	37.8	24.4	-13.4
Finland	23.6	26.6	+3.0
France	616.1	500.1	-116.0
Germany	610.6	639.2	+28.6
Ireland	92.9	67.5	-25.4
Italy	243.1	114.7	-128.4
Luxembourg	12.9	30.2	+17.3
Netherlands	223.8	386.5	+162.7
Norway	32.9	7.7	-25.2
Spain	197.1	40.1	-157.0
Switzerland	83.0	n.a.	n.a.
United Kingdom	1,191.9	n.a.	n.a.
Europe	4,184.5	3,474.9	-709.6

Note: Employment balance "+" favors the United States
Source: Bureau of Economic Analysis
[1] Majority-owned non-bank affiliates

top five employers in the U.S. were firms from the United Kingdom (949,300), Germany (653,900), France (516,000), the Netherlands (391,200) and Switzerland (396,900). European firms employed more than two-thirds of the 5.5 million U.S. workers on the payrolls of majority-owned bank and nonbank foreign affiliates in 2007.

In the aggregate, the transatlantic workforce directly employed by all U.S. and European foreign affiliates in 2007 was roughly 8.7 million strong. That said, as we have stressed in our last survey, these figures understate the employment effects of mutual investment flows, since these numbers are limited to direct employment, and do not account for indirect employment effects of nonequity arrangements such as strategic alliances, joint ventures and other deals. Moreover, affiliate employment figures do not include jobs supported by transatlantic trade flows. Trade-related employment is substantial in many U.S. states and many European regions.

In total, and adding in indirect employment, we estimate that the transatlantic work force numbers some 12-14 million workers. Europe is by far the most important source of "onshored" jobs in America, and the U.S. is by far the most important source of "onshored" jobs in Europe.

4. Research and Development (R&D) of Foreign Affiliates

While most multinationals still tend to cluster their R&D expenditures and activities in their home country, foreign affiliate R&D has become more prominent over the past decade as firms seek to share development costs, spread risks and tap into the intellectual talent of other nations. Alliances, cross-licensing of intellectual property, mergers and acquisitions and other forms of cooperation have become more prevalent characteristics of the transatlantic economy in the past decade. The internet, in particular, has powered greater transatlantic R&D.

Research and development among U.S. foreign affiliates totaled $35 billion in 2007. The bulk of such activity was carried out in the developed nations, where the largest pool of skilled labor resides. In 2007, U.S. affiliates sank $23 billion in research and development in Europe, or nearly 66% of total U.S. R&D expenditures abroad. The United Kingdom, Germany, France, and Sweden represented markets where R&D expenditures by U.S. affiliates were greatest. These four nations accounted for roughly 45% of U.S. global spending on R&D in 2007.

In the United States, meanwhile, expenditures on R&D performed by majority-owned non-bank foreign affiliates totaled nearly $40 billion in 2007, up nearly 15% from the prior year and accounting for roughly 15% of total R&D spending in the U.S. A significant share (78%) emanated from world-class leaders from Europe, given their interests in America's highly skilled labor force and first-class university infrastructure. Most of this investment took place among European firms in such research-intensive sectors as energy, chemicals, telecommunications, and automobiles. By country, British-owned affiliates ranked as the number one foreign source of R&D in the United States in 2007. British R&D in the U.S. totaled $10.5 billion in 2007, up roughly 50% from the prior year, accounting for 26% of total affiliate R&D in the United States. Swiss-owned affiliates accounted for the second largest percentage of affiliate R&D expenditures, with a 15% share in 2007. R&D of German affiliates came in third, totaling $5.6 billion (14%), and was mainly concentrated in transportation equipment, pharmaceuticals and machinery.

5. Intra-Firm Trade of Foreign Affiliates

While we have frequently highlighted the fact that cross-border trade is a secondary means of delivering goods and services across the Atlantic, the modes of delivery—affiliate sales and trade—should not be viewed independently. They are more complements than substitutes, since foreign investment and affiliate sales increasingly drive cross-border trade flows. Indeed, a substantial share of transatlantic trade is considered intra-firm trade or related-party trade, which is cross-border trade that stays within the ambit of the company.

For instance, it is trade involving BMW or Mercedes of Germany sending parts to BMW of South Carolina or Mercedes of Alabama, or when LaFarage or Michelin send intermedi-

Related Party Trade, 2008

	US Imports: "Related Party Trade," as % of Total	US Exports: "Related Party Trade," as % of Total
European Union	59.7	31.2
Germany	66.8	35.7
France	51.1	31.8
Ireland	88.7	29.7
Netherlands	64.8	45.4
United Kingdom	56.2	23.7

Source: U.S. Census Bureau

ate components to their plants in the Greater Cincinnati area, or when 3M ships components for its office products or communications sectors from St. Paul to affiliates in Germany or UK. The tight linkages between European parent companies and their U.S. affiliates is reflected in the fact nearly 60% of U.S. imports from the European Union consisted of related party trade in 2008. The percentage was even higher in the case of Germany (67%). Meanwhile, roughly 31% of U.S. exports to the EU in 2008 represented related-party trade. 45% of total U.S. exports to the Netherlands in 2008 was classified as related-party trade.

6. Foreign Affiliate Sales

U.S. foreign affiliate sales (goods and services) were nearly $5 trillion in 2007, well in excess of U.S. exports of $1.6 trillion. Europe accounted for more than half of total global foreign affiliate sales, with sales topping $2.8 trillion in 2007, up 15% from the prior year. Reflecting just how important Europe is to corporate America, sale of U.S. affiliates in Europe were roughly double comparable sales in the entire Asia/Pacific region. Affiliate sales in the United Kingdom ($672 billion) exceeded aggregate sales in Latin America. While U.S. affiliate sales in China have soared over the past decade, they do so from a low base, and still remain well below comparable sales in Europe. For instance, U.S. affiliate sales of $146 billion in China in 2007 were slightly below sales to Italy ($155 billion) and well below those in Germany ($357 billion) or France ($228 billion).

Affiliate sales are also the primary means by which European firms deliver goods and services to consumers in the United States. In 2007, for instance, majority-owned nonbank European affiliate sales in the U.S. ($1.8 trillion) were roughly three times larger than U.S. imports from Europe ($577 billion). In the case of Germany, foreign affiliate sales in the United States totaled $383 billion in 2007, nearly three times U.S. imports of goods and services from Germany the same year. For virtually all nations in Europe, foreign affiliate sales were easily in excess of their U.S. imports in 2007.

7. Foreign Affiliate Profits

The transatlantic economy enjoyed a profits boom between 2002 and 2007, but the tide turned in the second half of 2007 and into 2008. Looking just at 2008, U.S. affiliates in Europe earned a $173 billion, down slightly from 2007 but more than three times the level of the cyclical lows of 2001, when slow growth on both sides of the Atlantic resulted in a transatlantic profits downturn. In the first half of 2008, U.S. affiliate income from Europe rose 9% from the same period a year ago but then the bottom fell out—affiliate income plunged along with the economic downturn that swept Europe in late 2008. The profits picture was not any prettier in 2009—indeed, in the first nine months of 2009 versus the same period a year earlier, affiliate income earned in Europe plummeted 25%, with steep declines registered in most major markets. A slight rebound is expected in 2010, helped by Europe's economic recovery and the general weakness of the dollar relative to the euro. However, we do not expect affiliate profits to reach their pre-crisis levels until 2011 or 2012. That said, on a global basis, Europe remains the most profitable region of the world for U.S. multinationals, with Europe accounting for half of total global affiliate earnings in 2007 and 2008.

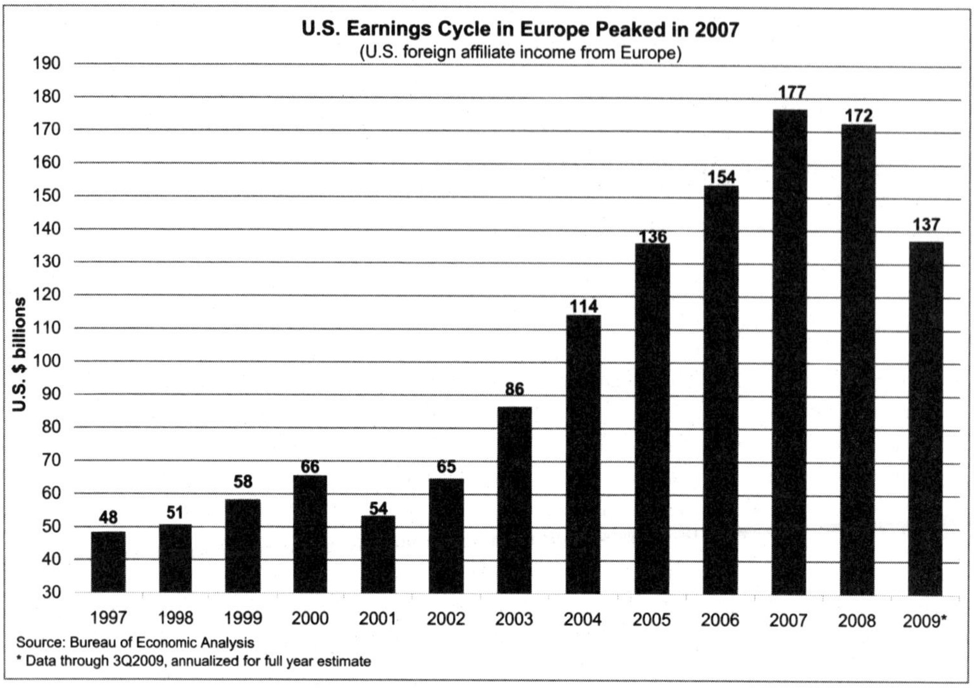

Just how important Europe is to the global earnings of U.S. multinationals is reflected by the following: in 2008, U.S. affiliate income from Europe was more than double the total earnings from Latin America and Asia. It is interesting to note that combined U.S. affiliate income from China and India in 2008 ($7.7 billion) was nearly 20% less than what affiliates earned in Germany ($9.4 billion) in the same year. Affiliates earned nearly three times in Ireland in 2008 than they did in India and China combined, although affiliate income in Ireland is expected to have declined last year. The affiliate earnings environment, on both sides of the Atlantic, will be very challenging in 2010.

Similarly, the United States remains the most important market in the world in terms of earnings for many European multinationals. Profits of European foreign affiliates in the United States actually rose by 19% in 2008, but fells by almost the same amount in 2009. As the U.S. economy has struggled over 2009 and U.S. corporate earnings have decelerated, the earnings of many European affiliates have deteriorated in line with their U.S. counterparts.

8. Transatlantic Service Linkages

As we have remarked in the past, services in particular represent the sleeping giant of the transatlantic economy, or the one key area where there exists significant opportunities to strengthen and deepen transatlantic commercial ties.[2]

[2] For a closer examination of the transatlantic services economy, see Daniel S. Hamilton and Joseph P. Quinlan, eds., *Sleeping Giant: Awakening the Transatlantic Services Economy* (Washington, DC: Center for Transatlantic Relations, 2007).

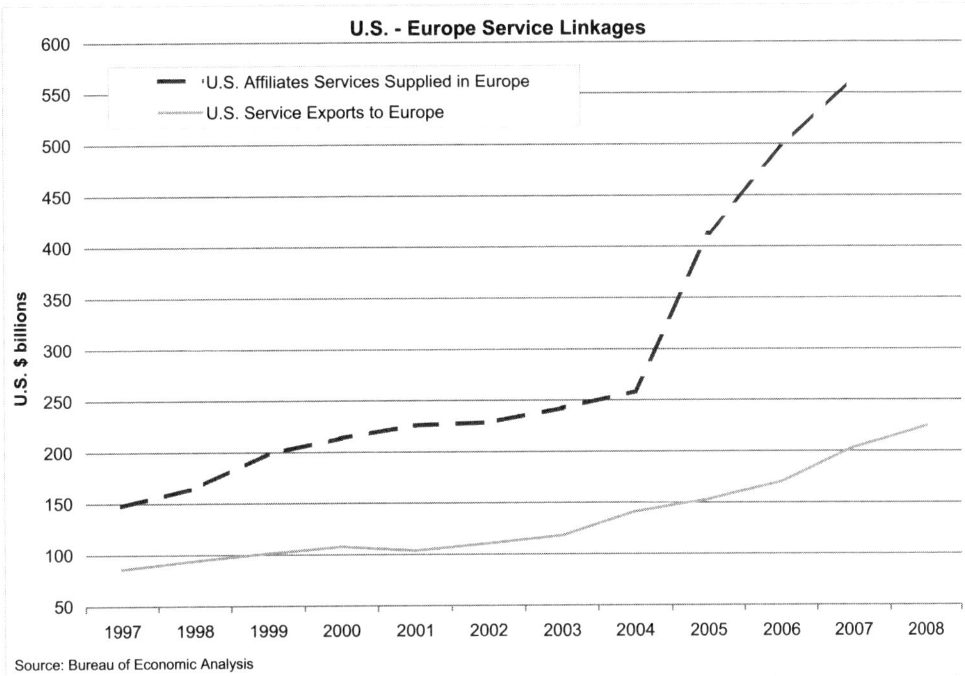

The services economies of the United States and Europe have become even more intertwined over the past year, with cross-border trade in services and sales through affiliates posting strong gains in the past year. By sector, transatlantic linkages continue to deepen in financial services, insurance, education, telecommunications, utilities, advertising, and computer services. Sectors such as aviation are gradually being liberalized and deregulated.

Starting with trade in services, five out of the top ten export markets for U.S. services in 2007 (the last year of available data) were in Europe. The United Kingdom ranked Number 1, followed by Germany (4th), Ireland (6th), France (7th), and Switzerland (8th). Thanks to a variety of factors—stronger growth, the weaker dollar, EU enlargement, industry reform and deregulation—U.S. services exports to Europe more than doubled between 1998 and 2008, rising from around $99 billion to nearly $230 billion in 2008. The bulk of these gains were in exports of "other private services," or in such value-added activities like computer processing, engineering, advertising and related activities. In this category, the U.S. posted a $51 billion trade surplus with Europe in 2008.

U.S. services imports from Europe, meanwhile, expanded just as fast as exports in the last decade. Imports doubled between 1998 and 2008, climbing from $79 billion to $133 billion in 2007. The same five nations that ranked in the top ten U.S. export markets also ranked among the top ten services providers to the U.S. On a regional basis, Europe accounted for 43% of total U.S. services exports and for 44% of total U.S. services imports in 2008.

Meanwhile, while the U.S. recorded a $120 billion deficit in goods exports with Europe in 2008, nearly 47% of the goods deficit was offset by America's $51 billion surplus in services. That was up substantially from the year before ($42 billion). The U.S. enjoys a sizable sur-

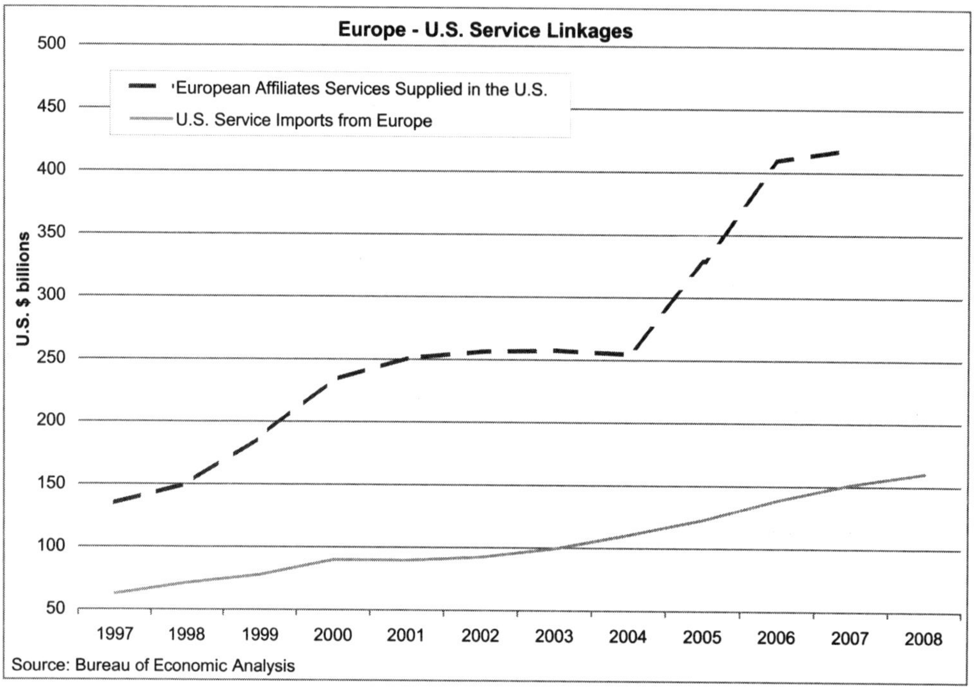

plus in "other private services," notably in activities associated with "business, professional and technical services." By activity, the U.S. registered a surplus in financial services, computer and information services, management consulting, legal services, construction engineering, and operational leasing with Europe in 2008.

Beyond trade, there are the foreign affiliate sales of services, or the delivery of transatlantic services by U.S. and European foreign affiliates. Sales of affiliates have exploded on both sides of the Atlantic over the past decade; indeed, affiliate sales of services have not only supplemented trade in services but also become the overwhelming mode of delivery in a rather short period of time.

Sales of services of U.S. foreign affiliate in the European Union rose again in 2007, the last year of available data. Sales rose to a record $565 billion, nearly double the level in 2002; meanwhile services sales were nearly triple U.S. service exports to Europe in the same year. The United Kingdom accounts for the bulk of U.S. services sales in Europe. In 2007, the UK accounted for around 38% of all U.S. affiliate sales of services in Europe. On a global basis, Europe accounted for 55% of total U.S. services sales.

Again, U.S. affiliate sales of services in the EU exceeded sales of services by U.S. affiliates of European firms. The latter totaled $419 billion in 2007. However, on a country basis, French, German, and Dutch affiliates sold more services in the U.S. in 2007 than American affiliates sold in France, Germany, and the Netherlands. Of particular note, European affiliate sales of services were nearly triple U.S. services imports—a fact that underscores the ever widening presence of European services leaders in the U.S. economy.

America's FDI Roots in Europe
(Billions of $)

Industry	US FDI to Europe	% of Industry Total
European Total	1,810	57%
Mining	39	25%
Manufacturing	260	51%
Food	27	66%
Chemicals	62	58%
Primary and fabricated metals	13	53%
Machinery	22	59%
Computers and electronic products	28	37%
Electrical equipment, appliances, and components	16	67%
Transportation equipment	24	46%
Wholesale trade	100	56%
Information	81	66%
Depository institutions	81	57%
Finance (except depository institutions) and insurance	328	52%
Professional, scientific, and technical services	54	66%
Other industries	117	55%

Europe's FDI Roots in the US
(Billions of $)

Industry	US FDI from Europe	% of Industry Total
Total from Europe	1,623	71%
Manufacturing	618	78%
Food	20	77%
Chemicals	190	87%
Primary and fabricated metals	37	75%
Machinery	51	67%
Computers and electronic products	41	65%
Electrical equipment, appliances, and components	19	81%
Transportation equipment	26	40%
Wholesale trade	168	54%
Retail trade	28	64%
Information	142	90%
Depository institutions	71	60%
Finance (except depository institutions) and insurance	178	71%
Real estate and rental and leasing	20	38%
Professional, scientific, and technical services	49	79%
Other industries	349	72%

Note: Historical-cost basis, 2008
Source: Bureau of Economic Analysis

In the end, these eight indices convey a more complete and complex picture of global engagement than simple tallies of exports and imports. Foreign direct investment and foreign affiliate sales, not trade, represent the backbone of the transatlantic economy. The eight variables just highlighted underscore the depth and breadth of U.S.-European bilateral relations.

Chapter 3

European Commerce and the 50 States: A State-by-State Comparison

Not unexpectedly, capital inflows from Europe to the United States plunged in 2009, a consequence of the U.S. financial crisis and economic recession. With the transatlantic economy reeling from what the IMF has called a "once-in-a-century event," both U.S. and European corporations pared their capital outlays at home and abroad in 2009. Due to a steep decline in final demand, depressed corporate earnings, and tight credit conditions, foreign direct investment from Europe to the United States plunged 48% in the first nine months of 2009 from the same period a year earlier.

As the accompanying chart illustrates, the declines were broadly based by country, with notably steep declines registered among such nations as the United Kingdom, Switzerland, and the Netherlands. Inflows from France were nearly flat at +0.1%. Inflows from Germany bucked the trend, however, rising 96%, but that was not enough to offset overall declines from Europe.

Notwithstanding the cyclical decline in investment in the recession-racked United States, Corporate Europe's capital stock in the United States remains quite extensive and expansive. European investment in the U.S. (measured as the stock of gross property, plant and

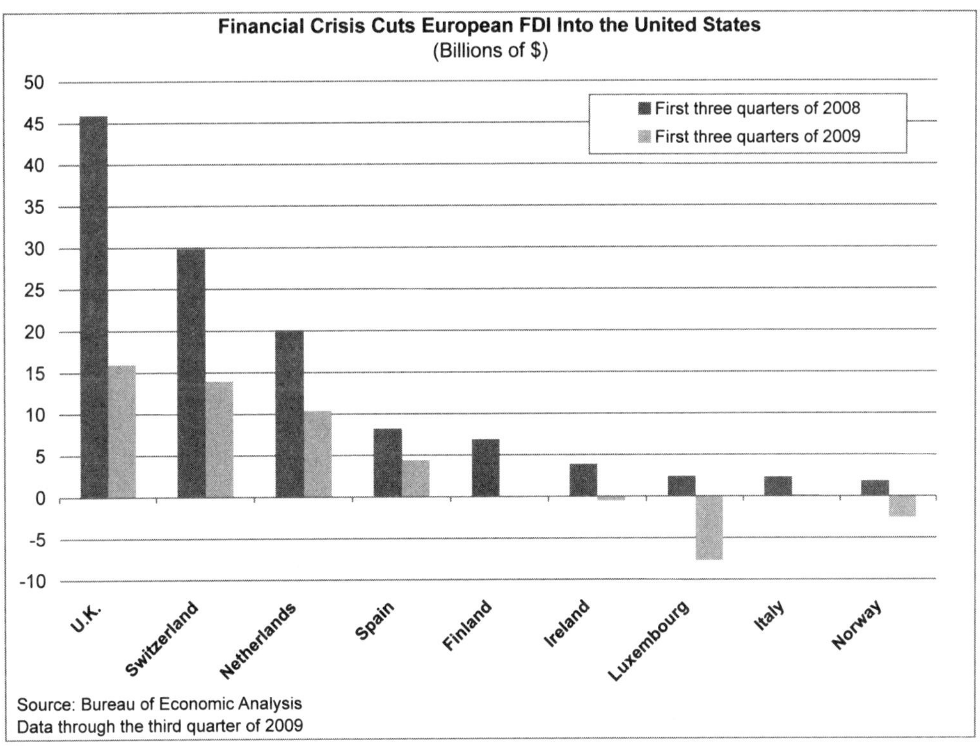

equipment owned by European[1] foreign affiliates in the United States) totaled $623.5 billion in 2007, the last year of available data. Another variable that measures Europe's investment stock in the U.S.—foreign investment based on a historic cost basis—portrays an even larger presence. In 2008, for instance, Europe's investment stakes in the U.S. totaled a record $1.6 trillion, a 7.6% rise from 2007 and nearly double the level a decade earlier. Corporate Europe accounted for 71% of total foreign direct investment (FDI) in the U.S. in 2008 ($2.3 trillion). Over the entire last decade, European firms invested roughly $1.2 trillion into the United States, roughly double aggregate investment over the 1990s. Whereas Europe accounted for roughly 76% of total U.S. investment inflows over the 1990-1999 period, Europe's share declined slightly to 73% in the last decade. FDI inflows from just the major European countries alone account for over half of total FDI into every region of the United States except the Rocky Mountains (41.6%) and the Far West (31.7%).

Nonetheless, no other region of the world has invested as much in the United States nor created as many American jobs as Corporate Europe, a state of affairs we don't expect to change any time soon. "Onshoring" by foreign companies, i.e., supporting American jobs, represents an integral part of the U.S. economy.

That said, at the regional and state level, Europe's investment stock in the U.S. continues to ebb and flow. Corporate Europe's investment position is in constant flux, reflecting general economic conditions in the U.S., as well as industry- and company-specific dynamics. Not surprisingly, as the U.S. recession unfolded in 2008 and lingered in 2009, various European firms with operations in the United States had to adjust to a much more difficult operating environment. When economic circumstances change, so too do the strategies of firms.

While our figures include 2007, the last year of available data, we have little doubt that Europe's investment at the U.S. state and local level underwent dramatic change over the last two years. Some regions and states are losing European investment, or seeing their stock of investment decline, while others are seeing their stock of investment gain. These shifts of investment can be quite significant for local communities.

European Investment in the United States: Regional, Industry and State Preferences

European investment can be found in all fifty states, although at the regional level, the bias remains towards the Southeast and Mideast areas of the country. Together the two regions account for one-third of all EU FDI in the United States. The Southeast's share of European[2] investment was roughly 17% in 2007, up from a share of 16.2% the year before. Overall the Southeast remains the most attractive investment destination for many European firms due to attractive land costs, relatively low unit labor costs, minimal union participation, first-class infrastructure and aggressive state incentives (including tax holidays in many cases). The Mideast also registered an increase in its share of European investment, with the region attracting 16.6% of total European investment in 2007 versus a share of

---

1 European investment includes France, Germany, Netherlands, Switzerland, and the United Kingdom. Due to a need to align resources with current funding levels, the U.S. Bureau of Economic Analysis has reduced its coverage to major investing countries.

2 Year-over-year comparisons only include investment from France, Germany, Netherlands, Switzerland, and the United Kingdom in order to keep the comparisons consistent.

European* Foreign Direct Investment in the U.S.
By geographic region, 2007

Region	U.S. $ billions	% of Total European* Investment	% of Total FDI in the Region
Southeast	105.5	16.9%	55.8%
Mideast	103.4	16.6%	56.6%
Great Lakes	71.6	11.5%	55.4%
Southwest	63.1	10.1%	43.1%
Far West	61.2	9.8%	31.7%
New England	29.1	4.7%	50.1%
Plains	19.8	3.2%	56.0%
Rocky Mountains	9.6	1.5%	41.6%

Source: Bureau of Economic Analysis

*European direct investment includes France, Germany, Netherlands, Switzerland, and the United Kingdom
Due to a need to align resources with current funding levels, the U.S. Bureau of Economic Analysis has reduced its coverage to major investing countries.

14.4% in 2006. The Mideast is particularly attractive for financial services, pharmaceuticals and R&D intensive investments.

The share of the Great Lakes continues to fall and dropped significantly in 2007. In 2006, the Great Lakes accounted for 15.4% of total European investment in the United States, but in 2007 its share plunged to 11.5%. The decline reflects the consolidation and the rationalization of the U.S. auto industry over the past few years, with many European automobile affiliates part of the process. The de-merging of DaimlerChrysler is one example of this dynamic, resulting in less European capital stock in the Great Lakes region. Given all of the above, it is noteworthy that three regions of the U.S. (the Southeast, Mideast, and Great Lakes) accounted for roughly 45% of total European investment in 2007.

Reflecting past trends, British, French and German foreign investors remain the largest and most prominent European investors in the United States. On a state-by-state basis, Canada was the top foreign investor in fifteen U.S. states in this year's survey, followed by Japan, number one in twelve states. The United Kingdom and Germany tied for third, number one in ten states, followed by France, which was number one in three states.

The geographic preference of French and German firms was the Southeast in 2007. Over the course of the past decade German firms have shifted their overall investment preferences from the Great Lakes to the Southeast. British firms showed a strong bias towards the Mideast and Great Lakes. In addition to these regional nuances, the rate of investment also varied by nationality. For instance, in 2007, German investment in U.S. property, plant and equipment fell 17.6% from the prior year; meanwhile, French investment climbed 12.3%, while investment from British firms rose 13%.

British affiliates operating in the U.S. increased their American payrolls by 7.4% in 2007, with some 949,300 U.S. jobs directly provided by British firms. French affiliates increased their U.S. payrolls by 3.6% in 2007, directly providing 516,000 jobs for U.S.-based workers. Employment levels among German affiliates fell 7.1%, but German companies still directly employed 653,900 U.S-based workers. Most Americans employed by European affiliates work in the services sector, and that is where most growth in European-sourced U.S. employment over the past decade has come from.

Gross Property, Plant, and Equipment of French Affiliates* in U.S. Regions, 2007
(Millions of $, % of total in region)

Southeast	18,613	10%
Mideast	15,824	9%
Southwest	12,664	9%
Great Lakes	8,207	6%
Far West	7,095	4%
Plains	3,735	11%
New England	2,997	5%
Rocky Mountains	1,003	4%
Total	74,542	6%

Source: Bureau of Economic Analysis

Overall Direct Employment of French Affiliates* in U.S. Regions, 2007
(Thousands of employees, % of total in region)

Mideast	117.5	11%
Southeast	114.7	9%
Great Lakes	78.9	9%
Far West	75.4	9%
Southwest	53.2	10%
New England	31.5	8%
Plains	25.9	8%
Rocky Mountains	17.6	12%
Total	516.0	9%

Source: Bureau of Economic Analysis

Manufacturing Employment of French Affiliates* in U.S. Regions, 2007
(Thousands of employees, % of total in region)

Southeast	46.0	10%
Great Lakes	24.2	7%
Mideast	20.1	10%
Far West	19.9	11%
Southwest	14.5	12%
New England	8.9	11%
Plains	7.6	6%
Rocky Mountains	2.5	7%
Total	144.0	9%

Source: Bureau of Economic Analysis
* All majority-owned affiliates

Gross Property, Plant, and Equipment of German Affiliates* in U.S. Regions, 2007
(Millions of $, % of total in region)

Southeast	44,358	23%
Mideast	32,479	18%
Great Lakes	22,783	18%
Far West	16,828	9%
Southwest	15,667	11%
Plains	6,999	20%
New England	3,837	7%
Rocky Mountains	1,023	4%
Total	199,493	16%

Source: Bureau of Economic Analysis

Overall Direct Employment of German Affiliates* in U.S. Regions, 2007
(Thousands of employees, % of total in region)

Southeast	160.5	12%
Mideast	140.3	13%
Great Lakes	130.1	15%
Far West	94.0	12%
Southwest	48.4	9%
New England	34.6	9%
Plains	33.1	11%
Rocky Mountains	11.2	7%
Total	653.9	12%

Source: Bureau of Economic Analysis

Manufacturing Employment of German Affiliates* in U.S. Regions, 2007
(Thousands of employees, % of total in region)

Southeast	66.8	14%
Great Lakes	45.6	14%
Mideast	24.3	12%
Far West	14.6	8%
New England	13.8	17%
Plains	10.7	9%
Southwest	7.9	7%
Rocky Mountains	0.7	2%
Total	187.9	12%

Source: Bureau of Economic Analysis

Gross Property, Plant, and Equipment of British Affiliates* in U.S. Regions, 2007
(Millions of $, % of total in region)

Mideast	33,767	18%
Great Lakes	31,547	24%
Southeast	24,230	13%
Southwest	20,989	14%
Far West	18,236	9%
New England	12,612	22%
Plains	4,478	13%
Rocky Mountains	4,325	19%
Total	221,265	17%

Source: Bureau of Economic Analysis

Overall Direct Employment of British Affiliates* in U.S. Regions, 2007
(Thousands of employees, % of total in region)

Mideast	217.6	20%
Southeast	197.3	15%
Great Lakes	169.5	19%
Far West	123.2	15%
Southwest	92.6	17%
New England	67.2	18%
Plains	47.6	15%
Rocky Mountains	27.8	19%
Total	949.3	17%

Source: Bureau of Economic Analysis

Manufacturing Employment of British Affiliates* in U.S. Regions, 2007
(Thousands of employees, % of total in region)

Great Lakes	57.8	17%
Southeast	42.8	9%
Mideast	33.6	17%
Far West	26.7	15%
Southwest	22.2	19%
Plains	14.1	12%
New England	9.9	12%
Rocky Mountains	4.3	12%
Total	219.1	14%

Source: Bureau of Economic Analysis

While services-sector jobs predominate, British manufacturing employment in the U.S. rose to 219,100 workers in 2007 from 211,200 the year before. Yet French affiliates decreased their U.S. manufacturing workforce by 3%, and German affiliates cut their U.S. manufacturing workforce by a whopping 22.5% in 2007; the German figure certainly reflects the de-merging of DaimlerChrysler.

As we noted earlier in this chapter, the data we are highlighting are for 2007; given the U.S. recession of 2008-2009, we highly suspect that most foreign affiliates in the United States have pared their American work forces further over the past twelve months. Indeed, with the U.S. employment hovering at 10%, there is little doubt the rising ranks of the unemployed include job cutbacks at European affiliates operating in the United States.

At the state level, the three most populous U.S. states—Texas, California and New York—maintained their rank as the top three destinations of European foreign investment. These three states account for nearly one-fourth of total European investment in the United States, just as they represent roughly one-fourth of the U.S. population. Each state has its own particular appeal to European investors: Texas is a magnet for energy and technology investment from Europe; Wall Street is a focus of many European banks and financial institutions; and Silicon Valley in California has long been a main attraction to European technology firms.

Michigan remains an important destination for European direct investment, but the consolidation and rationalization of the U.S. automotive industry has triggered a decline in European investment and European-supported jobs in the state. On the other hand, European investment in the Carolinas remains substantial: North Carolina first cracked the top ten list in 2005, with South Carolina right behind. Interestingly, on an aggregate basis the Carolinas ranked as the fourth-largest destination of European foreign direct investment, attracting nearly $28 billion in 2007. The key to this trend is Europe's expanding automobile manufacturing/assembly presence in both states.

In terms of jobs, European affiliates directly employed the most U.S. workers in California (303,600), New York (271,300) and Texas (210,700) in 2007.

Just as growing levels of foreign direct investment not only create jobs directly but also boost additional jobs indirectly through distributor networks and related support industries, so too the loss of foreign direct investments ripples through regional economies in terms of both direct and indirect job losses.

Trade Linkages: European Multinationals and American States

Virtually every U.S. state maintains cross-border trade ties with Europe. Indeed, Europe is a key export market for many U.S. states, a role that grants even more economic benefits to states, ranging from income growth to the creation of jobs. Since U.S. exports have been a key driver of economic growth over the past few years, rising exports to Europe were a critical ingredient of growth in both 2008 and 2009. However, the transatlantic economic recession has slowed the pace of bilateral trade between the U.S. and Europe over the past year.

For 2008, which our survey covers, U.S. exports to Europe remained quite strong. Indeed, 32 states posted double-digit export growth to Europe, among the strongest annual export performances in years. For the year, U.S. exports to Europe rose by 15%. All major U.S.

Ranking of U.S. States Benefiting from European* Foreign Direct Investment

Ranking of States by European* Direct Investment
(Billions of $, 2007)

U.S. State	European Direct Investment (FDI)
Texas	55.9
California	46.7
New York	44.2
New Jersey	25.0
Pennsylvania	22.3
Illinois	22.3
Indiana	18.0
Ohio	17.0
Massachusetts	16.7
North Carolina	14.0
South Carolina	13.9
Virginia	12.0
Florida	12.0
Alabama	11.9
Kentucky	11.8
Georgia	10.7
Michigan	9.4
Washington	9.1
Connecticut	8.7
Colorado	8.2
Missouri	8.0
Louisiana	7.8
Maryland	7.6
Tennessee	6.2
Arizona	5.4
Wisconsin	4.9
Minnesota	3.7
Iowa	3.6
Kansas	3.4
New Hampshire	2.7
Oregon	2.5
Delaware	2.4
Arkansas	2.3
Nevada	2.0
Mississippi	1.5
Oklahoma	1.4
West Virginia	1.4
Utah	1.0
Nebraska	0.9
Hawaii	0.9
Rhode Island	0.5
New Mexico	0.4
Maine	0.4
Idaho	0.4
South Dakota	0.2
Vermont	0.1
North Dakota	0.1
Wyoming	0.1
Alaska	0.03
Montana	0.03

Ranking of States by Jobs Supported Directly by European* Investment
(Thousands of employees, 2007)

U.S. State	Employees
California	303.6
New York	271.3
Texas	210.7
Pennsylvania	162.1
Illinois	154.7
New Jersey	143.3
Florida	118.4
Ohio	116.7
Massachusetts	102.7
North Carolina	97.8
Georgia	86.0
Indiana	78.7
Michigan	78.5
Virginia	76.2
Maryland	70.2
Connecticut	66.9
Tennessee	60.3
South Carolina	60.1
Missouri	46.5
Washington	45.8
Wisconsin	44.2
Minnesota	40.6
Colorado	38.2
Kentucky	37.8
Arizona	37.2
Alabama	33.7
Louisiana	28.8
Iowa	23.8
Oregon	23.6
Kansas	23.4
Utah	23.3
New Hampshire	19.6
Rhode Island	17.6
Delaware	16.5
Arkansas	15.3
Oklahoma	15.2
Nevada	15.2
Mississippi	10.0
West Virginia	9.8
Nebraska	9.4
Hawaii	8.6
Idaho	8.2
New Mexico	7.6
Maine	6.2
Vermont	4.3
Alaska	4.2
Wyoming	4.1
Montana	3.1
North Dakota	2.9
South Dakota	1.5

Source: Bureau of Economic Analysis

*European investment includes France, Germany, Netherlands, Switzerland, and the United Kingdom. Due to a need to align resources with current funding levels, the Bureau of Economic Analysis has reduced its coverage to major investing countries. We estimate that this statistical change underestimates the number of U.S. jobs directly generated by European FDI by at least 300,000.

Ranking of U.S. States Total Exports to Europe, by Value, 2008
(Billions of $)

U.S. State	2000	2008	% Change from 2007	% Change from 2000
California	27.9	32.3	7%	16%
Texas	12.3	31.4	21%	156%
New York	15.3	30.3	22%	98%
New Jersey	6.4	14.9	30%	134%
Massachusetts	8.0	13.1	21%	64%
Puerto Rico	5.6	13.1	19%	132%
Illinois	7.3	12.8	-5%	76%
Pennsylvania	4.7	9.4	20%	101%
Florida	3.9	9.2	35%	137%
Washington	13.1	9.0	-8%	-31%
South Carolina	2.8	8.9	25%	218%
Ohio	5.0	8.5	3%	70%
Louisiana	3.3	8.5	65%	158%
Georgia	4.0	8.3	17%	109%
Indiana	3.1	7.6	6%	141%
Virginia	3.8	7.3	13%	91%
Connecticut	3.5	6.6	7%	90%
North Carolina	4.6	6.3	14%	36%
Kentucky	3.1	6.1	6%	101%
Alabama	2.5	6.1	7%	147%
Michigan	5.0	5.7	7%	13%
Minnesota	3.3	5.6	-2%	72%
Tennessee	2.7	5.4	7%	102%
Utah	1.3	5.0	25%	272%
Wisconsin	2.4	4.6	7%	90%
Arizona	2.9	4.3	0%	46%
Maryland	1.8	3.9	40%	120%
Nevada	0.3	3.5	6%	1103%
Kansas	1.1	3.4	15%	209%
Iowa	1.2	2.7	33%	134%
Oregon	1.9	2.5	14%	32%
Missouri	1.5	2.3	16%	56%
Delaware	0.5	2.1	25%	298%
West Virginia	0.7	2.0	70%	182%
Colorado	2.3	1.8	8%	-21%
Mississippi	0.8	1.5	46%	94%
Arkansas	0.6	1.5	-7%	140%
New Hampshire	0.9	1.2	10%	28%
Oklahoma	0.6	0.9	11%	49%
Nebraska	0.4	0.9	29%	119%
Alaska	0.2	0.8	-17%	227%
Rhode Island	0.3	0.8	45%	125%
North Dakota	0.2	0.7	21%	253%
Idaho	0.9	0.5	12%	-45%
Vermont	0.9	0.4	14%	-56%
Maine	0.3	0.4	8%	42%
New Mexico	0.2	0.3	-1%	60%
South Dakota	0.2	0.2	10%	-11%
Montana	0.1	0.2	14%	112%
Wyoming	0.0	0.1	5%	206%
Hawaii	0.0	0.1	74%	290%
Unallocated	11.2	8.4	11%	-25%
U.S. Total	187.4	325.0	15%	73%

Source: Foreign Trade Division, U.S. Census Bureau

Ranking of U.S. States Total Exports to Europe, by Percentage Change, 2000-2008
(Billions of $)

U.S. State	2000	2007	2008	% Change from year ago	% Change from 2000
Nevada	0.3	3.3	3.5	6%	1103%
Delaware	0.5	1.7	2.1	25%	298%
Hawaii	0.0	0.0	0.1	74%	290%
Utah	1.3	4.0	5.0	25%	272%
North Dakota	0.2	0.5	0.7	21%	253%
Alaska	0.2	1.0	0.8	-17%	227%
South Carolina	2.8	7.1	8.9	25%	218%
Kansas	1.1	2.9	3.4	15%	209%
Wyoming	0.0	0.1	0.1	5%	206%
West Virginia	0.7	1.2	2.0	70%	182%
Louisiana	3.3	5.1	8.5	65%	158%
Texas	12.3	25.9	31.4	21%	156%
Alabama	2.5	5.7	6.1	7%	147%
Indiana	3.1	7.1	7.6	6%	141%
Arkansas	0.6	1.6	1.5	-7%	140%
Florida	3.9	6.8	9.2	35%	137%
Iowa	1.2	2.1	2.7	33%	134%
New Jersey	6.4	11.5	14.9	30%	134%
Puerto Rico	5.6	11.0	13.1	19%	132%
Rhode Island	0.3	0.5	0.8	45%	125%
Maryland	1.8	2.8	3.9	40%	120%
Nebraska	0.4	0.7	0.9	29%	119%
Montana	0.1	0.2	0.2	14%	112%
Georgia	4.0	7.1	8.3	17%	109%
Tennessee	2.7	5.1	5.4	7%	102%
Pennsylvania	4.7	7.9	9.4	20%	101%
Kentucky	3.1	5.8	6.1	6%	101%
New York	15.3	24.9	30.3	22%	98%
Mississippi	0.8	1.1	1.5	46%	94%
Virginia	3.8	6.5	7.3	13%	91%
Connecticut	3.5	6.2	6.6	7%	90%
Wisconsin	2.4	4.3	4.6	7%	90%
Illinois	7.3	13.6	12.8	-5%	76%
U.S. Total	187.4	283.1	325.0	15%	73%
Minnesota	3.3	5.7	5.6	-2%	72%
Ohio	5.0	8.3	8.5	3%	70%
Massachusetts	8.0	10.8	13.1	21%	64%
New Mexico	0.2	0.3	0.3	-1%	60%
Missouri	1.5	2.0	2.3	16%	56%
Oklahoma	0.6	0.8	0.9	11%	49%
Arizona	2.9	4.3	4.3	0%	46%
Maine	0.3	0.4	0.4	8%	42%
North Carolina	4.6	5.5	6.3	14%	36%
Oregon	1.9	2.2	2.5	14%	32%
New Hampshire	0.9	1.1	1.2	10%	28%
California	27.9	30.3	32.3	7%	16%
Michigan	5.0	5.3	5.7	7%	13%
South Dakota	0.2	0.2	0.2	10%	-11%
Colorado	2.3	1.7	1.8	8%	-21%
Unallocated	11.2	7.6	8.4	11%	-25%
Washington	13.1	9.8	9.0	-8%	-31%
Idaho	0.9	0.4	0.5	12%	-45%
Vermont	0.9	0.4	0.4	14%	-56%

Source: Foreign Trade Division, U.S. Census Bureau

exporting states to Europe have posted double or triple-digit percentage gains over the course of this decade except the state of Washington, which lost nearly a third of its European export market over the past decade.

California, the largest exporter among U.S. states, exported nearly $32.3 billion in goods to Europe in 2008, a 7% rise from the prior year. Europe represents one of the largest markets in the world for information technology, and technology firms in California and other states, like New York, Colorado and Oregon, have seen exports of computers and related parts to Europe expand sharply over the past few years. Texas and New York are also sizable exporters to Europe. In fact, while both states' exports to Europe at the beginning of the last decade were less than half of California's exports to Europe, by 2008 both states had boosted their exports so much they had pulled roughly even with California as leading U.S. exporters to Europe. Texas exports to Europe totaled $31.4 billion in 2008, while exports from New York were slightly lower at $30.3 billion. The composition of exports runs the gamut—from machinery to chemicals to pulp and paper.

Germany was the top European export market for 16 states in 2008. The United Kingdom was second, the top European export market for 13 states. In general, Europe is one of the largest markets in the world for a host of U.S. goods, ranging from agricultural products to high tech goods. By commodity, sharp increases were recorded for such exports as mineral fuels, crude material, processed foods, and chemicals.

The deep transatlantic linkages forged by investment and trade flows are underscored by the important ties such states as Alabama, Michigan and South Carolina have with European automobile manufacturers. In many cases, trade flows represent "related party" trade,

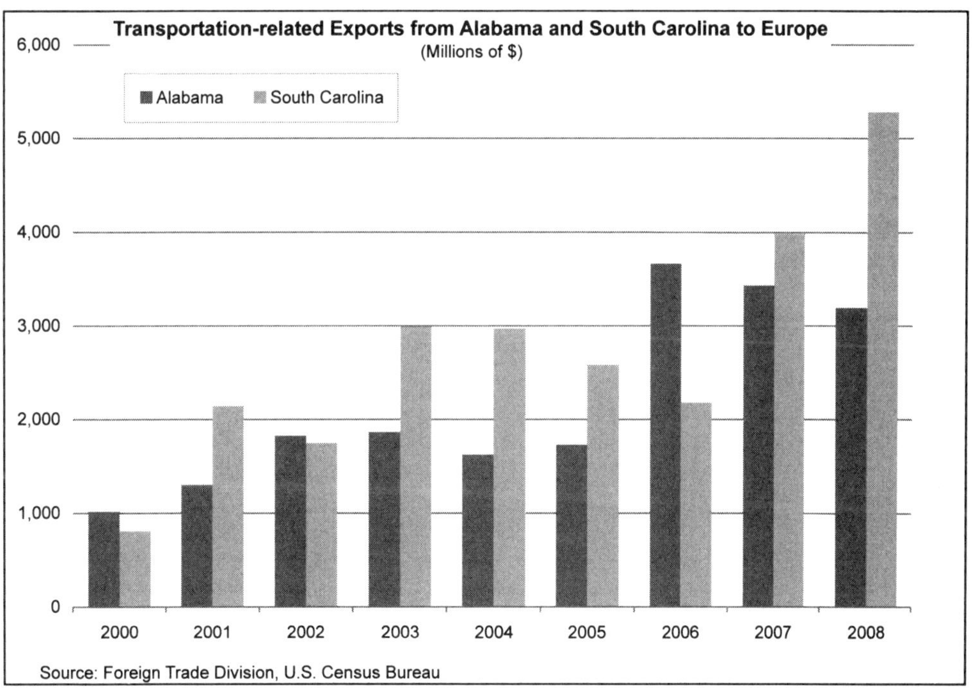

which are trade flows that stay within the ambit of the company. In this respect, European affiliates in the U.S. are significant exporters in their own right.

South Carolina and Alabama offer vivid examples of how U.S. exports can be boosted by European direct investment. In 2008 South Carolina's transportation-related exports to Europe were five times that of 2001, when the European investment wave had begun to develop momentum. Similarly in Alabama, assembling passenger cars and manufacturing auto parts have compensated for the loss of jobs in such traditional industries as mining, agriculture, and textiles. Alabama never produced an automobile prior to 1997, but it has become a major auto-producing state due to European, Japanese and Korean foreign direct investment. Due to the high volume of intra-party trade generated by European FDI, this has translated into high levels of Alabama exports to Europe.

These figures about investment flows and exports may be abstract, but they translate into real jobs for American workers. For all the talk about offshored American jobs, European investments create jobs in U.S. state and local economies. Moreover, those investments also tend to generate U.S. exports, opening additional markets to U.S. workers. Similarly, when European investments decline, this means job losses for American workers. The United States as a whole, and a substantial number of U.S. states and localities in particular, have developed a real stake in healthy, two-way transatlantic commerce.

Special Focus

European FDI Abroad: The U.S. versus the Rest of the World

While previous surveys have focused just on Europe's investment in the United States in isolation, the following presents a brief look at the EU's foreign direct investment position on a global basis.

The first point to highlight is that in terms of FDI flows and outward stock, the United States remains the primary destination of EU investment outside the EU itself. Based on data from Eurostat, the U.S. was the top recipient of extra-EU FDI outflows in 2008, which is the last year of available data. Outflows to the U.S. totaled €121 billion, 34.8% of the extra-EU27 total, followed by Switzerland (9.8%), Russia (7.4%) and Singapore (4.4%). In terms of capital stock, the EU's investment stock in the United States rose by 43% between 2000 and 2008, with the U.S. accounting for roughly one-third of extra-EU27 FDI stock abroad.

Of particular interest is the spread between European FDI in the United States on the one hand versus EU FDI in China and India on the other. Simply put, there is no comparison: in 2008, EU FDI in the U.S. totaled €1.1 trillion, versus total combined investment of €66.5 billion in China and India. EU FDI in China totaled €47.2 billion in 2008, while EU FDI in India tallied just €19.3 billion.

What is particularly striking from the latest figures is that EU FDI outflows to the BRICs are focused primarily on Russia, and then Brazil, rather than China or India. EU FDI outflows to Russia in 2007 and 2008 totaled €42.8 billion, roughly three times EU FDI to

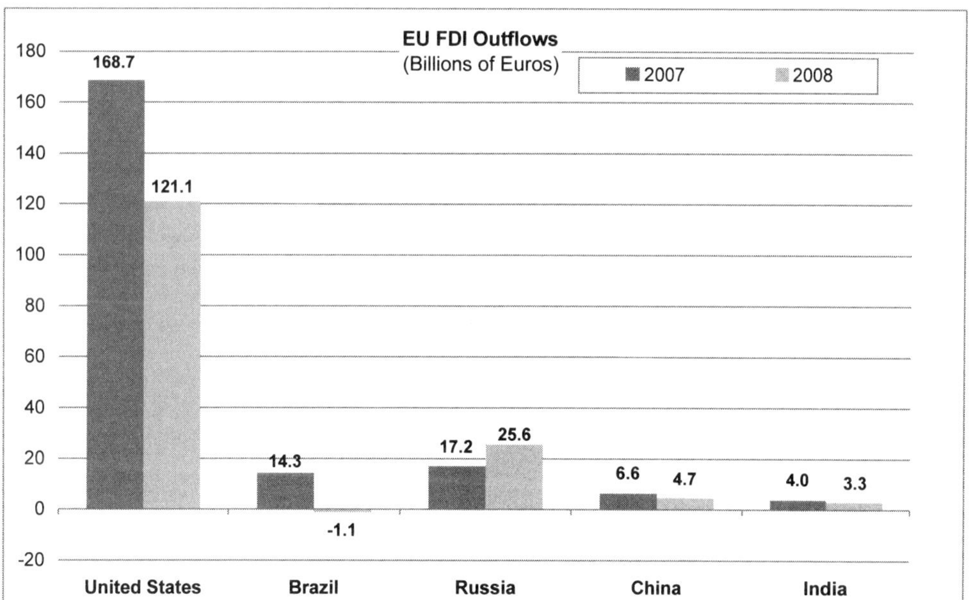

Source: Eurostat
Data for 2008 preliminary
* China does not include Hong Kong

EU FDI Assets
Billions of Euros

	2000	2001	2002	2003	2004	2005	2006	2007	2008
United States	752	915	760	748	732	845	949	1,006	1,075
Brazil	75	73	44	59	70	74	92	114	111
Russia	7	11	10	15	21	33	51	70	91
China*	15	19	20	19	21	28	33	40	47
India	6	6	6	7	8	11	12	16	19
BRICs	104	110	81	99	121	145	188	241	269

Source: Eurostat
*China does not include Hong Kong

Brazil, four times EU FDI to China and six times EU FDI to India. EU FDI outflows to Russia in 2007-2008, in turn, represented only about one-seventh the value of EU FDI outflows to the United States in this period.

In terms of EU FDI assets in each country, again the gap between EU investment assets in the U.S. and the BRICs is huge. EU investment assets in the U.S. are nearly 33% of extra-EU27 investment stock. EU investment assets in Brazil were roughly one-tenth of those in the United States in 2008. EU investment assets in Russia were about 8% of those in the U.S. In China, the comparable figure was less than 5% of EU investment stock in the United States. India's total above was even smaller, coming in less than 1% of extra-EU27 investment stock in 2008. All told, EU investment assets in the BRICs are one-quarter of EU investment assets in the United States.

The bottom line is that U.S. and European multinationals continue to show a strong preference for each other's market when it comes to investing overseas. The notion that the U.S. and Europe are decamping from each other's markets for the low-cost destinations of China and India is wide of the mark. Between 2001 and 2008 EU FDI outflows to the BRICS represented only 8.3% of global EU FDI outflows outside the EU27, and most of that was to Russia, not China and India. U.S. FDI outflows to the BRICS during this same period accounted for only 4.5% of global U.S. FDI outflows.

As we highlight in the next chapter, however, both U.S. and European firms are gradually increasing their exposure to the developing nations. That's hardly surprising given the growth differential between the slow-growth, mature economies of the west versus the fast-growth, emerging markets of Asia, Latin America, the Middle East and Africa.

EU FDI Assets
Percent of extra-EU27 total

	2004	2005	2006	2007
United States	36.2%	34.8%	34.6%	31.9%
Brazil	3.5%	3.1%	3.4%	3.6%
Russia	1.0%	1.4%	1.8%	2.2%
China	1.1%	1.1%	1.2%	1.3%
India	0.4%	0.4%	0.5%	0.5%
BRICs	6.0%	6.0%	6.8%	7.7%

Source: Eurostat

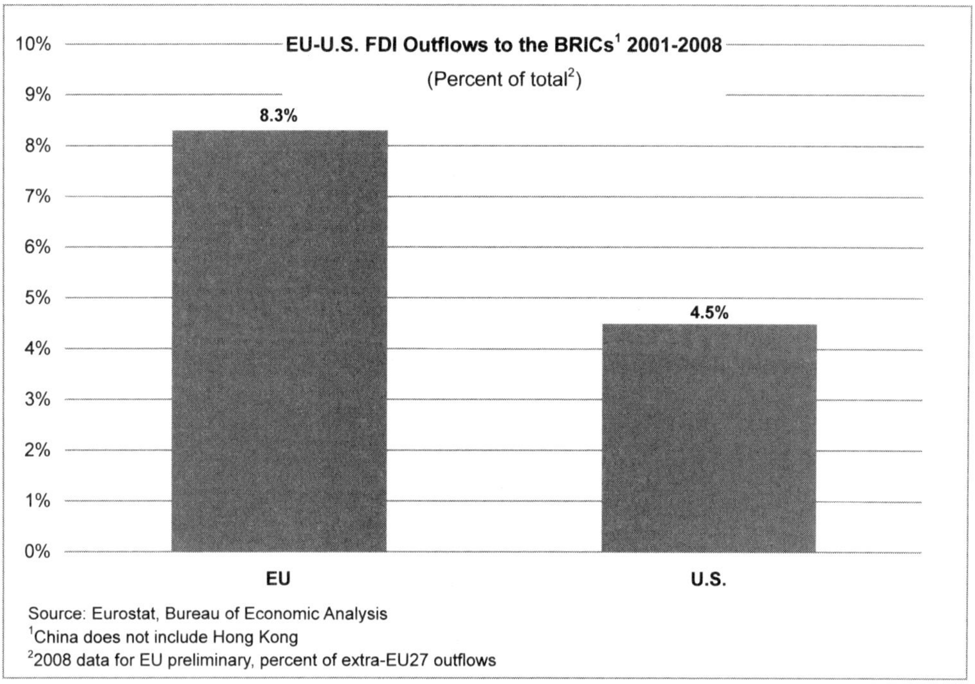

Over the near-term, however, European investment in many U.S. regions and states will continue to play a key role in promoting growth and creating jobs in American states and localities. Although European investment inflows to the U.S. declined in 2009, this should be viewed as a cyclical factor rather than a structural shift.

Alabama and Europe

Employment, Investment, and Trade Linkages

Employment

European* investment in Alabama supported 33,700 jobs in 2007; 48% of the jobs were in manufacturing.

Investment

Of the $22 billion invested in Alabama in 2007, 54%, or $11.9 billion came from Europe*.

Sources of FDI within Alabama, 2007	
Country	**FDI ($ Millions)**
Japan	4,316
Germany	4,152
United Kingdom	2,598
France	2,209
Netherlands	1,498

Trade

In 2008, Europe purchased $6.1 billion worth of goods from Alabama.
Nearly 50% of total exports represented transportation equipment, reflecting the state's linkages with European auto manufacturers.

Top European Export Markets, 2008	
Country	**Exports ($ Millions)**
Germany	3,181
United Kingdom	650
France	309
Netherlands	297
Poland	259

Top Ten Exports to Europe ($ Millions)

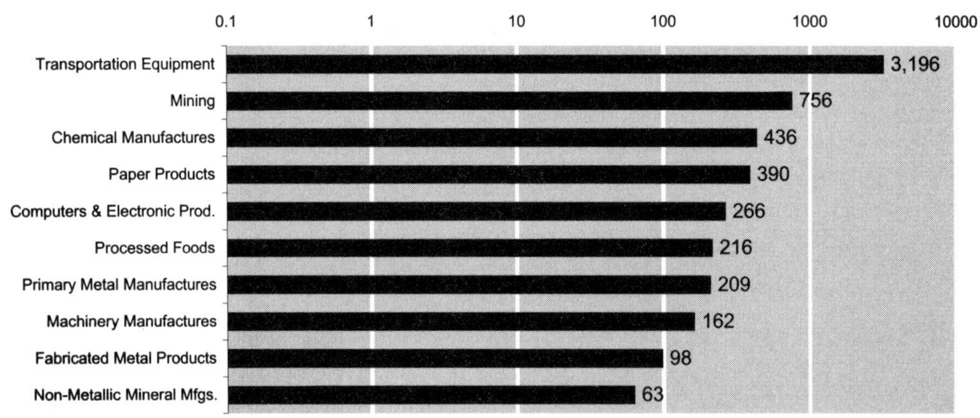

Source: Bureau of Economic Analysis; Foreign Trade Division, U.S. Census Bureau
*European investment includes France, Germany, Netherlands, Switzerland, and the United Kingdom
Due to a need to align resources with current funding levels, the Bureau of Economic Analysis has reduced its coverage to major investing countries.

Alaska and Europe

Employment, Investment, and Trade Linkages

Employment

European* investment in Alaska supported 4,200 jobs in 2007, of which 2% were in manufacturing.

Investment

Alaska received $34.3 billion of investment in 2007, the amount from Europe* is not available.

Sources of FDI within Alaska, 2007	
Country	**FDI ($ Millions)**
Canada	1,849
Japan	891
Germany	17
Switzerland	12

Trade

In 2008, Europe purchased $794 million worth of goods from Alaska.
The bulk of exports consist of primary commodities.

Top European Export Markets, 2008	
Country	**Exports ($ Millions)**
Germany	208
Switzerland	148
Netherlands	105
Portugal	59
France	44

Top Ten Exports to Europe ($ Millions)

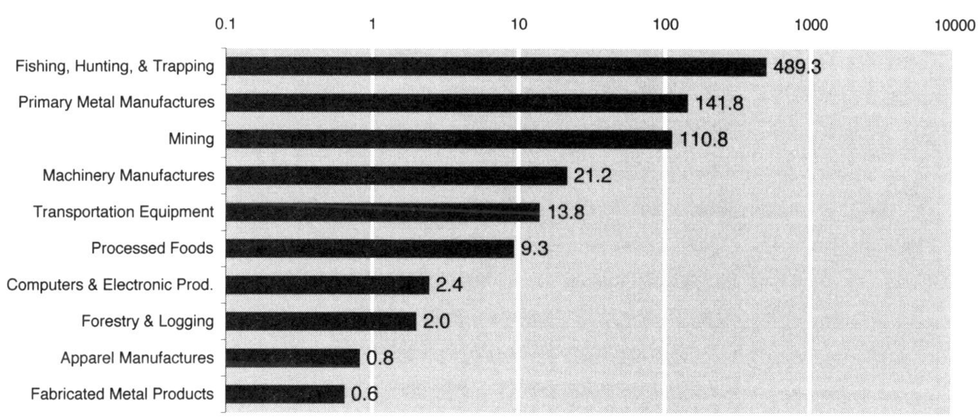

Source: Bureau of Economic Analysis; Foreign Trade Division, U.S. Census Bureau
*European investment includes France, Germany, Netherlands, Switzerland, and the United Kingdom
Due to a need to align resources with current funding levels, the Bureau of Economic Analysis has reduced its coverage to major investing countries.

Arizona and Europe

Employment, Investment, and Trade Linkages

Employment

European* investment in Arizona supported 37,200 jobs in 2007; 3,500 were in manufacturing.

Investment

Of the $13.1 billion invested in Arizona in 2007, 41%, or $5.4 billion came from Europe*.

Sources of FDI within Arizona, 2007	
Country	**FDI ($ Millions)**
Germany	2,600
Canada	1,737
Japan	1,646
Netherlands	1,197
United Kingdom	958

Trade

In 2008, Europe purchased $4.3 billion worth of goods from Arizona.
Nearly third of the state's exports consist of transportation equipment.

Top European Export Markets, 2008	
Country	**Exports ($ Millions)**
United Kingdom	1,013
Germany	964
France	608
Netherlands	372
Poland	299

Top Ten Exports to Europe ($ Millions)

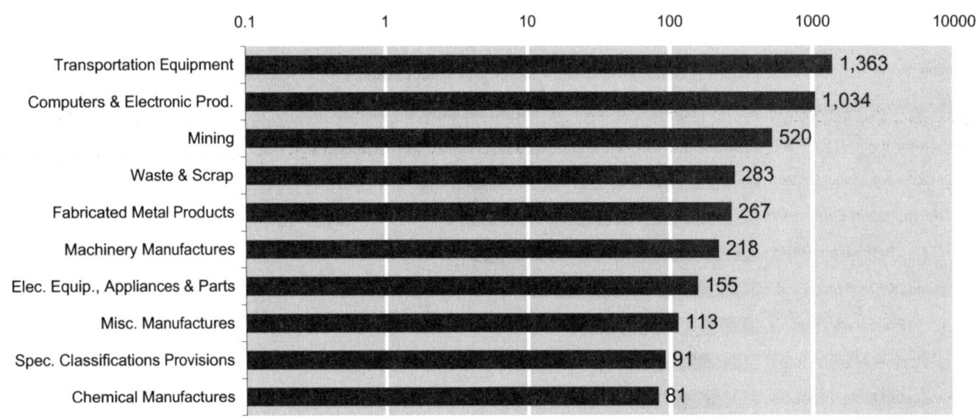

Source: Bureau of Economic Analysis; Foreign Trade Division, U.S. Census Bureau
*European investment includes France, Germany, Netherlands, Switzerland, and the United Kingdom
Due to a need to align resources with current funding levels, the Bureau of Economic Analysis has reduced its coverage to major investing countries.

Arkansas and Europe

Employment, Investment, and Trade Linkages

Employment

European* investment in Arkansas supported 15,300 jobs in 2007, half of which were in manufacturing.

Investment

Of the $5 billion invested in Arkansas in 2007, 46%, or $2.3 billion came from Europe*.

Sources of FDI within Arkansas, 2007

Country	FDI ($ Millions)
France	1,190
Japan	695
Switzerland	473
United Kingdom	319
Germany	227

Trade

In 2008, Europe purchased $1.5 billion worth of goods from Arkansas. Transportation equipment was the top export to the continent.

Top European Export Markets, 2008

Country	Exports ($ Millions)
Switzerland	259
United Kingdom	168
Italy	144
Belgium	144
France	130

Top Ten Exports to Europe ($ Millions)

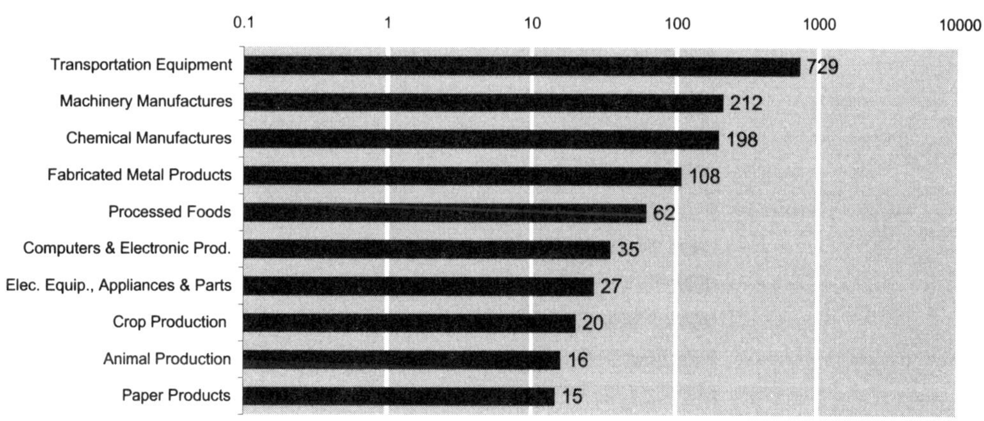

Source: Bureau of Economic Analysis; Foreign Trade Division, U.S. Census Bureau
*European investment includes France, Germany, Netherlands, Switzerland, and the United Kingdom
Due to a need to align resources with current funding levels, the Bureau of Economic Analysis has reduced its coverage to major investing countries.

California and Europe

Employment, Investment, and Trade Linkages

Employment

European* investment in California supported 303,600 jobs in 2007; roughly one-quarter of those jobs were in manufacturing activities.

Investment

Of the $110.2 billion invested in California in 2007, 42%, or $46.7 billion came from Europe*.

Sources of FDI within California, 2007	
Country	**FDI ($ Millions)**
Japan	26,412
United Kingdom	14,464
Germany	10,798
Switzerland	10,465
Netherlands	5,835

Trade

In 2008, Europe purchased $32.3 billion worth of goods from California.
Nearly 30% of Californian exports to Europe consist of high-tech goods.

Top European Export Markets, 2008	
Country	**Exports ($ Millions)**
Germany	5,759
United Kingdom	5,538
Netherlands	4,348
France	2,701
Belgium	2,444

Top Ten Exports to Europe ($ Millions)

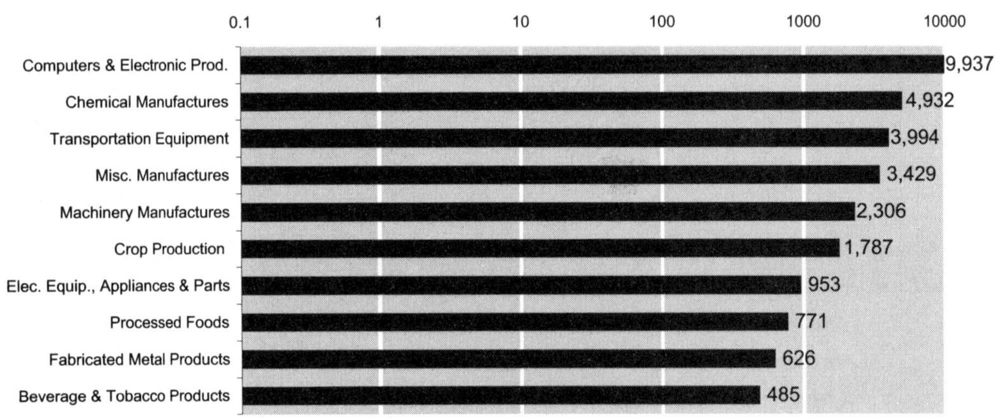

Source: Bureau of Economic Analysis; Foreign Trade Division, U.S. Census Bureau
*European investment includes France, Germany, Netherlands, Switzerland, and the United Kingdom
Due to a need to align resources with current funding levels, the Bureau of Economic Analysis has reduced its coverage to major investing countries.

Colorado and Europe

Employment, Investment, and Trade Linkages

Employment

European* investment in Colorado supported 38,200 jobs in 2007, of which 5,900 were in manufacturing.

Investment

Of the investment into Colorado in 2007, $8.2 billion came from Europe*.

Sources of FDI within Colorado, 2007	
Country	**FDI ($ Millions)**
Canada	18,840
United Kingdom	4,160
Switzerland	1,936
Netherlands	1,002
Japan	709

Trade

In 2008, Europe purchased $1.8 billion worth of goods from Colorado. Thirty percent of the state's exports consist of high-tech goods like computers and electronic products.

Top European Export Markets, 2008	
Country	**Exports ($ Millions)**
Netherlands	404
Germany	284
United Kingdom	231
France	198
Belgium	180

Top Ten Exports to Europe ($ Millions)

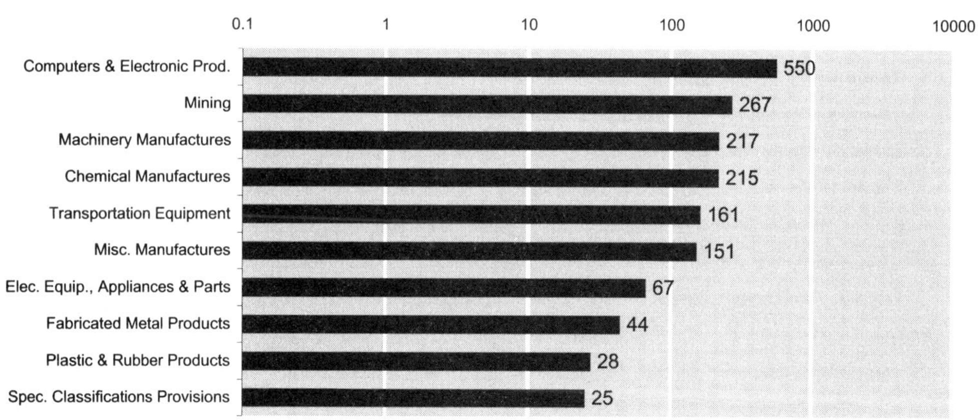

Source: Bureau of Economic Analysis; Foreign Trade Division, U.S. Census Bureau
*European investment includes France, Germany, Netherlands, Switzerland, and the United Kingdom
Due to a need to align resources with current funding levels, the Bureau of Economic Analysis has reduced its coverage to major investing countries.

Connecticut and Europe

Employment, Investment, and Trade Linkages

Employment

European* investment in Connecticut supported 66,900 jobs in 2007, with 22% in manufacturing.

Investment

Of the $13.6 billion invested in Connecticut in 2007, 64%, or $8.7 billion came from Europe*.

Sources of FDI within Connecticut, 2007	
Country	**FDI ($ Millions)**
United Kingdom	2,623
Netherlands	2,222
Switzerland	1,644
Germany	1,524
Japan	950

Trade

In 2008, Europe purchased $6.6 billion worth of goods from Connecticut. Exports are heavily skewed toward transportation equipment.

Top European Export Markets, 2008	
Country	**Exports ($ Millions)**
France	1,734
Germany	1,454
United Kingdom	875
Belgium	523
Netherlands	404

Top Ten Exports to Europe ($ Millions)

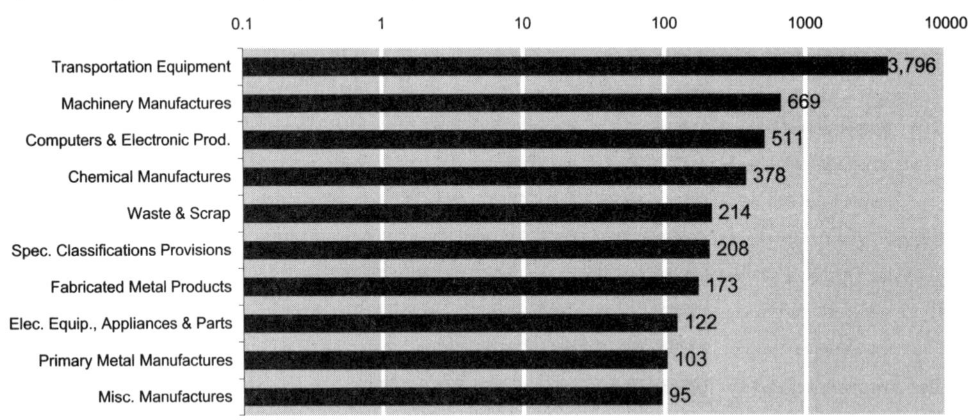

Source: Bureau of Economic Analysis; Foreign Trade Division, U.S. Census Bureau
*European investment includes France, Germany, Netherlands, Switzerland, and the United Kingdom
Due to a need to align resources with current funding levels, the Bureau of Economic Analysis has reduced its coverage to major investing countries.

Delaware and Europe

Employment, Investment, and Trade Linkages

Employment

European* investment in Delaware supported 16,500 jobs in 2007, 400 of which were in manufacturing.

Investment

Of the $4.3 billion invested in Delaware in 2007, 56%, or $2.4 billion came from Europe*.

Sources of FDI within Delaware, 2007	
Country	**FDI ($ Millions)**
United Kingdom	1,961
Canada	622
France	225
Japan	171
Germany	119

Trade

In 2008, Europe purchased $2.1 billion worth of goods from Delaware. Chemical exports are Delaware's primary export to Europe.

Top European Export Markets, 2008	
Country	**Exports ($ Millions)**
United Kingdom	1,099
Germany	486
Netherlands	118
Belgium	103
Portugal	39

Top Ten Exports to Europe ($ Millions)

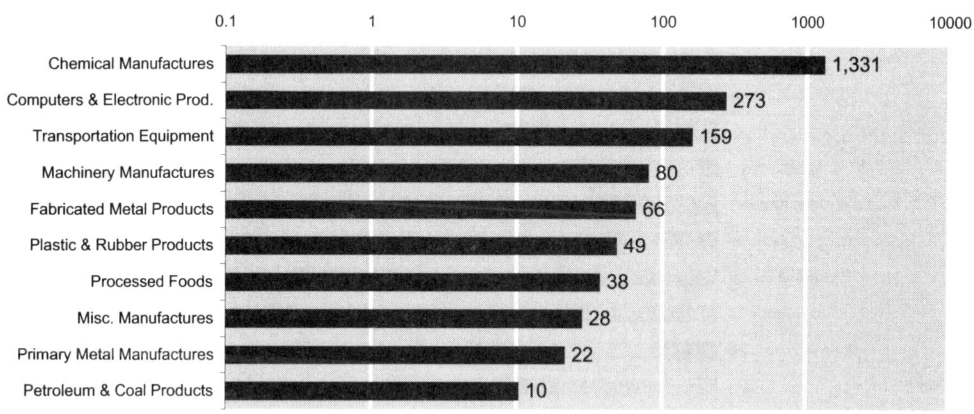

Source: Bureau of Economic Analysis; Foreign Trade Division, U.S. Census Bureau
*European investment includes France, Germany, Netherlands, Switzerland, and the United Kingdom
Due to a need to align resources with current funding levels, the Bureau of Economic Analysis has reduced its coverage to major investing countries.

Florida and Europe

Employment, Investment, and Trade Linkages

Employment

European* investment in Florida supported 118,400 jobs in 2007. Ten percent of these jobs were in manufacturing.

Investment

Of the $33.6 billion invested in Florida in 2007, 36%, or $12 billion came from Europe*.

Sources of FDI within Florida, 2007	
Country	**FDI ($ Millions)**
Japan	4,159
Germany	4,128
United Kingdom	3,877
Canada	3,358
France	1,531

Trade

In 2008, Europe purchased $9.2 billion worth of goods from Florida.
Transportation equipment accounts for 30% of Florida's total exports to the continent.

Top European Export Markets, 2008	
Country	**Exports ($ Millions)**
Switzerland	1,657
United Kingdom	1,347
Germany	1,322
Netherlands	906
Italy	613

Top Ten Exports to Europe ($ Millions)

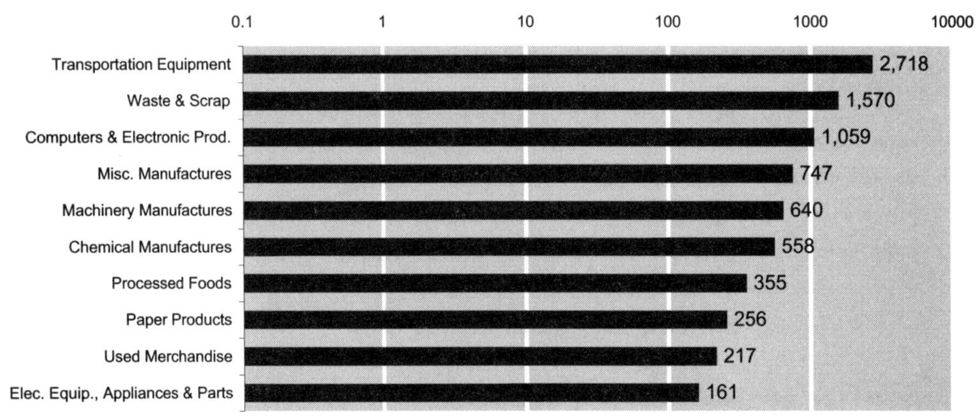

Source: Bureau of Economic Analysis; Foreign Trade Division, U.S. Census Bureau
*European investment includes France, Germany, Netherlands, Switzerland, and the United Kingdom
Due to a need to align resources with current funding levels, the Bureau of Economic Analysis has reduced its coverage to major investing countries.

Georgia and Europe

Employment, Investment, and Trade Linkages

Employment

European* investment in Georgia supported 86,000 jobs in 2007; a bit less than one-quarter of these were in manufacturing.

Investment

Of the investment into Georgia in 2007, $10.7 billion came from Europe*.

Sources of FDI within Georgia, 2007	
Country	**FDI ($ Millions)**
Japan	4,952
Germany	4,325
Canada	2,384
France	2,310
United Kingdom	1,842

Trade

In 2008, Europe purchased $8.3 billion worth of goods from Georgia. Exports are broadly diversified among such exports as transportation equipment, machinery and chemical manufactures.

Top European Export Markets, 2008	
Country	**Exports ($ Millions)**
United Kingdom	1,327
Germany	1,281
Netherlands	940
Belgium	785
Italy	573

Top Ten Exports to Europe ($ Millions)

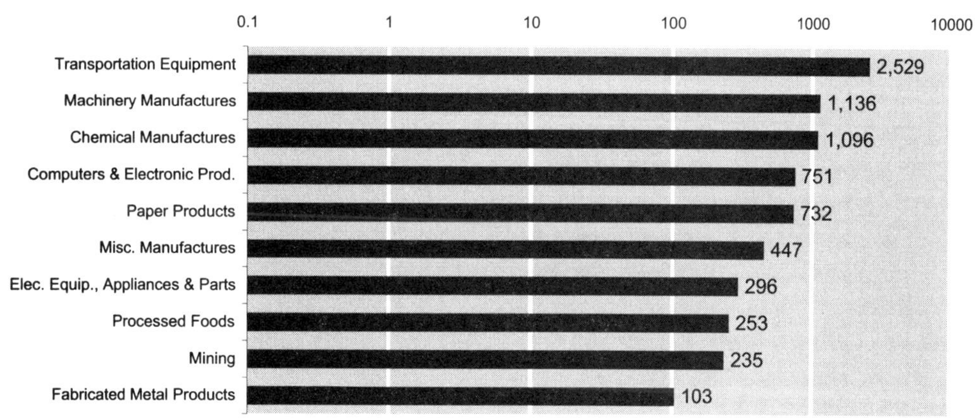

Source: Bureau of Economic Analysis; Foreign Trade Division, U.S. Census Bureau
*European investment includes France, Germany, Netherlands, Switzerland, and the United Kingdom
Due to a need to align resources with current funding levels, the Bureau of Economic Analysis has reduced its coverage to major investing countries.

Hawaii and Europe

Employment, Investment, and Trade Linkages

Employment

European* investment in Hawaii supported 8,600 jobs in 2007, only 800 of which were in manufacturing.

Investment

Of the $6.2 billion invested in Hawaii in 2007, 15%, or $0.9 billion came from Europe*.

Sources of FDI within Hawaii, 2007	
Country	**FDI ($ Millions)**
Japan	4,371
France	600
Germany	213
Canada	105
Switzerland	40

Trade

In 2008, Europe purchased $59 million worth of goods from Hawaii. Transportation equipment accounts for more than half of total exports.

Top European Export Markets, 2008	
Country	**Exports ($ Millions)**
Netherlands	23
United Kingdom	14
Germany	8
France	6
Sweden	2

Top Ten Exports to Europe ($ Millions)

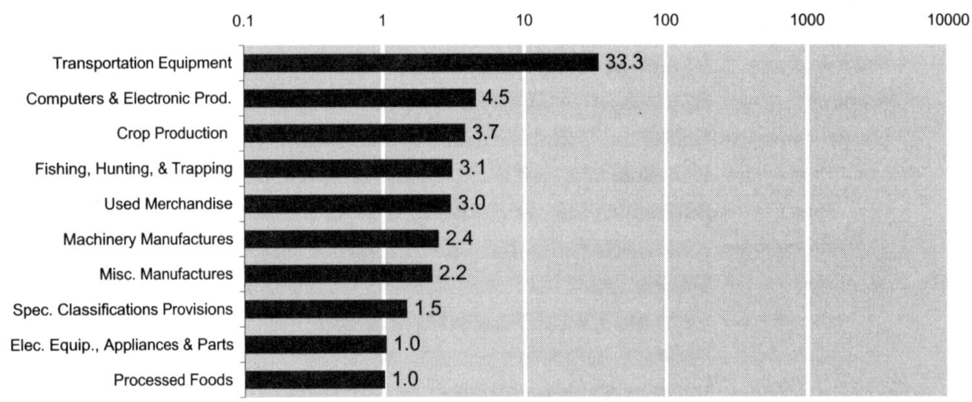

Source: Bureau of Economic Analysis; Foreign Trade Division, U.S. Census Bureau
*European investment includes France, Germany, Netherlands, Switzerland, and the United Kingdom
Due to a need to align resources with current funding levels, the Bureau of Economic Analysis has reduced its coverage to major investing countries.

Idaho and Europe

Employment, Investment, and Trade Linkages

Employment

European* investment in Idaho supported 8,200 jobs in 2007; nearly one-fifth of these were in manufacturing.

Investment

Of the $2 billion invested in Idaho in 2007, nearly 20%, or $0.4 billion came from Europe*.

Sources of FDI within Idaho, 2007	
Country	**FDI ($ Millions)**
Canada	575
United Kingdom	165
Switzerland	94
Germany	91
Japan	76

Trade

In 2008, Europe purchased $494 million worth of goods from Idaho. Exports are mostly concentrated in computers and electronic products.

Top European Export Markets, 2008	
Country	**Exports ($ Millions)**
United Kingdom	121
France	107
Netherlands	73
Italy	40
Germany	33

Top Ten Exports to Europe ($ Millions)

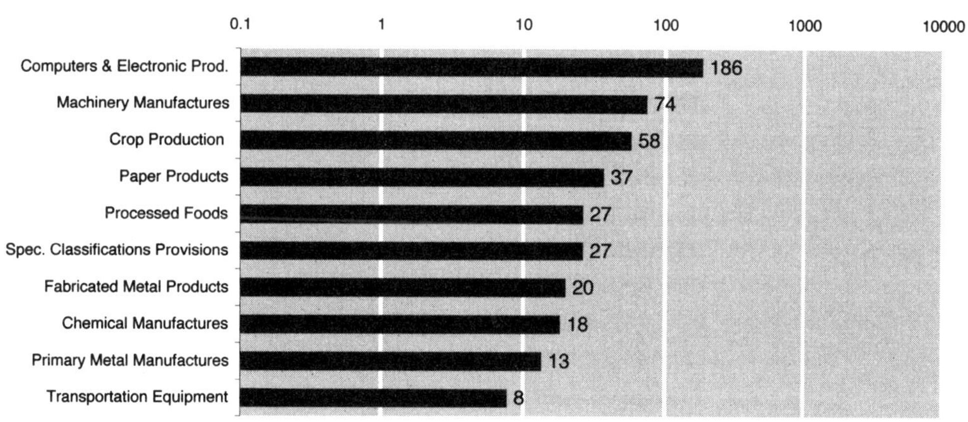

Source: Bureau of Economic Analysis; Foreign Trade Division, U.S. Census Bureau
*European investment includes France, Germany, Netherlands, Switzerland, and the United Kingdom
Due to a need to align resources with current funding levels, the Bureau of Economic Analysis has reduced its coverage to major investing countries.

Illinois and Europe

Employment, Investment, and Trade Linkages

Employment

European* investment in Illinois supported 154,700 jobs in 2007; 22% of the workforce was employed in manufacturing activities.

Investment

Of the $49.2 billion invested in Illinois in 2007, 45%, or $22.3 billion came from Europe*.

Sources of FDI within Illinois, 2007	
Country	**FDI ($ Millions)**
United Kingdom	8,633
Japan	8,447
Germany	7,560
Canada	6,262
France	2,335

Trade

In 2008, Europe purchased $12.8 billion worth of goods from Illinois. Machinery is a key export, followed by chemicals and computers.

Top European Export Markets, 2008	
Country	**Exports ($ Millions)**
Germany	2,224
Netherlands	1,854
United Kingdom	1,852
Belgium	1,652
France	1,302

Top Ten Exports to Europe ($ Millions)

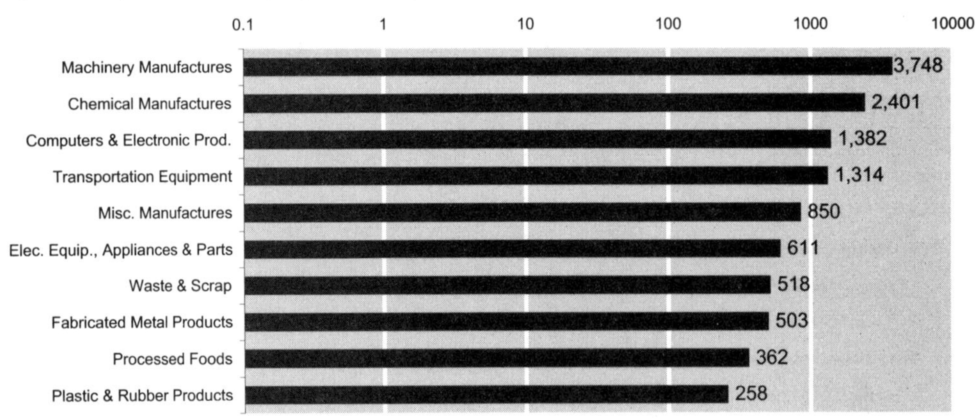

Source: Bureau of Economic Analysis; Foreign Trade Division, U.S. Census Bureau
*European investment includes France, Germany, Netherlands, Switzerland, and the United Kingdom
Due to a need to align resources with current funding levels, the Bureau of Economic Analysis has reduced its coverage to major investing countries.

Indiana and Europe

Employment, Investment, and Trade Linkages

Employment

European* investment in Indiana supported 78,700 jobs in 2007; a little more than half of these were in manufacturing.

Investment

Of the investment into Indiana in 2007, $18 billion came from Europe*.

Sources of FDI within Indiana, 2007	
Country	**FDI ($ Millions)**
United Kingdom	11,366
Japan	11,179
Germany	3,556
France	1,434
Canada	1,378

Trade

In 2008, Europe purchased $7.6 billion worth of goods from Indiana. Exports are heavily skewed toward chemicals.

Top European Export Markets, 2008	
Country	**Exports ($ Millions)**
United Kingdom	1,979
France	1,419
Germany	1,271
Netherlands	481
Belgium	479

Top Ten Exports to Europe ($ Millions)

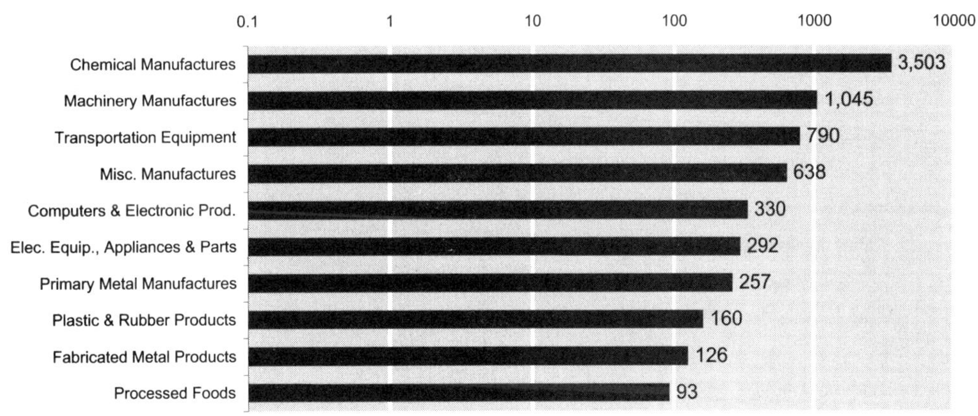

Source: Bureau of Economic Analysis; Foreign Trade Division, U.S. Census Bureau
*European investment includes France, Germany, Netherlands, Switzerland, and the United Kingdom
Due to a need to align resources with current funding levels, the Bureau of Economic Analysis has reduced its coverage to major investing countries.

Iowa and Europe
Employment, Investment, and Trade Linkages

Employment
European* investment in Iowa supported 23,800 jobs in 2007, one-third of which were in manufacturing.

Investment
Of the $8.4 billion invested in Iowa in 2007, 43%, or $3.6 billion came from Europe*.

Sources of FDI within Iowa, 2007	
Country	**FDI ($ Millions)**
France	1,162
Japan	1,091
Germany	1,081
Canada	976
United Kingdom	665

Trade
In 2008, Europe purchased $2.7 billion worth of goods from Iowa. Machinery manufactures account for 50% of total exports.

Top European Export Markets, 2008	
Country	**Exports ($ Millions)**
Germany	573
United Kingdom	333
France	317
Netherlands	200
Belgium	102

Top Ten Exports to Europe ($ Millions)

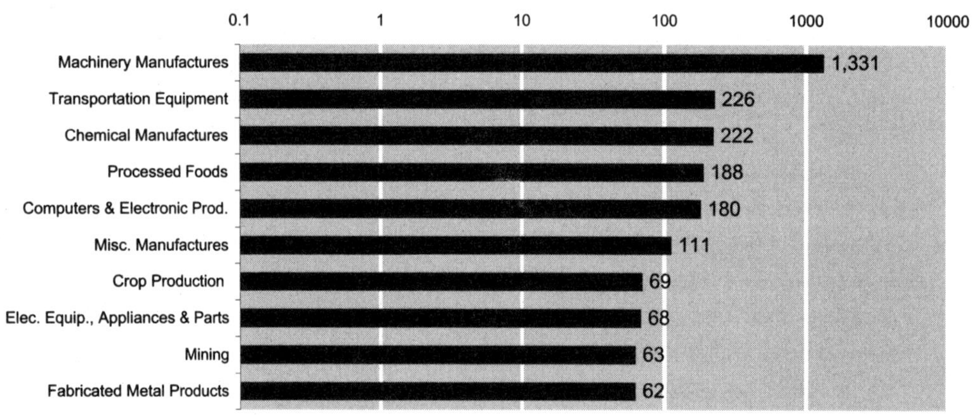

Source: Bureau of Economic Analysis; Foreign Trade Division, U.S. Census Bureau
*European investment includes France, Germany, Netherlands, Switzerland, and the United Kingdom
Due to a need to align resources with current funding levels, the Bureau of Economic Analysis has reduced its coverage to major investing countries.

Kansas and Europe

Employment, Investment, and Trade Linkages

Employment

European* investment in Kansas supported 23,400 jobs in 2007, one-fourth of which were in the manufacturing sector.

Investment

Of the $8 billion invested in Kansas in 2007, 43%, or $3.4 billion came from Europe*.

Sources of FDI within Kansas, 2007	
Country	**FDI ($ Millions)**
Canada	1,857
Germany	897
France	895
United Kingdom	894
Netherlands	474

Trade

In 2008, Europe purchased $3.4 billion worth of goods from Kansas. More than 60% of the state's exports consist of transportation equipment.

Top European Export Markets, 2008	
Country	**Exports ($ Millions)**
Germany	631
United Kingdom	597
Portugal	237
France	234
Austria	152

Top Ten Exports to Europe ($ Millions)

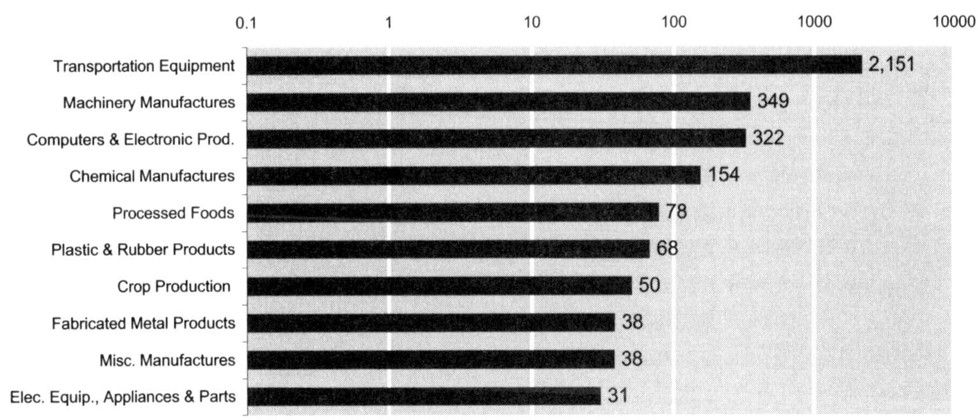

Source: Bureau of Economic Analysis; Foreign Trade Division, U.S. Census Bureau
*European investment includes France, Germany, Netherlands, Switzerland, and the United Kingdom
Due to a need to align resources with current funding levels, the Bureau of Economic Analysis has reduced its coverage to major investing countries.

Kentucky and Europe

Employment, Investment, and Trade Linkages

Employment

European* investment in Kentucky supported 37,800 jobs in 2007, nearly 40% of which were in manufacturing.

Investment

Of the $28.3 billion invested in Kentucky in 2007, 42%, or $11.8 billion came from Europe*.

Sources of FDI within Kentucky, 2007	
Country	**FDI ($ Millions)**
Japan	11,230
Germany	8,486
Netherlands	1,216
Canada	1,118
France	1,029

Trade

In 2008, Europe purchased $6.1 billion worth of goods from Kentucky. Reflecting the large presence of automobile manufacturers in the state, Kentucky's top export to Europe is transportation equipment.

Top European Export Markets, 2008	
Country	**Exports ($ Millions)**
France	1,939
United Kingdom	1,162
Germany	752
Netherlands	644
Belgium	379

Top Ten Exports to Europe ($ Millions)

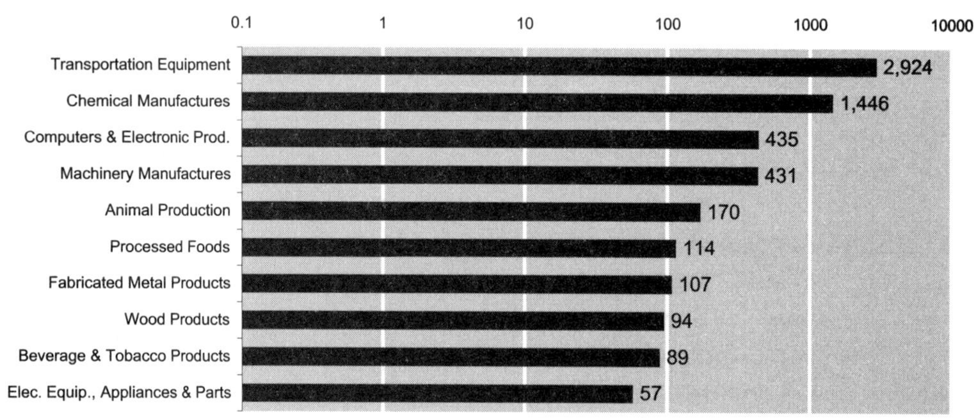

Source: Bureau of Economic Analysis; Foreign Trade Division, U.S. Census Bureau
*European investment includes France, Germany, Netherlands, Switzerland, and the United Kingdom
Due to a need to align resources with current funding levels, the Bureau of Economic Analysis has reduced its coverage to major investing countries.

Louisiana and Europe

Employment, Investment, and Trade Linkages

Employment

European* investment in Louisiana supported 28,800 jobs in 2007, 15% of which were in the manufacturing sector.

Investment

Of the $30.7 billion invested in Louisiana in 2007, 25%, or $7.8 billion came from Europe*.

Sources of FDI within Louisiana, 2007	
Country	**FDI ($ Millions)**
Germany	3,297
United Kingdom	2,548
France	1,982
Canada	1,828
Japan	1,494

Trade

In 2008, Europe purchased $8.5 billion worth of goods from Louisiana. The state's exports consist of a mix of petroleum and coal products, chemicals and agricultural products.

Top European Export Markets, 2008	
Country	**Exports ($ Millions)**
Netherlands	2,245
Germany	1,300
Belgium	918
Spain	573
United Kingdom	518

Top Ten Exports to Europe ($ Millions)

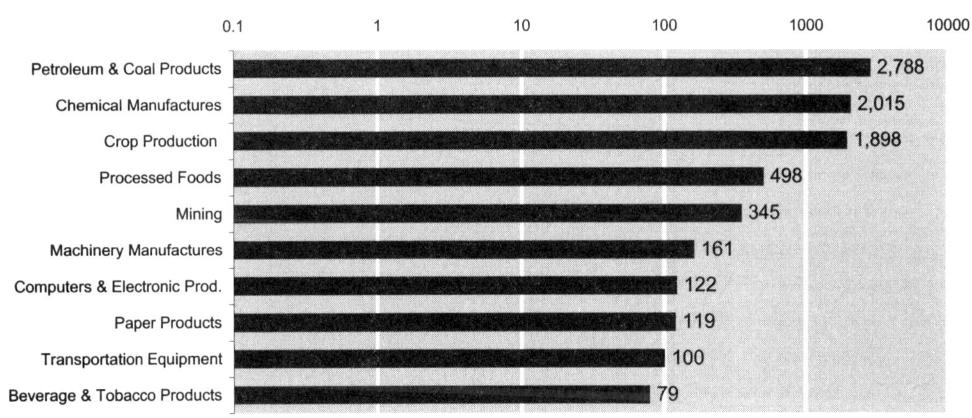

Source: Bureau of Economic Analysis; Foreign Trade Division, U.S. Census Bureau
*European investment includes France, Germany, Netherlands, Switzerland, and the United Kingdom
Due to a need to align resources with current funding levels, the Bureau of Economic Analysis has reduced its coverage to major investing countries.

Maine and Europe

Employment, Investment, and Trade Linkages

Employment

European* investment in Maine supported 6,200 jobs in 2007, nearly 30% of which were in the manufacturing sector.

Investment

Of the $6.3 billion invested in Maine in 2007, 6%, or $0.4 billion came from Europe*.

Sources of FDI within Maine, 2007	
Country	**FDI ($ Millions)**
Canada	2,300
Germany	173
Japan	151
United Kingdom	106
France	59

Trade

In 2008, Europe purchased $412 million worth of goods from Maine.
Paper and transportation equipment are the state's top exports to Europe.

Top European Export Markets, 2008	
Country	**Exports ($ Millions)**
Belgium	77
Netherlands	61
United Kingdom	50
Germany	44
France	43

Top Ten Exports to Europe ($ Millions)

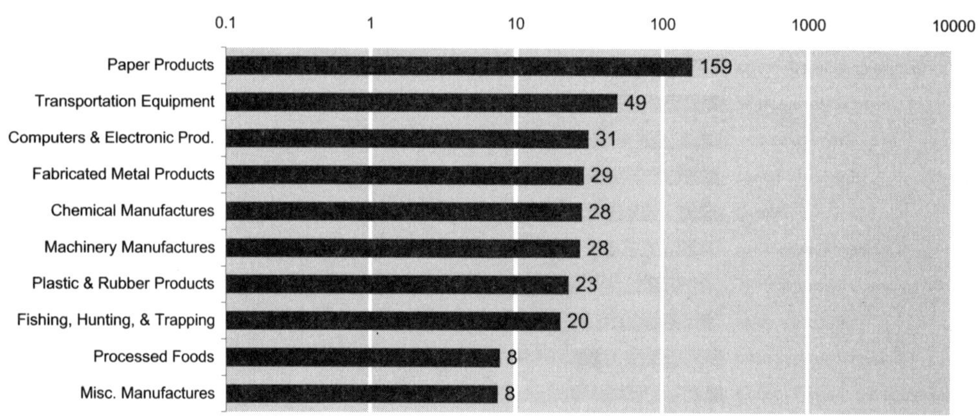

Source: Bureau of Economic Analysis; Foreign Trade Division, U.S. Census Bureau
*European investment includes France, Germany, Netherlands, Switzerland, and the United Kingdom
Due to a need to align resources with current funding levels, the Bureau of Economic Analysis has reduced its coverage to major investing countries.

Maryland and Europe

Employment, Investment, and Trade Linkages

Employment

European* investment in Maryland supported 70,200 jobs in 2007; the bulk of employment was in services while only 18% was in manufacturing.

Investment

Of the $13.5 billion invested in Maryland in 2007, 56%, or $7.6 billion came from Europe*.

Sources of FDI within Maryland, 2007	
Country	**FDI ($ Millions)**
United Kingdom	2,442
Netherlands	1,876
Germany	1,734
Japan	1,375
Canada	1,017

Trade

In 2008, Europe purchased $3.9 billion worth of goods from Maryland. Top exports are transportation equipment, computers and chemicals.

Top European Export Markets, 2008	
Country	**Exports ($ Millions)**
Belgium	524
Netherlands	516
Germany	497
United Kingdom	462
France	322

Top Ten Exports to Europe ($ Millions)

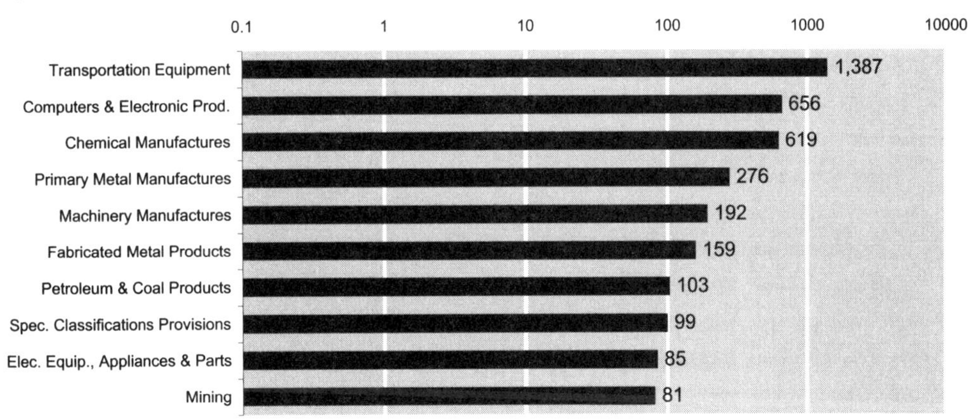

Source: Bureau of Economic Analysis; Foreign Trade Division, U.S. Census Bureau

*European investment includes France, Germany, Netherlands, Switzerland, and the United Kingdom

Due to a need to align resources with current funding levels, the Bureau of Economic Analysis has reduced its coverage to major investing countries.

Massachusetts and Europe

Employment, Investment, and Trade Linkages

Employment

European* investment in Massachusetts supported 102,700 jobs in 2007, 16% of which were in the manufacturing sector.

Investment

Of the $26.3 billion invested in Massachusetts in 2007, 64%, or $16.7 billion came from Europe*.

Sources of FDI within Massachusetts, 2007	
Country	**FDI ($ Millions)**
United Kingdom	8,803
Canada	3,425
Netherlands	3,037
Japan	2,146
France	1,786

Trade

In 2008, Europe purchased $13.1 billion worth of goods from Massachusetts. Nearly a third of exports to Europe consist of chemical manufactures followed by computers and electronic products.

Top European Export Markets, 2008	
Country	**Exports ($ Millions)**
United Kingdom	3,504
Netherlands	2,675
Germany	2,489
France	944
Italy	580

Top Ten Exports to Europe ($ Millions)

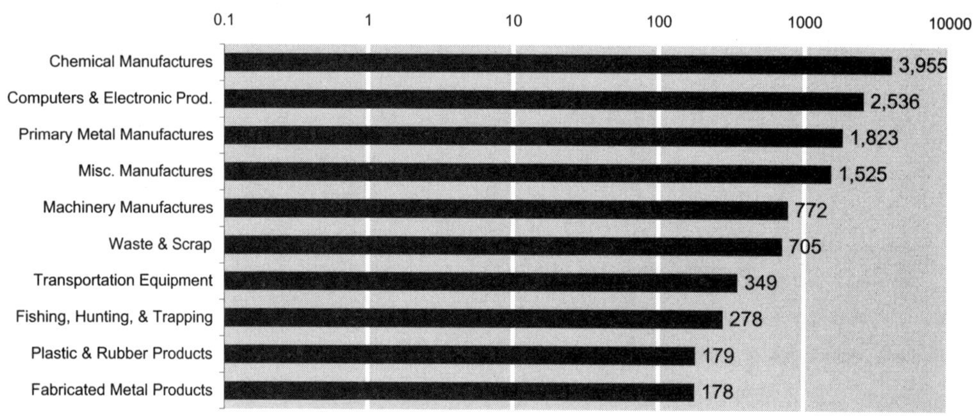

Source: Bureau of Economic Analysis; Foreign Trade Division, U.S. Census Bureau
*European investment includes France, Germany, Netherlands, Switzerland, and the United Kingdom
Due to a need to align resources with current funding levels, the Bureau of Economic Analysis has reduced its coverage to major investing countries.

Michigan and Europe

Employment, Investment, and Trade Linkages

Employment

European* investment in Michigan supported 78,500 jobs in 2007, a third were related to manufacturing.

Investment

Of the $22.7 billion invested in Michigan in 2007, 42%, or $9.4 billion came from Europe*.

Sources of FDI within Michigan, 2007	
Country	**FDI ($ Millions)**
Japan	6,342
Germany	4,606
Canada	4,022
United Kingdom	1,839
France	1,664

Trade

In 2008, Europe purchased $5.7 billion worth of goods from Michigan. Not surprisingly, transportation equipment makes up a fourth of Michigan's exports to Europe.

Top European Export Markets, 2008	
Country	**Exports ($ Millions)**
Germany	1,562
United Kingdom	694
France	627
Belgium	532
Netherlands	490

Top Ten Exports to Europe ($ Millions)

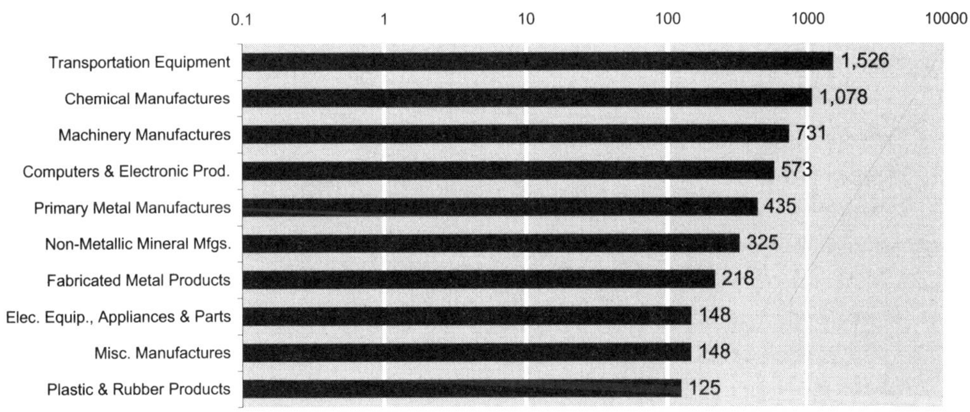

Source: Bureau of Economic Analysis; Foreign Trade Division, U.S. Census Bureau
*European investment includes France, Germany, Netherlands, Switzerland, and the United Kingdom
Due to a need to align resources with current funding levels, the Bureau of Economic Analysis has reduced its coverage to major investing countries.

Minnesota and Europe

Employment, Investment, and Trade Linkages

Employment

European* investment in Minnesota supported 40,600 jobs in 2007, 23% were in manufacturing activities.

Investment

Of the $16.3 billion invested in Minnesota in 2007, 23%, or $3.7 billion came from Europe*.

Sources of FDI within Minnesota, 2007	
Country	**FDI ($ Millions)**
Canada	5,099
Germany	1,403
United Kingdom	969
Switzerland	688
Japan	444

Trade

In 2008, Europe purchased $5.6 billion worth of goods from Minnesota. Computers and electronic products and miscellaneous manufactures rank as the top export to Europe.

Top European Export Markets, 2008	
Country	**Exports ($ Millions)**
Ireland	885
United Kingdom	778
Germany	764
Belgium	663
Netherlands	602

Top Ten Exports to Europe ($ Millions)

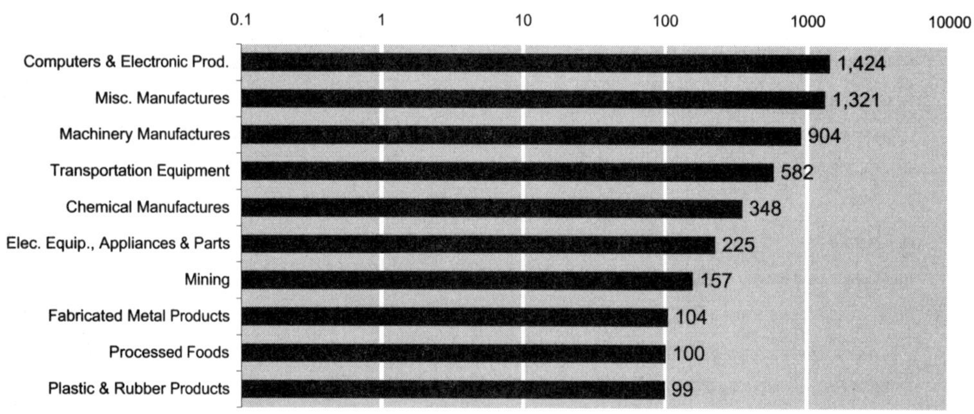

Source: Bureau of Economic Analysis; Foreign Trade Division, U.S. Census Bureau
*European investment includes France, Germany, Netherlands, Switzerland, and the United Kingdom
Due to a need to align resources with current funding levels, the Bureau of Economic Analysis has reduced its coverage to major investing countries.

Mississippi and Europe

Employment, Investment, and Trade Linkages

Employment

European* investment in Mississippi supported 10,000 jobs in 2007, nearly one-fourth were in manufacturing activities.

Investment

Of the $11 billion invested in Mississippi in 2007, 14%, or $1.5 billion came from Europe*.

Sources of FDI within Mississippi, 2007	
Country	**FDI ($ Millions)**
Japan	2,127
Canada	1,630
United Kingdom	1,072
Germany	206
Netherlands	165

Trade

In 2008, Europe purchased $1.5 billion worth of goods from Mississippi. Petroleum products and chemicals rank as the top exports to Europe.

Top European Export Markets, 2008	
Country	**Exports ($ Millions)**
Belgium	250
United Kingdom	218
Netherlands	132
Germany	122
Italy	86

Top Ten Exports to Europe ($ Millions)

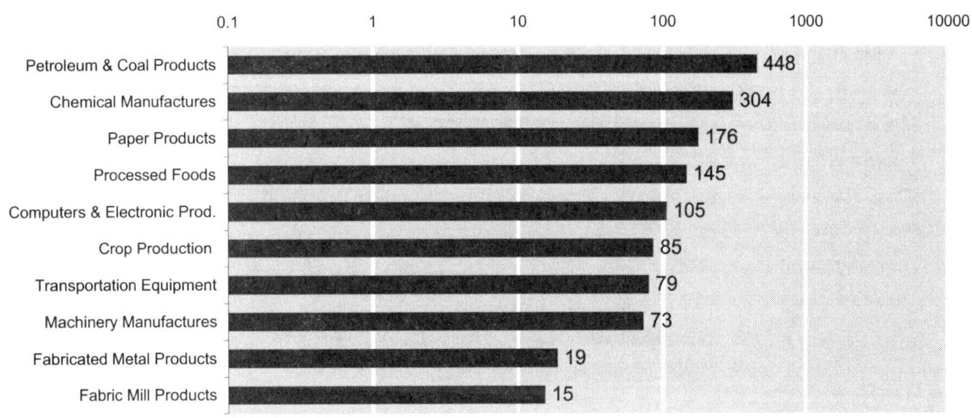

Source: Bureau of Economic Analysis; Foreign Trade Division, U.S. Census Bureau
*European investment includes France, Germany, Netherlands, Switzerland, and the United Kingdom
Due to a need to align resources with current funding levels, the Bureau of Economic Analysis has reduced its coverage to major investing countries.

Missouri and Europe

Employment, Investment, and Trade Linkages

Employment

European* investment in Missouri supported 46,500 jobs in 2007, nearly a third were in manufacturing.

Investment

Of the investment in Missouri in 2007, $8 billion came from Europe*.

Sources of FDI within Missouri, 2007	
Country	**FDI ($ Millions)**
Germany	3,351
United Kingdom	1,693
Japan	1,490
France	1,224
Switzerland	1,158

Trade

In 2008, Europe purchased $2.3 billion worth of goods from Missouri. Top exports include chemicals, machinery and transportation equipment.

Top European Export Markets, 2008	
Country	**Exports ($ Millions)**
Germany	386
United Kingdom	366
Belgium	333
Netherlands	312
France	149

Top Ten Exports to Europe ($ Millions)

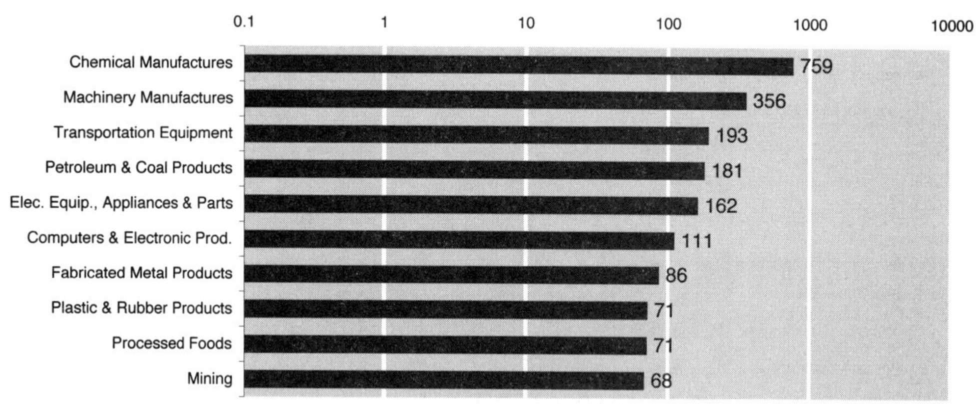

Source: Bureau of Economic Analysis; Foreign Trade Division, U.S. Census Bureau
*European investment includes France, Germany, Netherlands, Switzerland, and the United Kingdom
Due to a need to align resources with current funding levels, the Bureau of Economic Analysis has reduced its coverage to major investing countries.

Montana and Europe

Employment, Investment, and Trade Linkages

Employment

European* investment in Montana supported 3,100 jobs in 2007, one-third of which were in manufacturing.

Investment

Of the $3.2 billion invested in Montana in 2007, less than 1%, or $25 million came from Europe*.

Sources of FDI within Montana, 2007	
Country	**FDI ($ Millions)**
Canada	1,151
Germany	14
Japan	13
France	10
Netherlands	1

Trade

In 2008, Europe purchased $204 million worth of goods from Montana. Exports are relatively small and skewed towards chemical, machinery goods and mining.

Top European Export Markets, 2008	
Country	**Exports ($ Millions)**
Netherlands	54
United Kingdom	34
Germany	23
France	20
Belgium	19

Top Ten Exports to Europe ($ Millions)

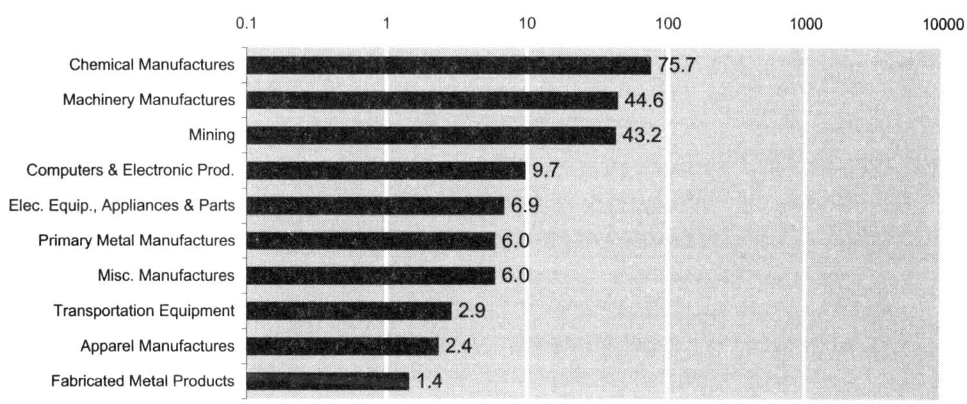

Source: Bureau of Economic Analysis; Foreign Trade Division, U.S. Census Bureau
*European investment includes France, Germany, Netherlands, Switzerland, and the United Kingdom
Due to a need to align resources with current funding levels, the Bureau of Economic Analysis has reduced its coverage to major investing countries.

Nebraska and Europe

Employment, Investment, and Trade Linkages

Employment

European* investment in Nebraska supported 9,400 jobs in 2007; nearly a third were in manufacturing.

Investment

Of the investment into Nebraska in 2007, $0.9 billion came from Europe*.

Sources of FDI within Nebraska, 2007	
Country	**FDI ($ Millions)**
Japan	671
Canada	588
Switzerland	444
Germany	187
France	149

Trade

In 2008, Europe purchased $898 million worth of goods from Nebraska. Top exports are machinery manufactures & processed foods.

Top European Export Markets, 2008	
Country	**Exports ($ Millions)**
Netherlands	121
Germany	92
France	87
Belgium	77
Italy	61

Top Ten Exports to Europe ($ Millions)

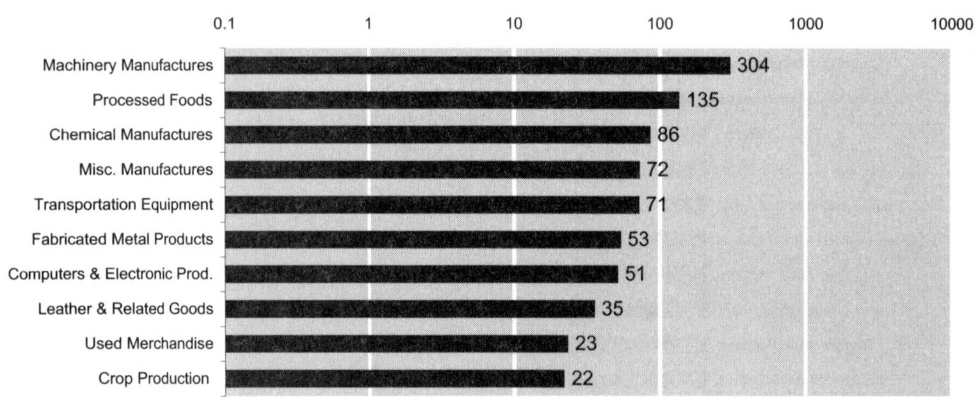

Source: Bureau of Economic Analysis; Foreign Trade Division, U.S. Census Bureau
*European investment includes France, Germany, Netherlands, Switzerland, and the United Kingdom
Due to a need to align resources with current funding levels, the Bureau of Economic Analysis has reduced its coverage to major investing countries.

Nevada and Europe

Employment, Investment, and Trade Linkages

Employment

European* investment in Nevada supported 15,200 jobs in 2007, 12% of which were in manufacturing.

Investment

Of the $9.7 billion invested in Nevada in 2007, 21%, or $2 billion came from Europe*.

Sources of FDI within Nevada, 2007	
Country	**FDI ($ Millions)**
Canada	5,661
United Kingdom	968
Japan	597
Germany	381
Switzerland	354

Trade

In 2008, Europe purchased $3.5 billion worth of goods from Nevada. Primary metal manufactures account for more than 80% of total exports.

Top European Export Markets, 2008	
Country	**Exports ($ Millions)**
Switzerland	2,875
Netherlands	106
United Kingdom	98
Germany	94
France	62

Top Ten Exports to Europe ($ Millions)

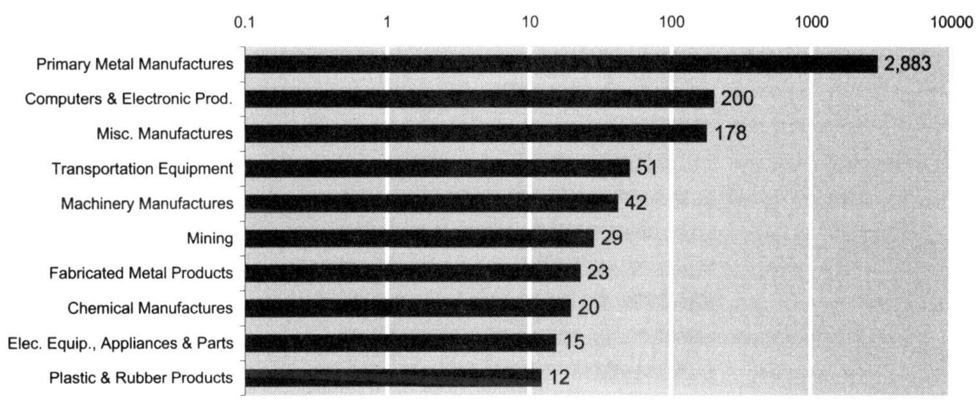

Source: Bureau of Economic Analysis; Foreign Trade Division, U.S. Census Bureau
*European investment includes France, Germany, Netherlands, Switzerland, and the United Kingdom
Due to a need to align resources with current funding levels, the Bureau of Economic Analysis has reduced its coverage to major investing countries.

New Hampshire and Europe

Employment, Investment, and Trade Linkages

Employment

European* investment in New Hampshire supported 19,600 jobs in 2007; a third of these jobs were in manufacturing.

Investment

Of the $5.1 billion invested in New Hampshire in 2007, 53%, or $2.7 billion came from Europe*.

Sources of FDI within New Hampshire, 2007

Country	FDI ($ Millions)
Canada	1,093
United Kingdom	1,023
Switzerland	657
Japan	535
Germany	400

Trade

In 2008, Europe purchased $1.2 billion worth of goods from New Hampshire. Computers and machinery are the top exports to Europe.

Top European Export Markets, 2008

Country	Exports ($ Millions)
Germany	262
United Kingdom	195
Netherlands	149
Italy	76
France	71

Top Ten Exports to Europe ($ Millions)

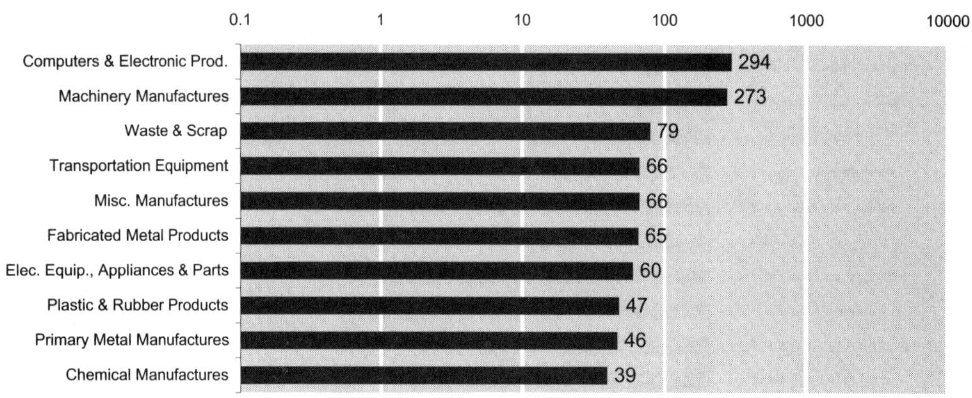

Source: Bureau of Economic Analysis; Foreign Trade Division, U.S. Census Bureau
*European investment includes France, Germany, Netherlands, Switzerland, and the United Kingdom
Due to a need to align resources with current funding levels, the Bureau of Economic Analysis has reduced its coverage to major investing countries.

New Jersey and Europe

Employment, Investment, and Trade Linkages

Employment

European* investment in New Jersey supported 143,300 jobs in 2007; one-fifth of the workforce was involved in manufacturing.

Investment

Of the $38.8 billion invested in New Jersey in 2007, 64%, or $25 billion came from Europe*.

Sources of FDI within New Jersey, 2007	
Country	**FDI ($ Millions)**
Germany	9,871
Japan	5,624
Switzerland	5,588
France	4,247
United Kingdom	3,508

Trade

In 2008, Europe purchased $14.9 billion worth of goods from New Jersey. Exports are diversified across several categories including: transportation equipment, chemicals, waste and scrap, and petroleum and coal products.

Top European Export Markets, 2008	
Country	**Exports ($ Millions)**
United Kingdom	2,863
Germany	1,906
Italy	1,372
Switzerland	1,086
Netherlands	1,062

Top Ten Exports to Europe ($ Millions)

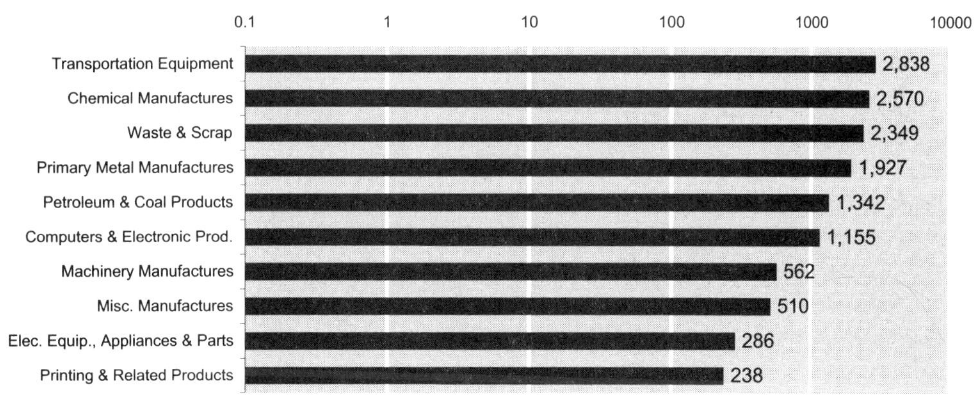

Source: Bureau of Economic Analysis; Foreign Trade Division, U.S. Census Bureau
*European investment includes France, Germany, Netherlands, Switzerland, and the United Kingdom
Due to a need to align resources with current funding levels, the Bureau of Economic Analysis has reduced its coverage to major investing countries.

New Mexico and Europe

Employment, Investment, and Trade Linkages

Employment

European* investment in New Mexico supported 7,600 jobs in 2007; 12% were in manufacturing activities.

Investment

Of the $4.1 billion invested in New Mexico in 2007, 10%, or $0.4 billion came from Europe*.

Sources of FDI within New Mexico, 2007	
Country	**FDI ($ Millions)**
Germany	242
Japan	129
Canada	116
France	70
Netherlands	49

Trade

In 2008, Europe purchased $285 million worth of goods from New Mexico. Exports are relatively small and are skewed toward computers and related goods.

Top European Export Markets, 2008	
Country	**Exports ($ Millions)**
Germany	64
United Kingdom	52
Ireland	32
France	29
Italy	24

Top Ten Exports to Europe ($ Millions)

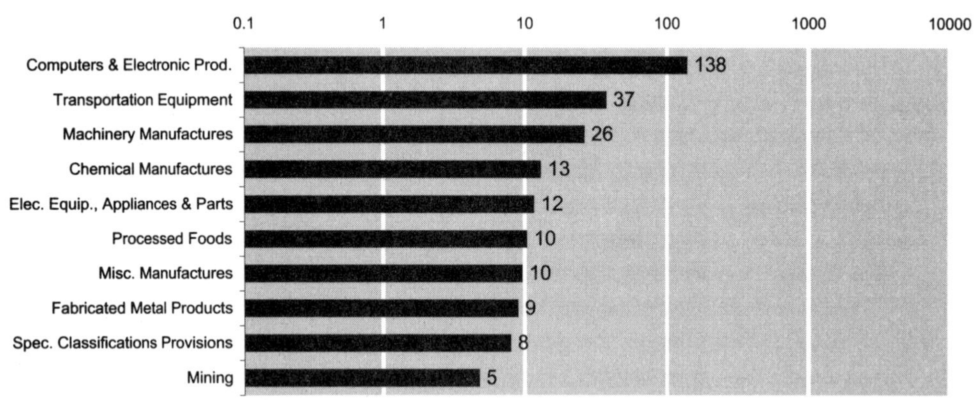

Source: Bureau of Economic Analysis; Foreign Trade Division, U.S. Census Bureau
*European investment includes France, Germany, Netherlands, Switzerland, and the United Kingdom
Due to a need to align resources with current funding levels, the Bureau of Economic Analysis has reduced its coverage to major investing countries.

New York and Europe
Employment, Investment, and Trade Linkages

Employment
European* investment in New York supported 271,300 jobs in 2007; most of the jobs were in services while 8% were in manufacturing activities.

Investment
Of the $82.6 billion invested in New York in 2007, 54%, or $44.2 billion came from Europe*.

Sources of FDI within New York, 2007	
Country	**FDI ($ Millions)**
United Kingdom	17,083
Germany	12,322
Canada	10,944
Japan	9,884
France	7,668

Trade
In 2008, Europe purchased $30.3 billion worth of goods from New York. Miscellaneous manufactures, used merchandise and primary metal manufactures are top export categories to Europe.

Top European Export Markets, 2008	
Country	**Exports ($ Millions)**
Switzerland	7,931
United Kingdom	5,502
Belgium	3,130
Germany	3,081
France	2,560

Top Ten Exports to Europe ($ Millions)

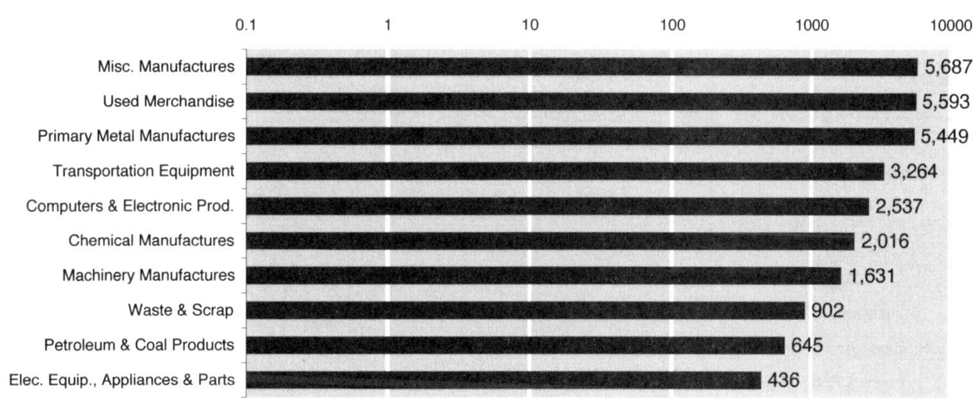

Source: Bureau of Economic Analysis; Foreign Trade Division, U.S. Census Bureau
*European investment includes France, Germany, Netherlands, Switzerland, and the United Kingdom
Due to a need to align resources with current funding levels, the Bureau of Economic Analysis has reduced its coverage to major investing countries.

North Carolina and Europe

Employment, Investment, and Trade Linkages

Employment

European* investment in North Carolina supported 97,800 jobs in 2007; nearly 40% of jobs were in manufacturing.

Investment

Of the $29.6 billion invested in North Carolina in 2007, 47%, or $14 billion came from Europe*.

Sources of FDI within North Carolina, 2007	
Country	**FDI ($ Millions)**
Germany	5,528
United Kingdom	5,243
Canada	3,741
Japan	3,510
France	1,257

Trade

In 2008, Europe purchased $6.3 billion worth of goods from North Carolina. Exports include such goods as chemicals, transportation equipment and machinery manufactures.

Top European Export Markets, 2008	
Country	**Exports ($ Millions)**
United Kingdom	1,045
Germany	1,040
France	1,001
Netherlands	902
Belgium	459

Top Ten Exports to Europe ($ Millions)

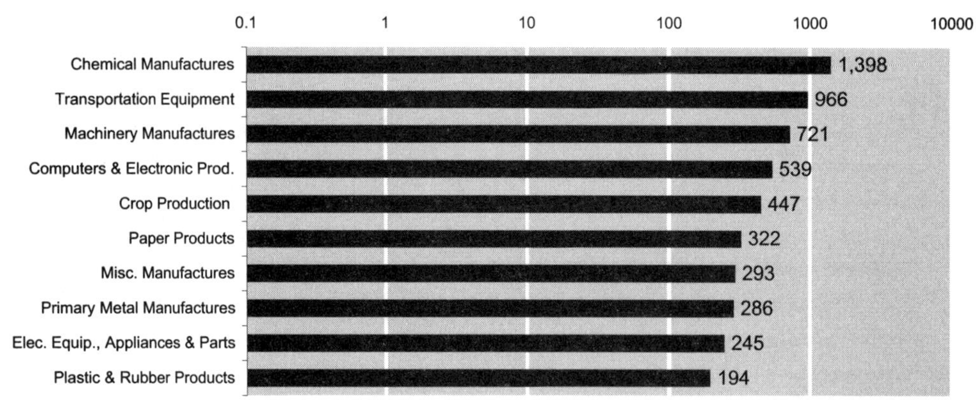

Source: Bureau of Economic Analysis; Foreign Trade Division, U.S. Census Bureau
*European investment includes France, Germany, Netherlands, Switzerland, and the United Kingdom
Due to a need to align resources with current funding levels, the Bureau of Economic Analysis has reduced its coverage to major investing countries.

North Dakota and Europe

Employment, Investment, and Trade Linkages

Employment

European* investment in North Dakota supported 2,900 jobs in 2007, 300 of which were in the manufacturing sector.

Investment

Of the $1.5 billion invested in North Dakota in 2007, 6%, or $0.1 billion came from Europe*.

Sources of FDI within North Dakota, 2007	
Country	**FDI ($ Millions)**
Canada	581
Germany	55
United Kingdom	28
Japan	19

Trade

In 2008, Europe purchased $655 million worth of goods from North Dakota. Three-fourths of the state's exports consists of machinery manufactures.

Top European Export Markets, 2008	
Country	**Exports ($ Millions)**
Belgium	95
Germany	94
United Kingdom	36
Spain	30
Czech Republic	28

Top Ten Exports to Europe ($ Millions)

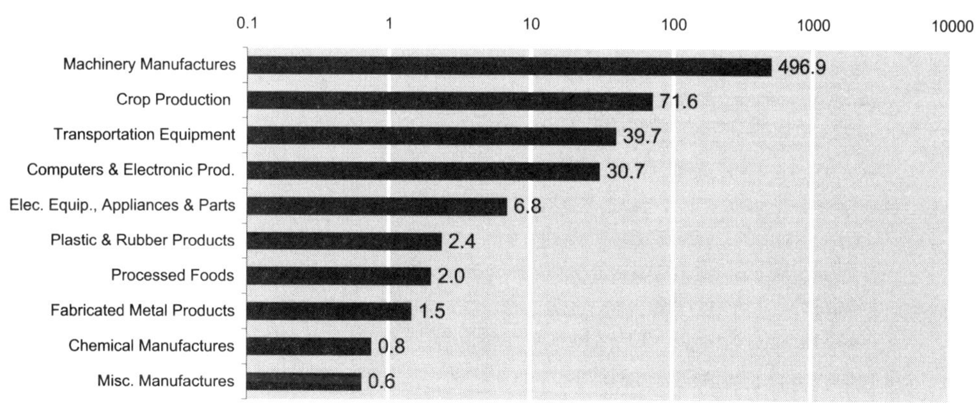

Source: Bureau of Economic Analysis; Foreign Trade Division, U.S. Census Bureau
*European investment includes France, Germany, Netherlands, Switzerland, and the United Kingdom
Due to a need to align resources with current funding levels, the Bureau of Economic Analysis has reduced its coverage to major investing countries.

Ohio and Europe

Employment, Investment, and Trade Linkages

Employment

European* investment in Ohio supported 116,700 jobs in 2007; nearly one-fourth of these jobs were employed in manufacturing activities.

Investment

Of the $42.9 billion invested in Ohio in 2007, 40%, or $17 billion came from Europe*.

Sources of FDI within Ohio, 2007	
Country	**FDI ($ Millions)**
Japan	15,230
United Kingdom	8,448
Germany	5,116
Canada	3,559
France	1,800

Trade

In 2008, Europe purchased $8.5 billion worth of goods from Ohio. Transportation equipment and machinery are the state's top exports to Europe.

Top European Export Markets, 2008	
Country	**Exports ($ Millions)**
Germany	1,478
United Kingdom	1,475
France	1,121
Belgium	727
Netherlands	697

Top Ten Exports to Europe ($ Billions)

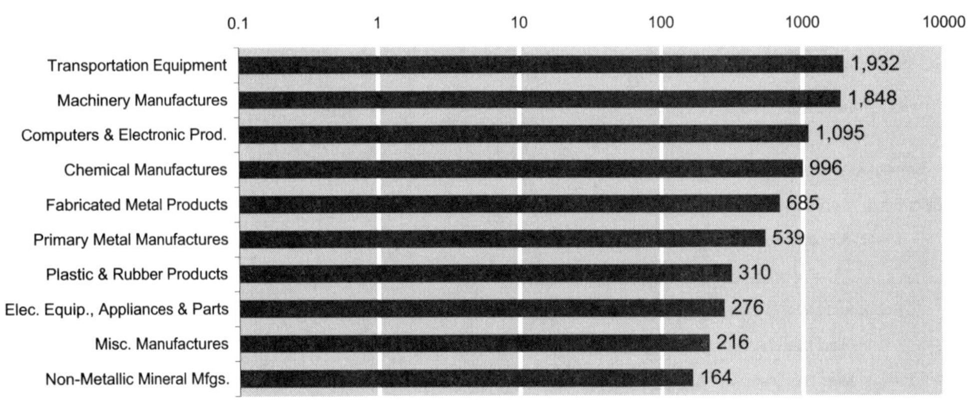

Source: Bureau of Economic Analysis; Foreign Trade Division, U.S. Census Bureau
*European investment includes France, Germany, Netherlands, Switzerland, and the United Kingdom
Due to a need to align resources with current funding levels, the Bureau of Economic Analysis has reduced its coverage to major investing countries.

Oklahoma and Europe

Employment, Investment, and Trade Linkages

Employment

European* investment in Oklahoma supported 15,200 jobs in 2007, one-third of which were in manufacturing activities.

Investment

Of the $10.1 billion invested in Oklahoma in 2007, 14%, or $1.4 billion came from Europe*.

Sources of FDI within Oklahoma, 2007	
Country	**FDI ($ Millions)**
France	830
Canada	539
Japan	427
Germany	412
Switzerland	188

Trade

In 2008, Europe purchased $933 million worth of goods from Oklahoma. Top exports include machinery, transportation equipment and computers.

Top European Export Markets, 2008	
Country	**Exports ($ Millions)**
Germany	150
Belgium	141
United Kingdom	120
Netherlands	67
Italy	51

Top Ten Exports to Europe ($ Millions)

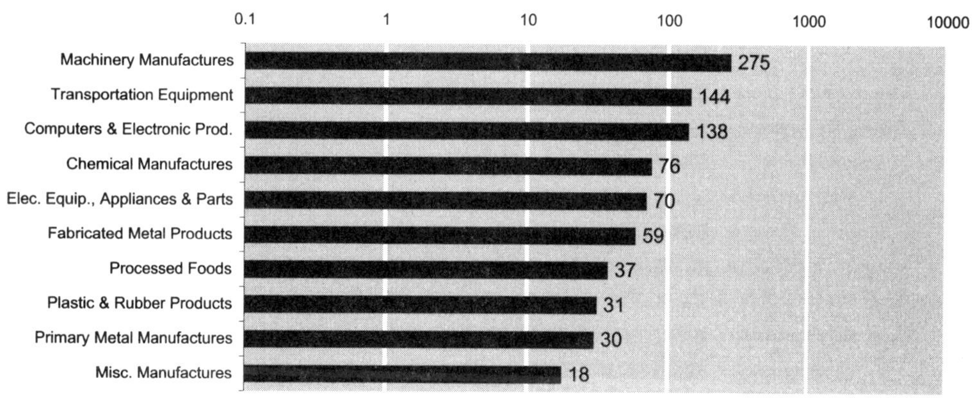

Source: Bureau of Economic Analysis; Foreign Trade Division, U.S. Census Bureau
*European investment includes France, Germany, Netherlands, Switzerland, and the United Kingdom
Due to a need to align resources with current funding levels, the Bureau of Economic Analysis has reduced its coverage to major investing countries.

Oregon and Europe

Employment, Investment, and Trade Linkages

Employment

European* investment in Oregon supported 23,600 jobs in 2007; 16% of these jobs were in manufacturing activities.

Investment

Of the $10.1 billion invested in Oregon in 2007, 25%, or $2.5 billion came from Europe*.

Sources of FDI within Oregon, 2007	
Country	**FDI ($ Millions)**
Canada	2,172
Germany	1,686
Japan	1,033
United Kingdom	355
Netherlands	180

Trade

In 2008, Europe purchased $2.5 billion worth of goods from Oregon. Roughly a third of Oregon's exports to Europe consist of computers and electronic products.

Top European Export Markets, 2008	
Country	**Exports ($ Millions)**
Germany	400
Netherlands	396
United Kingdom	338
France	295
Italy	158

Top Ten Exports to Europe ($ Millions)

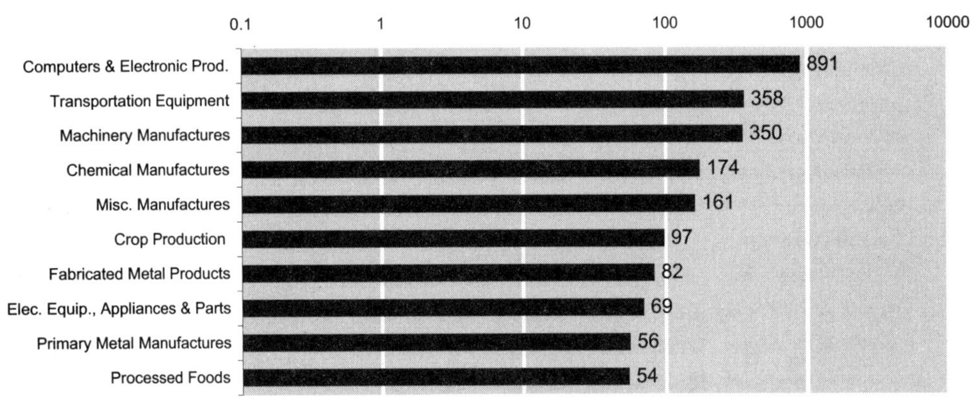

Source: Bureau of Economic Analysis; Foreign Trade Division, U.S. Census Bureau
*European investment includes France, Germany, Netherlands, Switzerland, and the United Kingdom
Due to a need to align resources with current funding levels, the Bureau of Economic Analysis has reduced its coverage to major investing countries.

Pennsylvania and Europe

Employment, Investment, and Trade Linkages

Employment

European* investment in Pennsylvania supported 162,100 jobs in 2007; one-fourth of these workers were involved in manufacturing.

Investment

Of the $37.8 billion invested in Pennsylvania in 2007, 59%, or $22.3 billion came from Europe*.

Sources of FDI within Pennsylvania, 2007	
Country	**FDI ($ Millions)**
United Kingdom	8,163
Germany	7,563
Canada	3,654
France	2,962
Japan	2,522

Trade

In 2008, Europe purchased $9.4 billion worth of goods from Pennsylvania. Exports are relatively diverse, ranging from chemicals & transportation equipment to machinery manufactures & primary metals

Top European Export Markets, 2008	
Country	**Exports ($ Millions)**
Belgium	1,649
United Kingdom	1,390
Germany	1,374
Netherlands	1,203
Italy	661

Top Ten Exports to Europe ($ Millions)

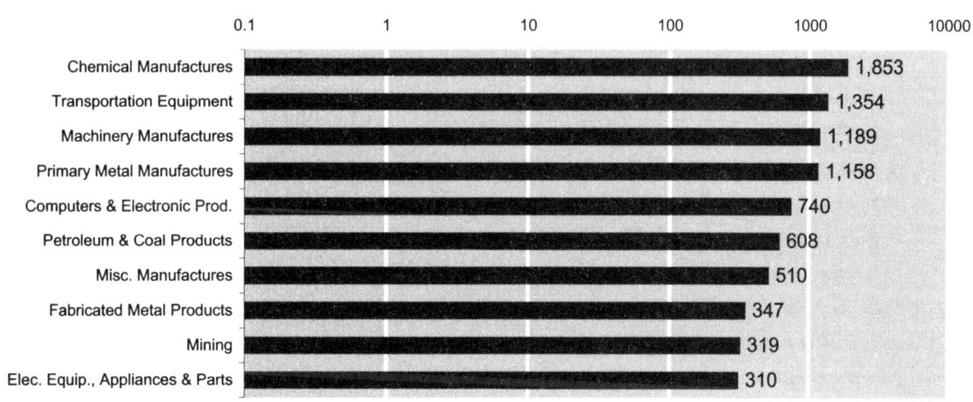

Source: Bureau of Economic Analysis; Foreign Trade Division, U.S. Census Bureau
*European investment includes France, Germany, Netherlands, Switzerland, and the United Kingdom
Due to a need to align resources with current funding levels, the Bureau of Economic Analysis has reduced its coverage to major investing countries.

Rhode Island and Europe

Employment, Investment, and Trade Linkages

Employment

European* investment in Rhode Island supported 17,600 jobs in 2007, 1,100 of which were in the manufacturing sector.

Investment

Of the $5.4 billion invested in Rhode Island in 2007, 9%, or $0.5 billion came from Europe*.

Sources of FDI within Rhode Island, 2007	
Country	**FDI ($ Millions)**
Germany	247
France	145
Switzerland	82
United Kingdom	n.a.
Netherlands	n.a.

Trade

In 2008, Europe purchased $759 million worth of goods from Rhode Island.
Top exports include waste and scrap, miscellaneous and machinery manufactures.

Top European Export Markets, 2008	
Country	**Exports ($ Millions)**
United Kingdom	173
Netherlands	126
Germany	109
Spain	46
Belgium	42

Top Ten Exports to Europe ($ Millions)

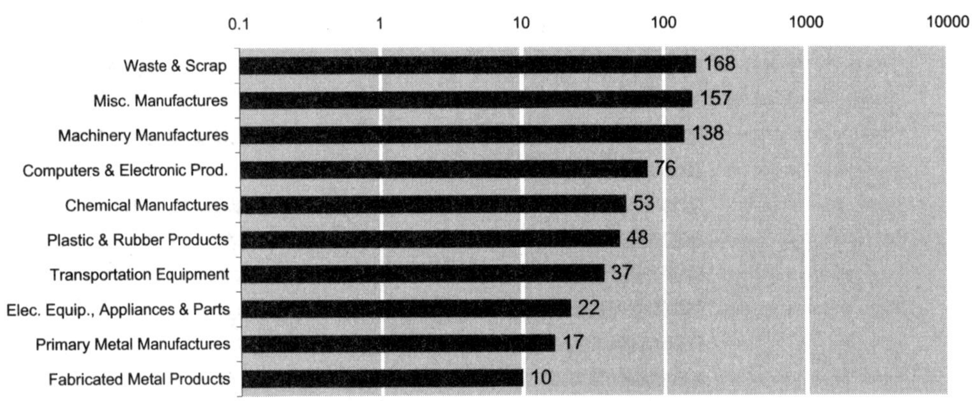

Source: Bureau of Economic Analysis; Foreign Trade Division, U.S. Census Bureau
*European investment includes France, Germany, Netherlands, Switzerland, and the United Kingdom
Due to a need to align resources with current funding levels, the Bureau of Economic Analysis has reduced its coverage to major investing countries.

South Carolina and Europe

Employment, Investment, and Trade Linkages

Employment

European* investment in South Carolina supported 60,100 jobs in 2007; nearly 50% of the jobs were in manufacturing.

Investment

Of the investment into South Carolina in 2007, $13.9 billion came from Europe*.

Sources of FDI within South Carolina, 2007	
Country	**FDI ($ Millions)**
Germany	5,438
Japan	4,121
France	3,810
United Kingdom	1,981
Switzerland	1,967

Trade

In 2008, Europe purchased $8.9 billion worth of goods from South Carolina. Nearly 60% of the state's exports consist of transportation equipment.

Top European Export Markets, 2008	
Country	**Exports ($ Millions)**
Germany	4,776
United Kingdom	1,189
France	611
Belgium	558
Netherlands	329

Top Ten Exports to Europe ($ Millions)

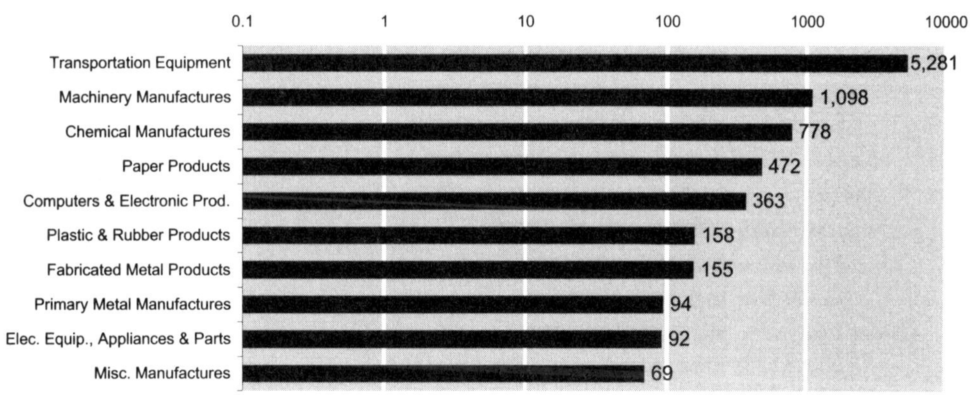

Source: Bureau of Economic Analysis; Foreign Trade Division, U.S. Census Bureau
*European investment includes France, Germany, Netherlands, Switzerland, and the United Kingdom
Due to a need to align resources with current funding levels, the Bureau of Economic Analysis has reduced its coverage to major investing countries.

South Dakota and Europe

Employment, Investment, and Trade Linkages

Employment

European* investment in South Dakota supported 1,500 jobs in 2007, one-third of which were in the manufacturing sector.

Investment

Of the $1.2 billion invested in South Dakota in 2007, 13%, or $0.2 billion came from Europe*.

Sources of FDI within South Dakota, 2007	
Country	**FDI ($ Millions)**
Canada	267
United Kingdom	105
Japan	34
Germany	25
Switzerland	12

Trade

In 2008, Europe purchased $207 million worth of goods from South Dakota. Machinery manufactures and computers & electronic products are the state's top exports to Europe.

Top European Export Markets, 2008	
Country	**Exports ($ Millions)**
Germany	69
United Kingdom	39
Belgium	14
Italy	13
France	12

Top Ten Exports to Europe ($ Millions)

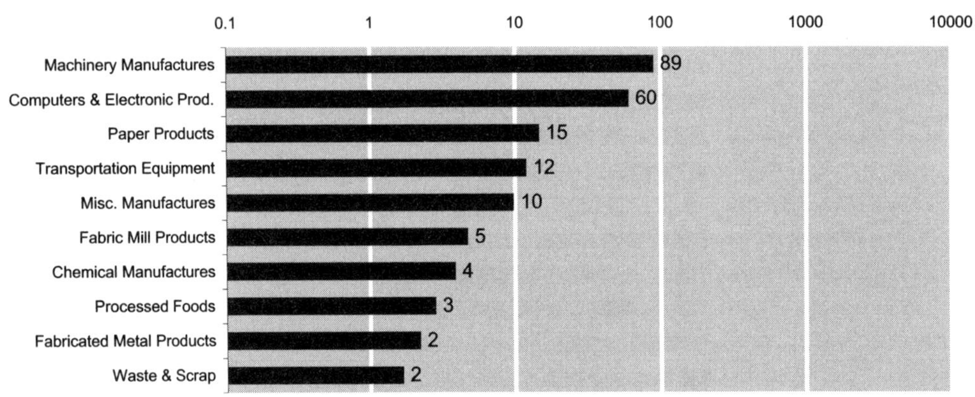

Source: Bureau of Economic Analysis; Foreign Trade Division, U.S. Census Bureau
*European investment includes France, Germany, Netherlands, Switzerland, and the United Kingdom
Due to a need to align resources with current funding levels, the Bureau of Economic Analysis has reduced its coverage to major investing countries.

Tennessee and Europe

Employment, Investment, and Trade Linkages

Employment

European* investment in Tennessee supported 60,300 jobs in 2007; just over one-third of the jobs were in manufacturing.

Investment

Of the $22.5 billion invested in Tennessee in 2007, 28%, or $6.2 billion came from Europe*.

Sources of FDI within Tennessee, 2007	
Country	**FDI ($ Millions)**
Japan	10,194
Germany	2,210
United Kingdom	2,192
Canada	2,003
France	921

Trade

In 2008, Europe purchased $5.4 billion worth of goods from Tennessee. Miscellaneous and chemical manufactures as well as transportation equipment make up the bulk of exports.

Top European Export Markets, 2008	
Country	**Exports ($ Millions)**
United Kingdom	1,032
Germany	811
Netherlands	694
Belgium	667
Italy	472

Top Ten Exports to Europe ($ Millions)

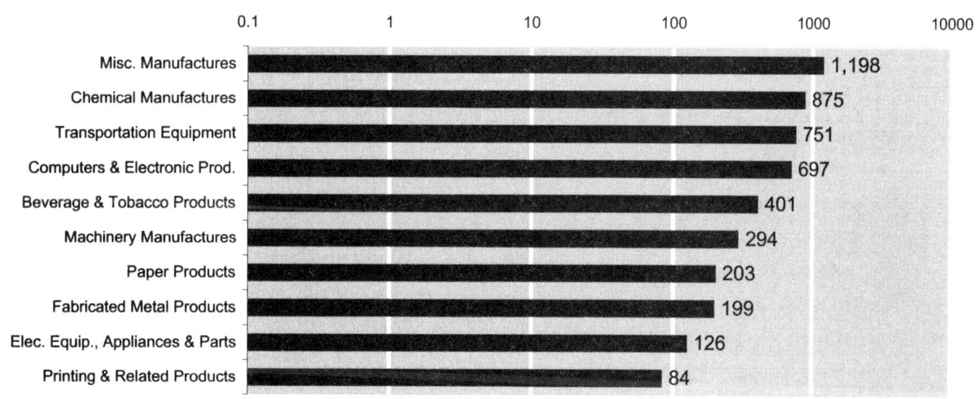

Source: Bureau of Economic Analysis; Foreign Trade Division, U.S. Census Bureau
*European investment includes France, Germany, Netherlands, Switzerland, and the United Kingdom
Due to a need to align resources with current funding levels, the Bureau of Economic Analysis has reduced its coverage to major investing countries.

Texas and Europe

Employment, Investment, and Trade Linkages

Employment

European* investment in Texas supported 210,700 jobs in 2007; roughly one-fourth of these jobs were in manufacturing.

Investment

Of the $119.3 billion invested in Texas in 2007, 47%, or $55.9 billion came from Europe*.

Sources of FDI within Texas, 2007	
Country	**FDI ($ Millions)**
United Kingdom	20,031
Germany	12,413
France	11,506
Japan	10,515
Netherlands	9,395

Trade

In 2008, Europe purchased $31.4 billion worth of goods from Texas. Exports are relatively diverse ranging from chemicals, petroleum, computers and machinery manufacturers.

Top European Export Markets, 2008	
Country	**Exports ($ Millions)**
Netherlands	7,063
Belgium	3,590
United Kingdom	3,542
Germany	2,854
France	2,411

Top Ten Exports to Europe ($ Billions)

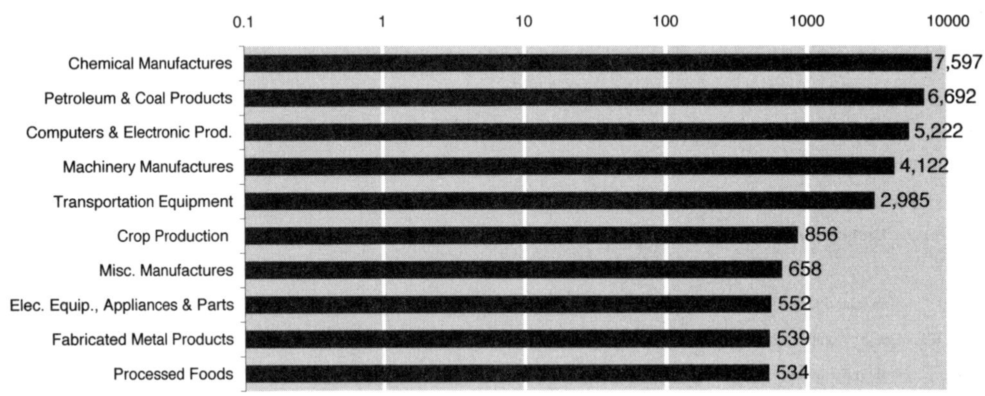

Source: Bureau of Economic Analysis; Foreign Trade Division, U.S. Census Bureau
*European investment includes France, Germany, Netherlands, Switzerland, and the United Kingdom
Due to a need to align resources with current funding levels, the Bureau of Economic Analysis has reduced its coverage to major investing countries.

Utah and Europe

Employment, Investment, and Trade Linkages

Employment

European* investment in Utah supported 23,300 jobs in 2007; 10% of these jobs were involved in manufacturing.

Investment

Of the $6.4 billion invested in Utah in 2007, 16%, or $1 billion came from Europe*.

Sources of FDI within Utah, 2007	
Country	**FDI ($ Millions)**
Germany	408
Japan	396
France	381
Canada	368
Netherlands	228

Trade

In 2008, Europe purchased $5 billion worth of goods from Utah. Primary metals dominate the state's exports to Europe.

Top European Export Markets, 2008	
Country	**Exports ($ Millions)**
United Kingdom	3,516
Belgium	543
Germany	234
Netherlands	176
France	87

Top Ten Exports to Europe ($ Millions)

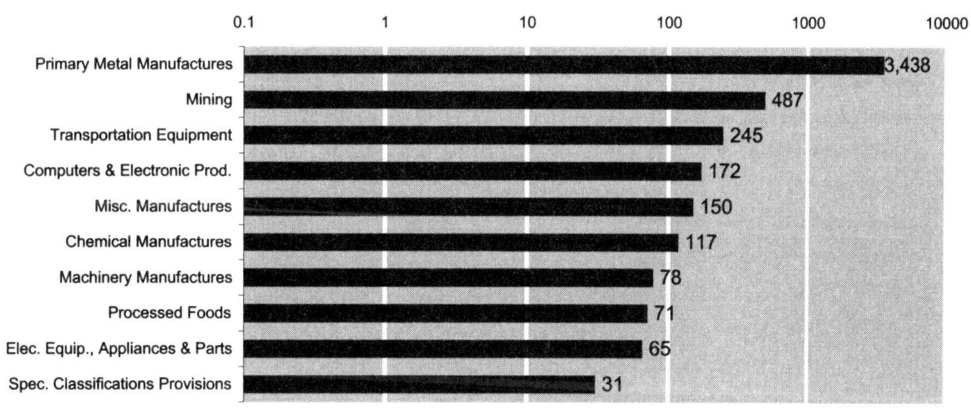

Source: Bureau of Economic Analysis; Foreign Trade Division, U.S. Census Bureau
*European investment includes France, Germany, Netherlands, Switzerland, and the United Kingdom
Due to a need to align resources with current funding levels, the Bureau of Economic Analysis has reduced its coverage to major investing countries.

Vermont and Europe

Employment, Investment, and Trade Linkages

Employment

European* investment in Vermont supported 4,300 jobs in 2007; nearly one-fifth of these jobs were in manufacturing.

Investment

Of the $1.5 billion invested in Vermont in 2007, 8%, or $0.1 billion came from Europe*.

Sources of FDI within Vermont, 2007	
Country	**FDI ($ Millions)**
United Kingdom	57
Germany	54
Switzerland	n.a.
Netherlands	n.a.
Japan	n.a.

Trade

In 2008, Europe purchased $417 million worth of goods from Vermont. Computers are and electronic products are the top export to Europe.

Top European Export Markets, 2008	
Country	**Exports ($ Millions)**
United Kingdom	116
Ireland	105
Germany	52
France	25
Belgium	21

Top Ten Exports to Europe ($ Millions)

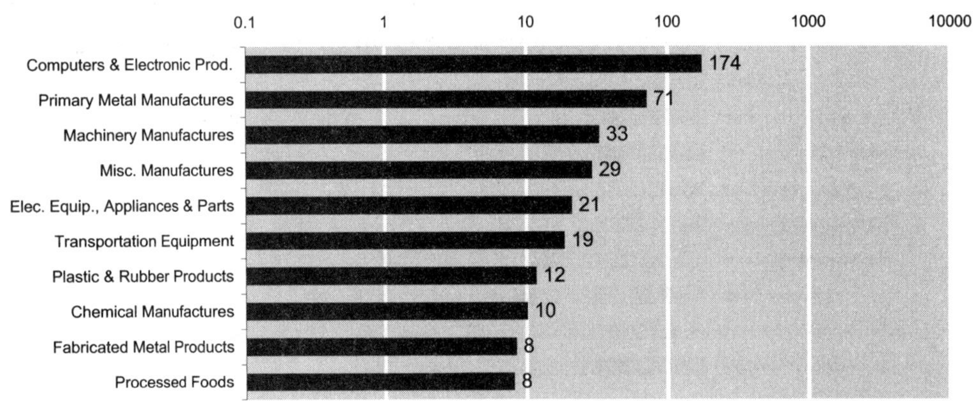

Source: Bureau of Economic Analysis; Foreign Trade Division, U.S. Census Bureau
*European investment includes France, Germany, Netherlands, Switzerland, and the United Kingdom
Due to a need to align resources with current funding levels, the Bureau of Economic Analysis has reduced its coverage to major investing countries.

Virginia and Europe

Employment, Investment, and Trade Linkages

Employment

European* investment in Virginia supported 76,200 jobs in 2007; roughly one-quarter were involved in manufacturing.

Investment

Of the investment into Virginia in 2007, $12 billion came from Europe*.

Sources of FDI within Virginia, 2007	
Country	**FDI ($ Millions)**
Germany	6,361
Japan	2,226
United Kingdom	1,846
Netherlands	1,563
France	1,524

Trade

In 2008, Europe purchased $7.3 billion worth of goods from Virginia. Top exports are spread across computers, transportation equipment and mining.

Top European Export Markets, 2008	
Country	**Exports ($ Millions)**
United Kingdom	1,173
Germany	965
Portugal	791
Belgium	698
Netherlands	597

Top Ten Exports to Europe ($ Millions)

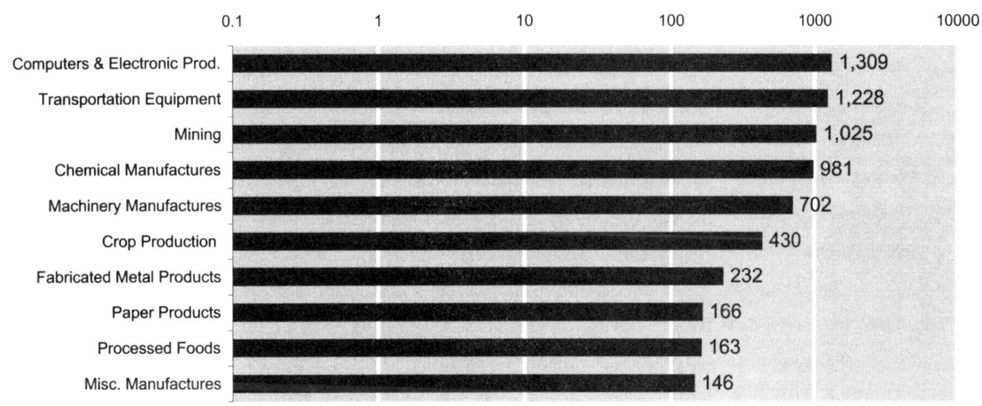

Source: Bureau of Economic Analysis; Foreign Trade Division, U.S. Census Bureau
*European investment includes France, Germany, Netherlands, Switzerland, and the United Kingdom
Due to a need to align resources with current funding levels, the Bureau of Economic Analysis has reduced its coverage to major investing countries.

Washington and Europe

Employment, Investment, and Trade Linkages

Employment

European* investment in Washington supported 45,800 jobs in 2007; only one-fifth of the jobs were involved in manufacturing.

Investment

Of the $22.4 billion invested in Washington in 2007, 41%, or $9.1 billion came from Europe*.

Sources of FDI within Washington, 2007	
Country	**FDI ($ Millions)**
Canada	5,316
Germany	3,733
Japan	3,203
United Kingdom	2,409
Netherlands	1,707

Trade

In 2008, Europe purchased $9 billion worth of goods from Washington. Transportation equipment dominates Washington's exports to Europe.

Top European Export Markets, 2008	
Country	**Exports ($ Millions)**
Netherlands	1,315
United Kingdom	1,289
Ireland	1,059
Germany	1,057
France	839

Top Ten Exports to Europe ($ Billions)

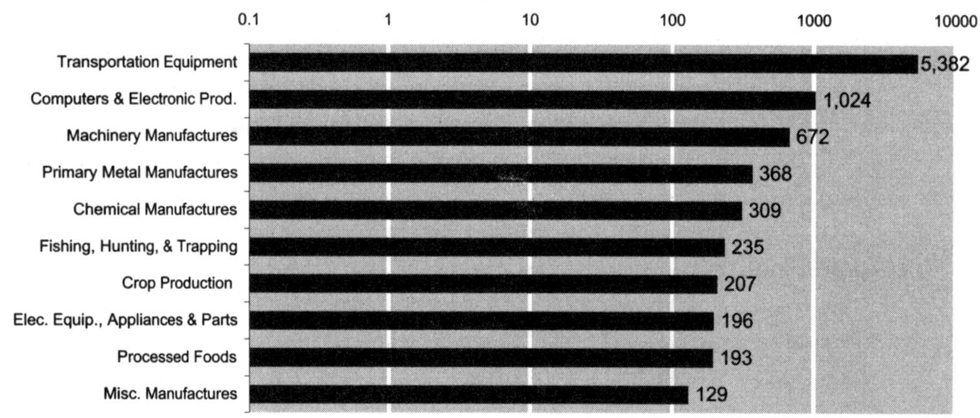

Source: Bureau of Economic Analysis; Foreign Trade Division, U.S. Census Bureau
*European investment includes France, Germany, Netherlands, Switzerland, and the United Kingdom
Due to a need to align resources with current funding levels, the Bureau of Economic Analysis has reduced its coverage to major investing countries.

West Virginia and Europe

Employment, Investment, and Trade Linkages

Employment

European* investment in West Virginia supported 9,800 jobs in 2007; roughly one-third were in manufacturing.

Investment

Of the $6.6 billion invested in West Virginia in 2007, 22%, or $1.4 billion came from Europe*.

Sources of FDI within West Virginia, 2007	
Country	**FDI ($ Millions)**
Japan	1,491
France	850
Canada	821
Switzerland	332
United Kingdom	141

Trade

In 2008, Europe purchased $2 billion worth of goods from West Virginia. Mining is the state's top export to Europe.

Top European Export Markets, 2008	
Country	**Exports ($ Millions)**
Belgium	323
Netherlands	302
France	290
United Kingdom	222
Italy	174

Top Ten Exports to Europe ($ Millions)

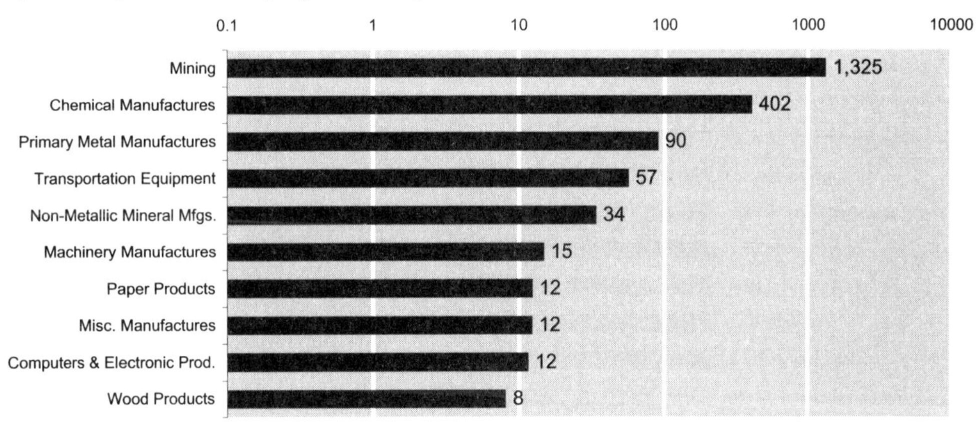

Source: Bureau of Economic Analysis; Foreign Trade Division, U.S. Census Bureau
*European investment includes France, Germany, Netherlands, Switzerland, and the United Kingdom
Due to a need to align resources with current funding levels, the Bureau of Economic Analysis has reduced its coverage to major investing countries.

Wisconsin and Europe

Employment, Investment, and Trade Linkages

Employment

European* investment in Wisconsin supported 44,200 jobs in 2007; manufacturing jobs accounted for 34% of the total.

Investment

Of the $14.5 billion invested in Wisconsin in 2007, 34%, or $4.9 billion came from Europe*.

Sources of FDI within Wisconsin, 2007	
Country	**FDI ($ Millions)**
Canada	5,154
Germany	1,945
United Kingdom	1,261
France	974
Japan	580

Trade

In 2008, Europe purchased $4.6 billion worth of goods from Wisconsin. Machinery and computers are the state's top exports to Europe.

Top European Export Markets, 2008	
Country	**Exports ($ Millions)**
Germany	790
United Kingdom	683
France	518
Belgium	414
Netherlands	366

Top Ten Exports to Europe ($ Millions)

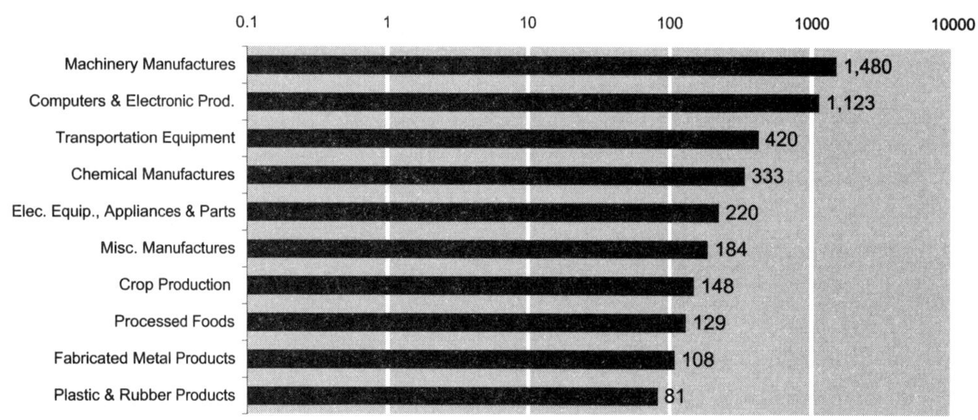

Source: Bureau of Economic Analysis; Foreign Trade Division, U.S. Census Bureau
*European investment includes France, Germany, Netherlands, Switzerland, and the United Kingdom
Due to a need to align resources with current funding levels, the Bureau of Economic Analysis has reduced its coverage to major investing countries.

Wyoming and Europe

Employment, Investment, and Trade Linkages

Employment

European* investment in Wyoming supported 4,100 jobs in 2007, 300 of which were in manufacturing.

Investment

Of the $11.5 billion invested in Wyoming in 2007, $0.1 billion came from Europe*.

Sources of FDI within Wyoming, 2007	
Country	**FDI ($ Millions)**
Canada	843
France	52
Japan	33
Switzerland	6
United Kingdom	n.a.

Trade

In 2008, Europe purchased $102 million worth of goods from Wyoming.
By a wide margin, chemicals are the top export to Europe.

Top European Export Markets, 2008	
Country	**Exports ($ Millions)**
Netherlands	21
Belgium	18
Spain	14
United Kingdom	9
France	9

Top Ten Exports to Europe ($ Millions)

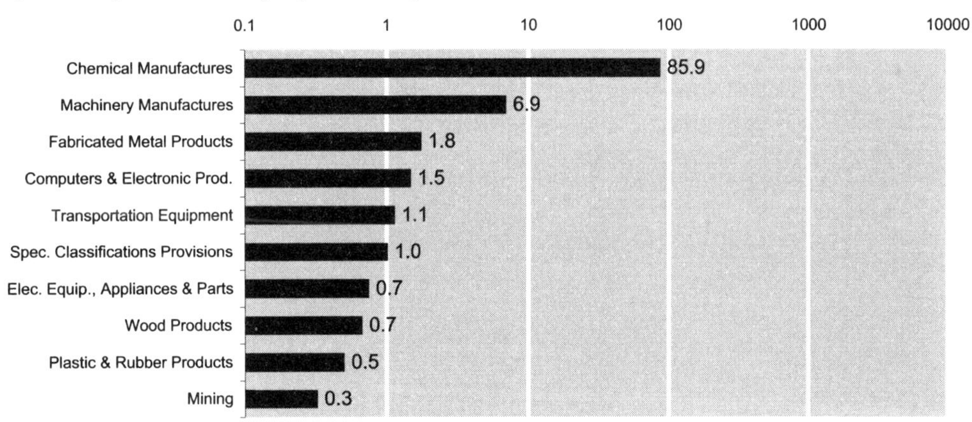

Source: Bureau of Economic Analysis; Foreign Trade Division, U.S. Census Bureau
*European investment includes France, Germany, Netherlands, Switzerland, and the United Kingdom
Due to a need to align resources with current funding levels, the Bureau of Economic Analysis has reduced its coverage to major investing countries.

Chapter 4

U.S. Commerce and Europe: A Country-by-Country Comparison

As the largest and one of the wealthiest economic entities in the world, the European Union (EU) remains a favorite destination for Corporate America. Europe possesses the main attributes that attract foreign investment in the first place—a wealthy consumer market, a transparent rule of law, a liberal investment environment, and a large pool of skilled labor. The successful enlargement of the Union, notably the integration of many central and eastern European nations, is another factor that makes Europe among the most favored destinations of U.S. foreign direct investment (FDI). Nestled among the nations of the "Old World" are some of the most dynamic and largest emerging markets in the world, including Poland, a nation at the forefront of this dynamic group. Finally, the EU's Single Market and single currency—while each incomplete and imperfect—are two more important factors that continue to draw more U.S. capital to Europe. Next to the United States, Europe is the closest economic entity in the world—in terms of size and scale—that resembles anything like a coherent, single market that is easily accessible to foreign firms looking to operate from within.

That said, global foreign direct investment flows are highly correlated to global growth. The stronger the global economy, the more robust global investment flows tend to be. Hence, over the 2003-2007 period, while the world economy expanded nearly 5% on an annual rate, global and transatlantic FDI flows were quite robust. In 2007, one year before the financial crisis hammered global economic growth, U.S. foreign direct investment to Europe hit an all-time high of $235 billion. Thereafter, however, U.S. investment declined along with the slumping global economy; U.S. foreign direct investment to Europe (including non-EU states like Switzerland, Norway, Russia and Turkey) dropped roughly 23% in 2008 and plunged by 44% in the first nine months of 2009 versus the same period a year earlier. As the accompanying chart highlights, U.S. FDI to most major markets declined in 2009 relative to 2008.

Over the first nine months of 2009 versus the same period a year earlier, U.S. FDI flows declined 124% to Spain, 65% to the United Kingdom, 43% to Germany, and 10% to Italy. U.S. FDI flows over this period also declined by 68% to Brazil and by 49% to India.

While these are considerable declines, they pale in comparison to the 185% drop in U.S. FDI flows to China over the same period. In fact, while U.S. FDI outflows to Europe declined during this period, they still totaled a positive $82.4 billion, whereas for the same period U.S. firms actually disinvested in China—there was a net reversal of U.S. FDI out of China of $6.3 billion. This disinvestment in China overshadowed smaller net investments in the other BRIC countries, so that overall, U.S. companies *disinvested* in the BRICs as a group.

Around the world, U.S. multinationals have been capital-constrained over the past two years, a consequence of one of the worst financial crises on record. Less capital in the way of earnings, bank lending and reinvested income have curtailed investment outlays, making it financially more difficult to expand offshore. This is a predictable outcome of the finan-

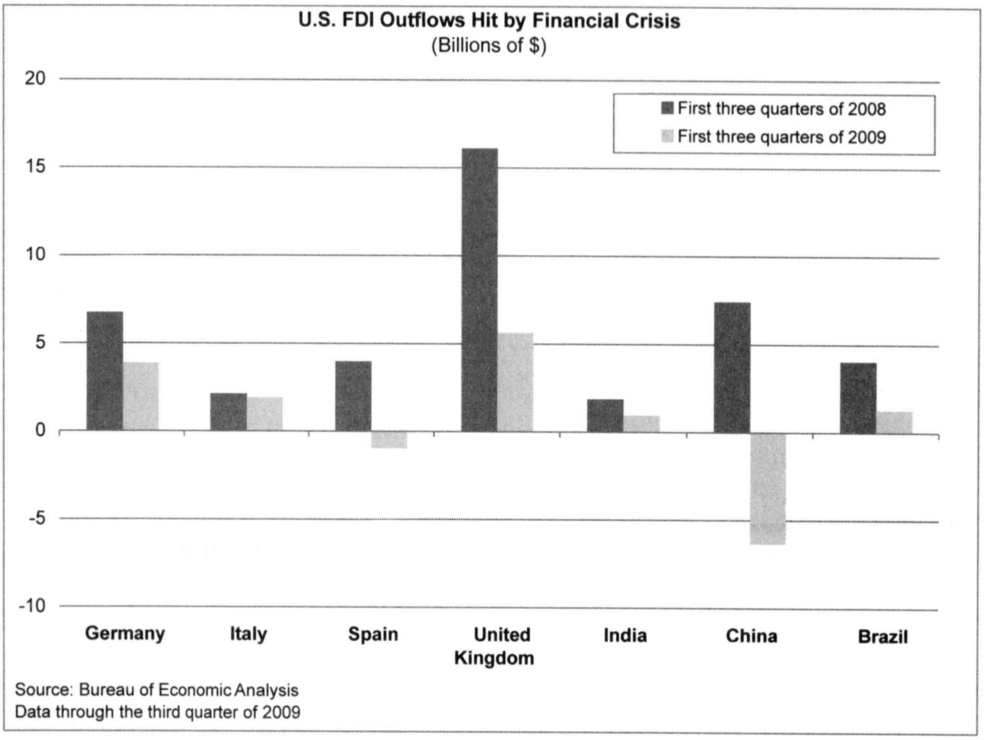
U.S. FDI Outflows Hit by Financial Crisis
(Billions of $)
First three quarters of 2008
First three quarters of 2009
20
15
10
5
0
-5
-10
Germany
Italy
Spain
United Kingdom
India
China
Brazil
Source: Bureau of Economic Analysis
Data through the third quarter of 2009

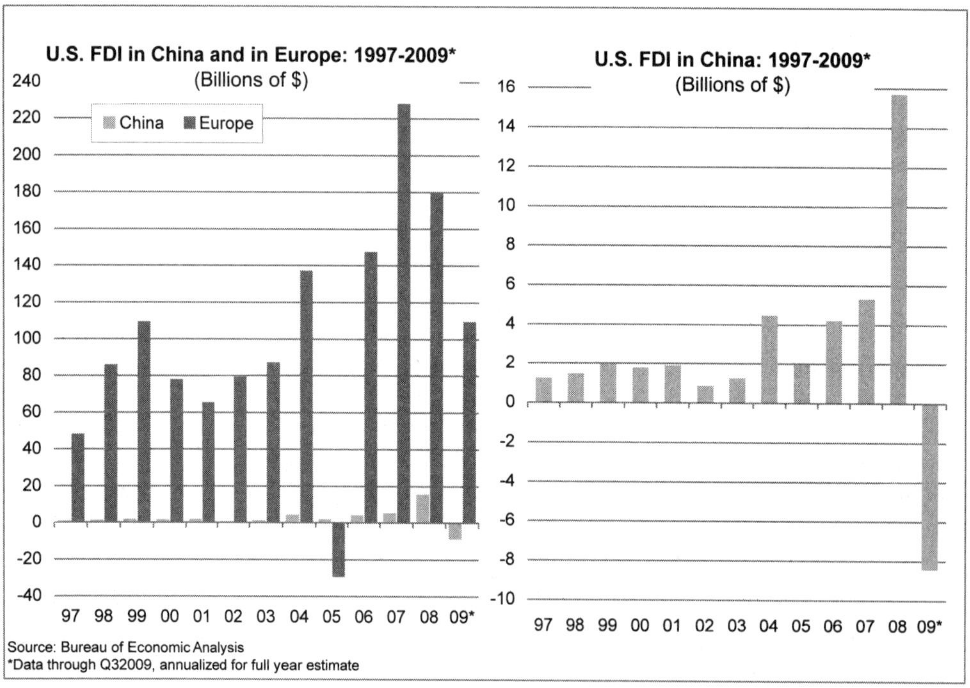
U.S. FDI in China and in Europe: 1997-2009*
(Billions of $)
China
Europe
240
220
200
180
160
140
120
100
80
60
40
20
0
-20
-40
97 98 99 00 01 02 03 04 05 06 07 08 09*
U.S. FDI in China: 1997-2009*
(Billions of $)
16
14
12
10
8
6
4
2
0
-2
-4
-6
-8
-10
97 98 99 00 01 02 03 04 05 06 07 08 09*
Source: Bureau of Economic Analysis
*Data through Q32009, annualized for full year estimate

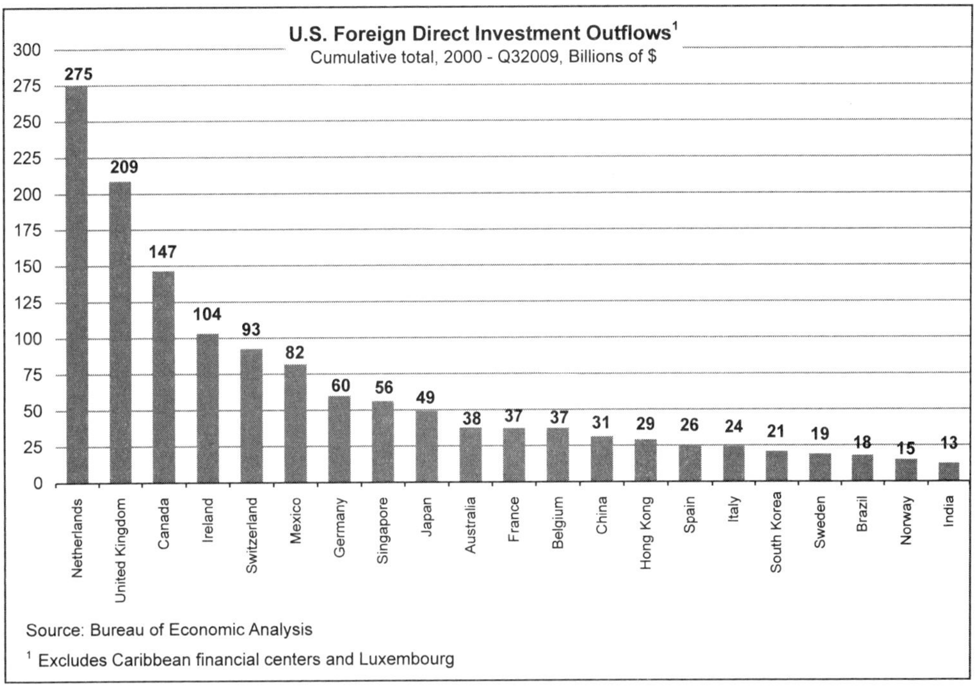

cial crisis. In aggregate, U.S. foreign direct investment dropped by an estimated 35% in 2009, one of the steepest annual declines on record.

Notwithstanding the plunge in investment, the direction of U.S. FDI has not noticeably changed over the past few years. U.S. investment to Europe considerably outweighs U.S. investment elsewhere in the world. That was the case in the 1960s, the 1970s, the 1980s and the 1990s. And things were no different in the first decade of the 21st century. Over the 2000-2009 period, U.S. companies sank roughly $1 trillion into Europe, a figure that equates to 60% of total U.S. investment (excluding flows to the Caribbean Islands) for the entire decade. This investment bias has remained despite all the talk about U.S. production facilities decamping America for lower cost locales like China and India.

Over the balance of the last decade, five out of the top ten overseas markets for U.S. investment were in Europe. In cumulative U.S. foreign investment outflows between 2000 and 2009, the Netherlands ranked first. The United Kingdom ranked second, Ireland fourth, Switzerland fifth, and Germany seventh. France ranked eleventh, Belgium twelfth, and Spain fifteenth. Also ranking in the top ten were America's Nafta neighbors, Canada and Mexico, which ranked third and sixth, respectively. Meanwhile, Singapore ranked eighth, Japan ninth and Australia tenth.

Over the past decade, U.S. firms invested more in the Netherlands than in the United Kingdom, the long-time favored destination of U.S. firms. Behind this trend: the expanding economic presence and clout of the European Union, with more and more U.S. firms opting to invest directly in the continental EU rather than the UK, a traditional export platform for U.S. affiliates to greater Europe. Even though the UK is an EU member and part of the EU Single Market, other considerations may be weighing on U.S. investors. The eurozone, of which the UK is not a member, appears to have galvanized more firms to invest on the continent. EU enlargement, and the accompanying extension of EU production networks and commercial infrastructure, has caused the center of economic gravity in Europe to shift eastward within the EU, with Brussels playing an important role in economic policies and decision-making.

In this regard, the Netherlands is becoming an increasingly important and critical launching pad for Corporate America to the rest of Europe. As a key export platform and pan-regional distribution hub, the Netherlands' share of U.S. investment in Europe increased from around 15% in the 1990s to nearly 26% this past decade.

Other EU nations have also become increasingly attractive to U.S. firms. For instance, Ireland's share of U.S. investment to the EU rose from a share of 4.6% in the 1990s to just shy of 10% over the last decade. U.S. firms sank over $100 billion into the Irish economy in the 2000s, more than four times the level of the 1990s. Facilitating this rise in investment has been the nation's low-cost, English-speaking labor force, coupled with the country's low corporate tax rates. The formula has made Ireland among the most favored destinations in the world for Corporate America. Even in the face of a severe recession, we estimate that U.S. firms invested roughly $20 billion in Ireland in 2009, not far from the peak of $22 billion in 2008.

Other destinations have fared less well. The share of U.S. investment in France and Italy declined over the last decade, with the former accounting for 3.5% of total U.S. investment to the Europe and the latter just 2.3%. Germany's share also fell, dropping to 5.6% of the total from nearly 7% in the 1990s. Greater U.S. investment in new EU member states in central and eastern Europe has helped to re-order U.S. flows to Europe, with Poland, one of the largest consumer markets in Europe, of key interest to Corporate America.

U.S. Outward FDI Flows to Europe, By Country
(% of Europe Total, 1990 - 1999)

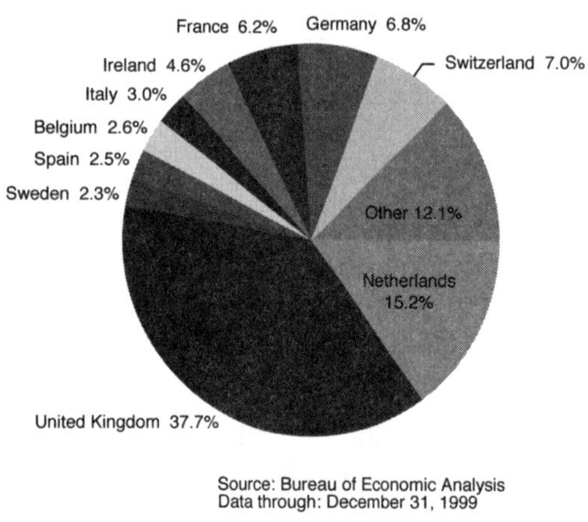

Source: Bureau of Economic Analysis
Data through: December 31, 1999

U.S. Outward FDI Flows to Europe, By Country
(% of Europe Total, 2000 - 3Q2009)

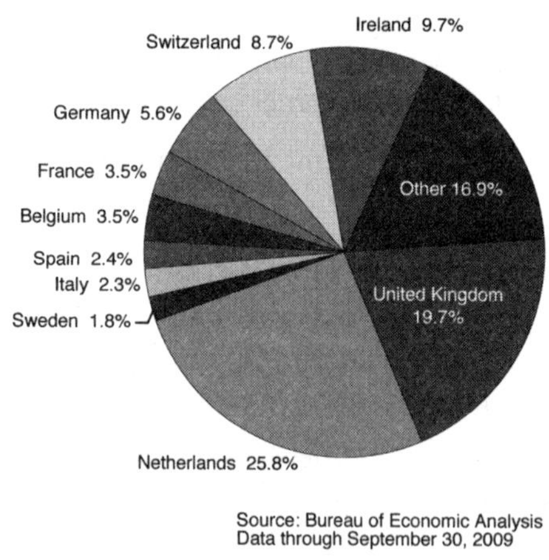

Source: Bureau of Economic Analysis
Data through September 30, 2009

U.S. Investment Outflows: Europe vs. the BRICs

Two myths are generating considerable heat and very little light in current U.S. debates about the activities of U.S. companies abroad. The first is that companies invest abroad only to export jobs out of the country. As we have demonstrated in our annual surveys, and as a consistent and credible body of academic research confirms, this is simply not true. Expansion by U.S. multinationals abroad tends to support jobs based in the United States. More investment and employment abroad is strongly correlated with more investment and employment in American parent companies. The occupations and skills of workers in U.S. foreign affiliates often complement, rather than substitute for jobs at parent firms. Between 1988 and 2007, the last year of available data, employment in affiliates rose by 5.3 million to 11.7 million (with most of them employed in Europe). Over that same period, employment in U.S. parent companies increased by nearly as much—4.3 million—to 22 million. Research repeatedly shows that foreign-affiliate expansion tends to expand U.S. parent activity. Procter & Gamble, for instance, calculates that one in five of its U.S. jobs—and two in five in Ohio—depend directly on its global business.[1]

The second myth is the commonplace assumption that when it comes to investing overseas, Corporate America is headed for the low-cost nations of Asia and Latin America. This is simply not true. Corporate America's global presence remains strongly rooted in Europe, a point we continue to emphasize in our annual surveys.

Take China for example. U.S. foreign direct investment to China increased sharply over the past decade, with U.S. firms investing roughly $31 billion into the Middle Kingdom between 2000 and 2009. This represents a significant rise from the prior decade, but some perspective is in order. China ranks 13th overall in terms of aggregate U.S. foreign direct investment in the 2000s, trailing a host of European nations such as Belgium, France, Germany, Switzerland, Ireland, the United Kingdom and the Netherlands. China did not only trail many European countries, it lagged by a wide margin. U.S. investment in Ireland over the 2000-2009 time period, for instance, was three times U.S. investment in China. American investment into the UK was nearly seven times larger than into China, and U.S. investment into the Netherlands was almost nine times greater than U.S. investment into China. To put the Netherlands in perspective, U.S. firms invested more in the Netherlands over the last decade than they invested in South and Central America, the Middle East, and Africa combined.

In relation to the other BRICs, the story is basically the same. America's cumulative investment in Brazil over the past decade ($18 billion) is roughly 70% of total U.S. investment in Spain. Russia has captured more U.S. investment since the start of this decade ($12 billion), but that is half the amount of U.S. investment in Italy. Finally, besides China, no nation has probably attracted as much attention and hope as India. Yet since 2000 U.S. firms have sunk roughly $13 billion into India—less than U.S. investment into Norway during the same period.

---

[1] Mihir A. Desai, C. Fritz Foley and James R. Hines, Jr., "Foreign Direct Investment And The Domestic Capital Stock," *American Economic Review*, 2005, v95(2,May), 33-38.; Carlos Lozada, "Does Overseas Investing Reduce Domestic Investment?" National Bureau of Economic Research, http://www.nber.org/digest/aug05/w11075.html; Theodore H. Moran, "American Multinationals and American Economic Interests: New Dimensions to an Old Debate," Peterson Institute for International Economics, March 17th, 2009, http://www.petersoninstitute.org/realtime/?p=550; Matthew Slaughter, "How to Destroy American Jobs," *Wall Street Journal*, February 3, 2010.

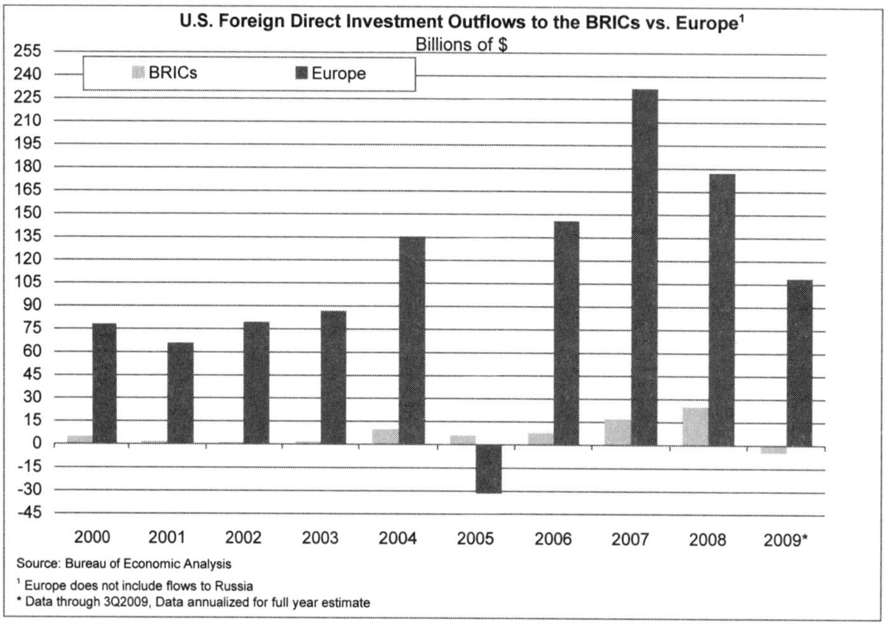

On a combined and cumulative basis, U.S. investment in the BRICs totaled roughly $74 billion last decade, up from a total of $48 billion in the 1990s. That represents a 53% increase—an impressive rise and indicative of the growing interest of Corporate America in key emerging markets. However, the total was less than U.S. investment in Ireland over the same period; moreover, what Corporate America sank in the BRICs last decade was just 8% of total U.S. investment into the European Union.

Viewed from a long-term perspective, or an historic-cost basis, in 2008 the U.S. investment position in Europe was 15 times larger than in the BRICs. In general, U.S. investment in Europe was nearly four times larger than corporate America's investment position in all of Asia at the end of 2008. U.S. investment stakes in Belgium at the end of 2008, $65 billion on a historic cost basis, were on par with the combined U.S. investment position in China and India, which totaled nearly $62 billion.

U.S. foreign affiliate sales in Europe remain robust, although the geographic distribution of affiliate sales has shifted over the past few decades. As the European Union has evolved over the past few decades, so have the strategies of U.S. affiliates operating in Europe. In particular, U.S. firms are increasingly slicing up their production chains across Europe, producing parts and components where it is most economical and cost-efficient, before final assembly.

This shift in strategy is evident from the accompanying table. Whereas in 1990, nearly 65% of U.S. affiliate sales were directed to local markets, the percentage dropped sharply, to 54%, by 2007. Exports to third parties—or other nations within the EU—have gained prominence. In 2007, for instance, nearly 40% of U.S. affiliate sales in Europe were classified as exports to third parties, up from 31% in 1990. The rise reflects the dispersion of U.S. manufacturing activities across Europe, notably between high-wage western Europe and low-cost eastern and central Europe. EU enlargement has allowed U.S. affiliates to slice up their production chains, and produce and assemble in various parts of the EU. Bel-

U.S. Affiliate Sales in Europe By Destination
% of total

Region	Calendar 1982: Local Market	Calendar 1982: Exports to 3rd Market	Calendar 1982: Exports to U.S.	Calendar 1990: Local Market	Calendar 1990: Exports to 3rd Market	Calendar 1990: Exports to U.S.	Calendar 2007: Local Market	Calendar 2007: Exports to 3rd Market	Calendar 2007: Exports to U.S.
World	**63.7%**	**25.6%**	**10.7%**	**67.0%**	**22.8%**	**10.2%**	**58.9%**	**30.6%**	**10.5%**
Europe	**61.4%**	**35.0%**	**3.6%**	**64.8%**	**31.2%**	**4.0%**	**53.9%**	**39.3%**	**6.7%**
Austria	na	na	na	77.8%	21.1%	1.1%	63.6%	33.9%	2.6%
Belgium	39.7%	57.2%	3.1%	41.5%	55.5%	3.0%	37.2%	57.7%	5.1%
Denmark	n.a.	n.a.	n.a.	75.7%	20.0%	4.3%	68.0%	20.8%	11.2%
Finland	97.6%	na	na	97.4%	2.3%	0.4%	64.4%	32.3%	3.3%
France	74.1%	24.0%	1.9%	72.4%	24.6%	3.0%	66.7%	29.6%	3.7%
Germany	69.8%	28.1%	2.1%	68.4%	29.0%	2.6%	61.9%	33.7%	4.5%
Ireland	n.a.	n.a.	5.3%	29.3%	64.9%	5.8%	25.5%	57.0%	17.4%
Italy	83.0%	16.0%	1.0%	82.3%	16.2%	1.5%	71.3%	25.6%	3.1%
Netherlands	44.1%	53.0%	2.9%	41.8%	55.7%	2.5%	42.2%	53.5%	4.3%
Norway	45.7%	41.7%	12.6%	n.a.	37.7%	n.a.	58.3%	39.1%	2.6%
Poland	n.a.	n.a.	n.a.	n.a.	n.a.	n.a.	61.1%	37.8%	1.1%
Portugal	76.6%	22.8%	0.6%	79.5%	20.1%	0.4%	77.0%	20.9%	2.0%
Spain	72.9%	25.8%	1.3%	74.7%	23.7%	1.7%	70.7%	26.9%	2.4%
Sweden	81.0%	18.1%	0.9%	78.8%	19.1%	2.1%	50.0%	39.2%	10.8%
Switzerland	12.4%	81.3%	6.3%	25.4%	63.5%	11.1%	18.7%	74.3%	6.9%
United Kingdom	68.3%	26.4%	5.3%	74.6%	20.3%	5.1%	67.5%	24.7%	7.9%

Source: Bureau of Economic Analysis

gium, Ireland and the Netherlands have emerged as significant export platforms for U.S. affiliates over the past few decades.

Honing in on Ireland, U.S. foreign affiliate sales totaled $24 billion in 2007, making Ireland one of the largest markets in the EU in terms of foreign affiliate sales. However, foreign affiliate sales to the local market accounted for just a quarter of the total in 2007; sales to third markets represented 57% of the total, while affiliate sales to the U.S. accounted for roughly 17-18% of the total.

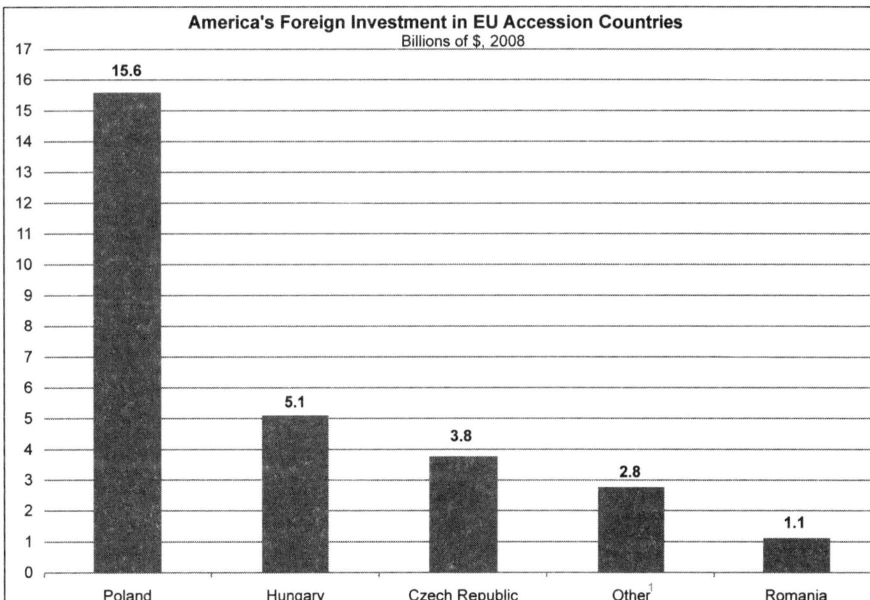

Source: Bureau of Economic Analysis

[1] Bulgaria, Cyprus, Estonia, Latvia, Lithuania, Malta, Slovakia, Slovenia

Belgium, the Netherlands and Switzerland are three more nations where U.S. affiliate sales are greater in third markets and the U.S. than in the local market. The same is true for Hungary, a low-cost center for production and distribution for many U.S. affiliates in the heart of Europe.

The accession of ten countries (Cyprus, Czech Republic, Estonia, Hungary, Lithuania, Latvia, Malta, Poland, Slovenia, and Slovakia) to the EU in 2004, along with the inclusion of Romania and Bulgaria at the start of 2007, presents a host of new and promising strategic opportunities for U.S. multinationals. Accession has helped to integrate these nations into the mainstream of transatlantic commerce and expanded the size of the Single European Market. The last two rounds of enlargement have increased the number of EU member states by over two-thirds, from 15 to 27; boosted the EU's population by nearly 20%; doubled its territory to over 2.5 million square miles; and nearly doubled its official languages. While the 12 new members add only about 5% to the overall output of the EU, they have been registering annual growth rates in excess of the EU annual average. U.S. multinationals have been very active in the accession states over the past decade, and are already well integrated into central and eastern Europe.

In particular, U.S. multinationals have been focused on the "Big Three" accession states—Poland, Hungary and the Czech Republic. Between 2000 and 2009, these nations, combined, attracted nearly $13 billion in U.S. capital, a greater amount than India ($12.7 billion) over the same period. In terms of profits—or affiliate income—U.S. affiliates earned $3.3 billion in the "Big Three" in 2008, nearly six times the level of 2000.

The following pages outline U.S.-sourced jobs, trade and investment for each of the members of the European Union. Norway and Switzerland are also included.

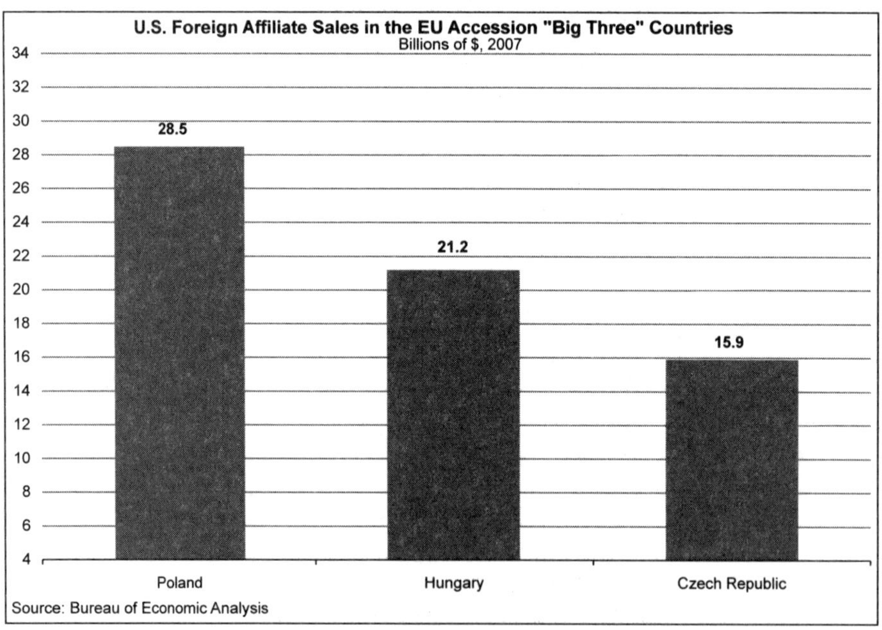

Source: Bureau of Economic Analysis

The Polish Bison and the Celtic Tiger[1]

Poland was Europe's lone star state of marginal economic growth in 2009, and in the Cushman & Wakefield *2009 European Cities Monitor*, Warsaw replaced Moscow as the city expected to see the biggest influx of investments by foreign companies in the next five years.

In its efforts to attract U.S. and foreign investments, Poland hopes to follow in the footsteps of the EU's previous star pupil, Ireland, which successfully lured U.S. and other foreign investors during the late 1990s and early 2000s. Although the two countries have very different geographic locations, they share many historical parallels—strong Catholic backbones, traditionally agriculture-based economies, struggles against occupiers, and citizens emigrating due to adverse economic and political conditions at home. Both countries also benefited greatly from EU accession and membership, using EU support funds to invest in areas such as infrastructure. Both countries also opened their economies and got their fiscal houses in order in the 1990s.

Some Poles are cautious about making too close a parallel with the Celtic Tiger. "I wouldn't say Poland is a Slavic tiger, because that would imply that the country has been making a huge jump, being very aggressive and going quite quickly," says Adam Zolnowski, a senior advisor for PricewaterhouseCoopers in Warsaw. "Poland is more like a bison, moving slowly but starting to gain speed."

In the current economic climate, it may be better to be a bison than a tiger. Poland is tempting companies today with the same types of enticements—EU membership, tax incentives, government grants and low wages—that Ireland used to attract foreign investors. Moreover, the estimated 800,000 Poles who left Poland for western Europe around the time of Poland's EU accession in 2004 are returning home in droves, just as many Irish did during the Celtic Tiger heyday. And as a much larger country—38 million residents compared with Ireland's 4 million—Poland's investment potential could be on an even greater trajectory.

Unlike Ireland, however, which continues to diversify from agriculture and manufacturing to high-value-chain activities, Poland's biggest investment draw remains manufacturing. According to the investment monitor *FDI Markets*, between January 2003 and July 2009 the manufacturing sector accounted for the largest number of foreign direct investment projects (735) in Poland, with an average growth of 17.3% a year.

Poland's rise as a source for U.S. investment can have real consequences for the Celtic Tiger. U.S. companies are not leaving Europe per se in terms of their investments, but they are shifting those investments around within the EU Single Market. U.S. PC manufacturer Dell, for instance, announced in 2009 that it was moving its European manufacturing base from Limerick, Ireland, to the western Polish city of Lodz to improve productivity and reduce costs. Ireland's loss has been Poland's gain – it is expected that the factory will employ up to 3,000 people during the next three years. While that means that nearly 2,000 jobs are moving west to east, Dell has transformed its Limerick facility into a key R&D center, including its Center of Competency for Communications and Network Product Development, and will retain 1,000 higher-level jobs there. Dell also employs more than 1,000 people at a sales, marketing and support center in South County, Dublin. The European-Middle East-Africa region accounts for 24% of Dell's revenue, behind the 62% accounted for by the Americas but well ahead of the Asia-Pacific's share of 14%. And while Ireland is concerned about the potential for more U.S-sourced jobs to leave Ireland, U.S FDI in Ireland grew from $36 billion in 2000 to $87 billion in 2008.

In short, even as Poland looks to Ireland, Ireland must also learn how to adapt to changing fortunes. John O'Brien, a member of the executive committee of Ireland's Industrial Development Agency (IDA), says that trying to attract foreign investors is a constant evolutionary process. "IBM came in here in the early 1990s largely to manufacture and employed about 2000 people," he says. "It still employs that number but only about 300 are doing the manufacturing and the rest have moved into services and R&D, so what you have to do is adapt pretty quickly to the changing circumstances."

As Poland draws lessons from Ireland, it would do well to consider not only how to mimic the Celtic Tiger's upswing but also how to avoid its downturn. Even as it attracts manufacturing investments, it will need to understand how to move to high-value-chain activities. Investment in higher education could prove critical. Ireland's investment in education and skills development—supported by EU funds—was a critical factor inducing high-value investors to commit to the country. And while Poland has boosted its ranks of college-age students enrolling in higher education, it still has a long way to go.

Ireland's low corporate rate of taxation—10% to 12.5% during the late 1990s—was an additional pull for investors. Poland's size and population will make such rates difficult. But it is using the example of Ireland's IDA to offer strategic grants to investors in flagship projects. It also benefits from EU funds to finance investment projects in the area of innovation. Poland's equivalent agency to IDA has a much lower budget, however, and is far more reliant on trade missions and embassies than its Irish sibling. Poland has adopted a more decentralized strategy, partnering with Polish regions that can promote their locales to investors.

---

[1] Drawn from Ginanne Brownell, "Europe's lone star," *FDIMagazine*, December 14, 2009, available at http://www.fdimagazine.com/news/fullstory.php/aid/3151/; and Lara Williams, "Dell looks east," *FDI Magazine*, February 14, 2009, available at http://fdimagazine.com/news/fullstory.php/aid/2663/Dell_looks_east_.html.

Special Focus:
The Race to the Developing Nations: The U.S. vs. Europe

The headlines have become commonplace—"Ford Unveils Small Car to Compete in India," "IBM Markets Wares in Africa," and "PC Makers Cultivate Buyers in Rural China." All three headlines appeared in late 2009 and speak volumes about the growing attractiveness of the emerging markets to companies in both the United States and Europe.

The common denominator to the headlines: a new race has begun, with U.S., European and Japanese firms scrambling to position themselves strategically in the developing nations. The stakes in this race are huge, since many large companies domiciled in slow-growth and saturated developed markets are increasingly dependent on younger, faster-growing developing markets for future earnings growth.

Against this backdrop, we would not be surprised at all to see more U.S. and European investment shift towards the developing nations in the coming decade. However, this should not be read as a sign that the U.S. and Europe are giving up on each other; rather, the coming shift reflects the simple yet glaring fact that many U.S. and European multinationals are behind the curve when it comes to having an in-country presence in many key emerging markets. Rather than having too much investment in the developing nations, as is commonly assumed, there is too little.

To this point, the bulk of America's global infrastructure—foreign capital stock, overseas workforce, R&D expenditures, foreign affiliates—is sunk in Europe, Canada and Japan. Of the nearly $2 trillion U.S. firms invested overseas in the last decade, nearly 70% was directed at the developed markets. U.S. investment in Ireland over the past ten years was roughly 35% greater than combined U.S. investment in the fabled BRIC nations.

Other key metrics tell a similar tale. According to figures from the Bureau of Economic Analysis, more than 80% of the R&D conducted by U.S. foreign affiliates takes place in the developed nations. This is despite all the chatter about the millions of science and engineering graduates being pumped out by Chinese and Indian universities each year.

Even on the employment front, the bias remains towards wealthy, high-wage nations. In 2007, the last year of available data, U.S. affiliates employed just over 10 million foreign workers worldwide, with 55% of this workforce toiling in the developed nations. Many in America blame China for declining U.S. manufacturing employment, even though the combined number of workers employed by U.S. affiliates in the United Kingdom is more than double those employed in China. On the whole, America's global manufacturing workforce is slowly shifting towards the developing world, although just over half of this cohort is still in Europe, Australia, Canada and Japan.

Moreover, when it comes to what matters most—corporate earnings—it is the developed nations that still yield the greatest windfall to U.S. multinationals, with the rich nations last decade accounting for nearly 70% of U.S. foreign affiliate income, a proxy for global earnings.

All of the above suggests that Corporate America's global infrastructure is presently configured for a bygone era when the developed nations, notably Europe, drove the global economy. Since the late 1950s, the principal focus of U.S. multinationals has been on the developed nations, a strategy that has served them well given the wealthy consumer markets and availability of skilled labor in these locations. Many other developed nations face the same

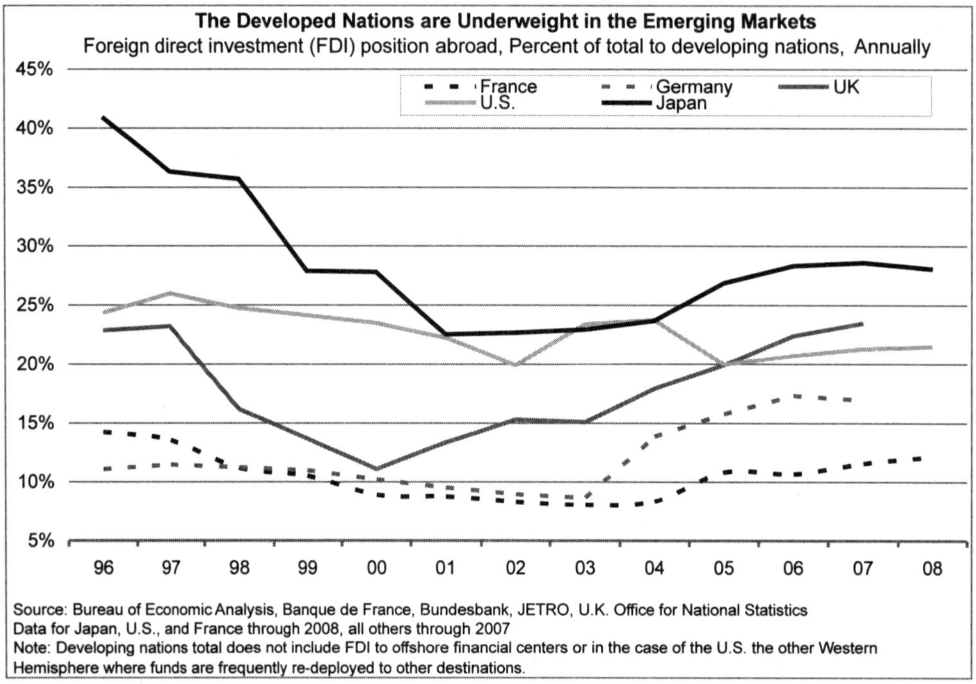

dilemma: they are overweight when it comes to investing in developed countries, and underweight when comes to investing in developing countries. This is true not just for the U.S., but for France, Germany, Japan and the United Kingdom as well.

In the years ahead, however, it is the developing nations that will drive global growth and come to possess the key endowments—expanding consumer markets, a skilled labor force, and critical natural resources—desired by both U.S. and European multinationals.

That said, the irony is that at precisely the moment when U.S. and European multinationals need to build out their presence in the developing nations, the latter have become pickier and somewhat less welcoming of foreign investment. U.S. oil companies, for instance, increasingly confront resource nationalism in a number of petro-states. Both U.S. and European firms have found it slow going in markets such as China and India. In general, a whiff of investment protectionism permeates many key developing nations at a time when Western multinationals are seeking to increase their local presence.

The bottom line: if the developing nations—with their burgeoning middle classes and massive infrastructure needs—represent the future of global economic activity, then many U.S. and European companies are not ready for the future. The race is on to correct this strategic gap. That said, however, we repeat again that should investment flows of the U.S. and Europe begin to shift more towards the developing nations, as we suspect, this should not be viewed as catastrophic for the transatlantic economy. The shift reflects the reality that the center of global economic activity is shifting from west to east, from the developed nations to the developing nations.

We think of the shift as the next (healthy) phase of globalization. To this point, whereas globalization over the 1980-2005 period was largely about the further integration of the

U.S. and Europe, going forward the next phase of globalization will be more about the further integration of the developing nations into the global economy. The transatlantic economy will remain first among equals in this scenario, although the spread of globalization to the other parts of the world, facilitated in part by rising U.S. and Europe investment levels, will become more prominent. This, in our opinion, represents a positive development for the transatlantic economy.

Austria & the United States

Investment and Trade Figures

Investment

Not surprisingly, America's direct investment position in Austria exceeds Austria's investment stakes in the U.S. American affiliates employed nearly three times as many workers in Austria than Austrian firms employed in the U.S.

Austria - U.S. Global Linkages, 2007 (Billions of $)	U.S. in Austria	Austria in U.S.
Foreign Direct Investment* (2008)	17.5	2.4
Total Assets of Affiliates	35.1	-
Foreign Affiliate Sales	22.2	-
Value Added of Affiliates	6.0	1.1
Affiliate Employees	39,600	13,300

*Based on a historic-cost basis, data for 2008; all data for majority-owned nonbank affiliates

Trade

On a global basis, the U.S. received $7.8 billion, or 4.3% of the total goods Austria exported to the world in 2008, but the share going to the U.S. rises to 14.1% of the global total after excluding intra-EU trade, this is down from a high of 21% in 2004. Imports of U.S. goods constituted $3.3 billion, or 1.8% of the total amount Austria imported from the world the same year and 8.0% when intra-EU imports were removed from the global total, down from a share of nearly 20% at the start of this decade.

Top Ten U.S. Imports from Austria, 2008 (in $ millions)

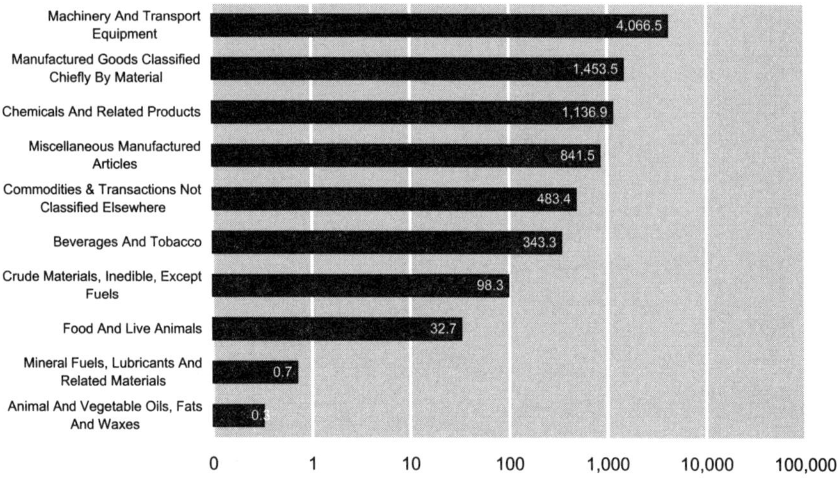

Source: Bureau of Economic Analysis, International Monetary Fund; Office of Trade and Industry Information

Belgium & the United States

Investment and Trade Figures

Investment

America's direct investment position in Belgium is more than three times larger than Belgium's investment stakes in the U.S. U.S. direct investments in Belgium are increasinly made in the services sector rather than the manufacturing sector though the latter is larger in terms of jobs supported. Belgium affiliates employed 10% more workers in the U.S. than U.S. affiliates in Belgium. Value added by U.S. affiliates in Belgium totaled $23.7 billion in 2007, nearly three times more than that of Belgium affiliates in the United States.

Belgium - U.S. Global Linkages, 2007

(Billions of $)

	U.S. in Belgium	Belgium in U.S.
Foreign Direct Investment* (2008)	65.1	18.6
Total Assets of Affiliates	288.9	-
Foreign Affiliate Sales	117.5	-
Value Added of Affiliates	23.7	8.3
Affiliate Employees	127,400	140,500

*Based on a historic-cost basis, data for 2008; all data for majority-owned nonbank affiliates

Trade

The U.S. accounted for 4.8%, or $23.1 billion, of total exports from Belgium in 2008. The share of total exports rises to 20.5% when intra-EU trade is excluded, down from a high of 31.5% in 2002. Chemicals and manufactured goods lead the way as the top export categories. Regarding imports, the U.S. supplied 5.6% of total imports by Belgium in 2008, although the share rises to 18.3% after accounting for intra-EU trade.

Top Ten U.S. Imports from Belgium, 2008 (in $ millions)

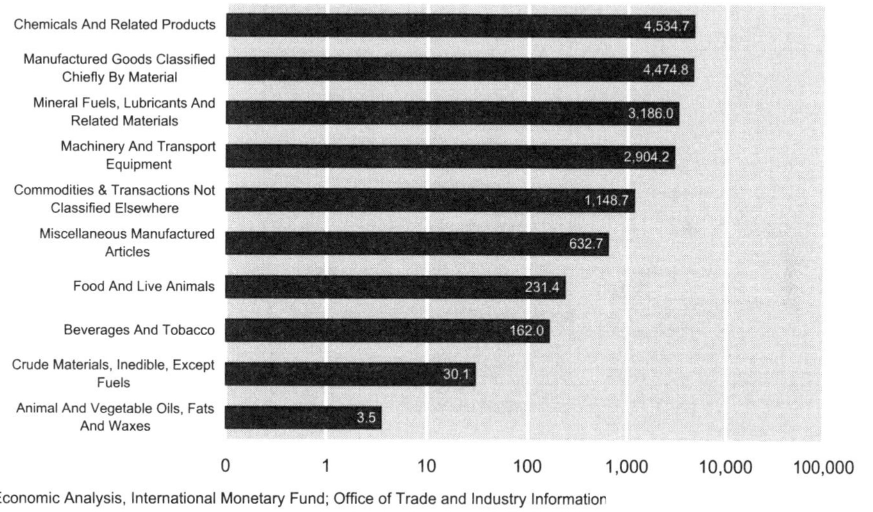

Source: Bureau of Economic Analysis, International Monetary Fund; Office of Trade and Industry Information

Bulgaria & the United States
Investment and Trade Figures

Investment
America's investment base in Bulgaria is rather small, with U.S. investment totaling $300 million in 2008. U.S. affiliates employed 3,300 workers in 2007, placing Bulgaria roughly in the middle of the EU12 in terms of employment.

Bulgaria - U.S. Global Linkages, 2007
(Billions of $)

	U.S. in Bulgaria	Bulgaria in U.S.
Foreign Direct Investment* (2008)	0.3	-
Total Assets of Affiliates	0.9	-
Foreign Affiliate Sales	0.3	-
Value Added of Affiliates	0.1	-
Affiliate Employees	3,300	-

*Based on a historic-cost basis, data for 2008; all data for majority-owned nonbank affiliates

Trade
The U.S. accounted for just 1.6% of Bulgaria's total exports in 2008; the percentage rises to just 3.4% when intra-EU trade is excluded from the total, down from a high of 13.4% in 2001. Imports from the U.S. are rather small, totaling just $410 million in 2008, only 2.2% of Bulgaria's extra-EU imports.

Top Ten U.S. Imports from Bulgaria, 2008 (in $ millions)

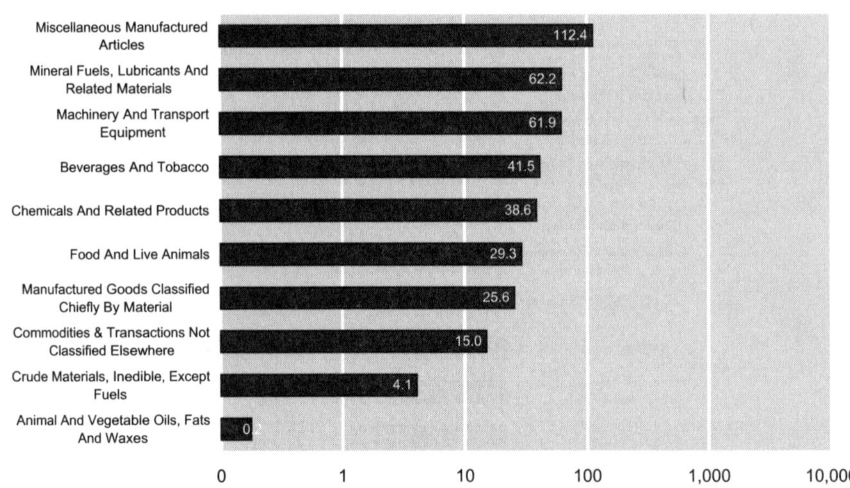

Source: Bureau of Economic Analysis, International Monetary Fund; Office of Trade and Industry Information

Cyprus & the United States

Investment and Trade Figures

Investment

Given the the country's small market the nation has not attracted much with regards to U.S. foreign direct investment relatively but it has nearly doubled to $1.1 billion in 2008 compared to investment levels seen in the middle of the decade.

Cyprus - U.S. Global Linkages, 2007 (Billions of $)	U.S. in Cyprus	Cyprus in U.S.
Foreign Direct Investment* (2008)	1.1	0.1
Total Assets of Affiliates	4.4	0.02
Foreign Affiliate Sales	1.4	0.00
Value Added of Affiliates	0.4	0.00
Affiliate Employees	1,500	-

*Based on a historic-cost basis, data for 2008; all data for majority-owned nonbank affiliates

Trade

Cyprus is an increasingly insignificant supplier of goods to the United States; the U.S. accounted for less than 1% of total exports in 2008. Imports from the U.S. were equally small in 2008, totaling $180 million, 1.7% of Cyprus' total imports from the world.

Top Ten U.S. Imports from Cyprus, 2008 (in $ millions)

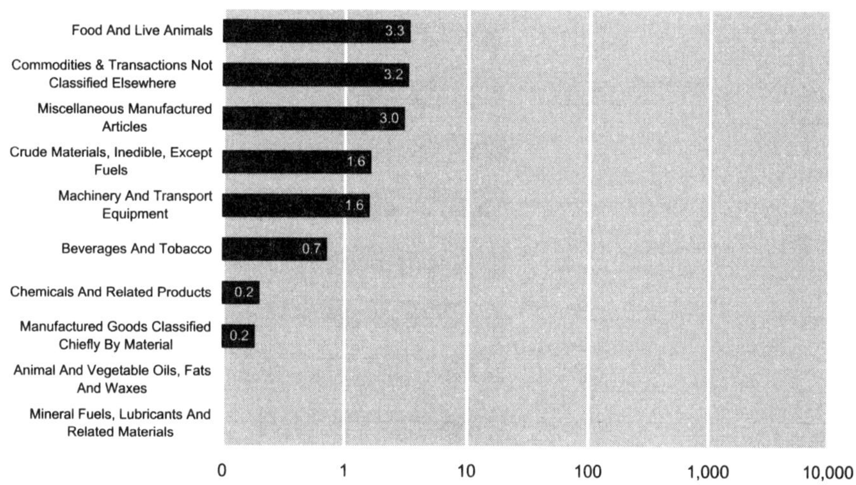

Source: Bureau of Economic Analysis, International Monetary Fund; Office of Trade and Industry Information

Czech Republic & the United States

Investment and Trade Figures

Investment

America's investment base in the Czech Republic is small but expanding, nearly doubling since 2004. U.S. foreign direct investment totaled $4.7 billion on a historic cost basis in 2008. Value added by U.S.-owned affiliates totaled $4.3 billion. Affiliate employment in the Czech Republic (73,000 workers) is among the highest in Eastern Europe. Foreign investment from the Czech Republic in the U.S. is still relatively very small.

Czech Republic - U.S. Global Linkages, 2007 (Billions of $)	U.S. in Czech Republic	Czech Republic in U.S.
Foreign Direct Investment* (2008)	4.7	0.02
Total Assets of Affiliates	15.3	0.004
Foreign Affiliate Sales	15.9	0.01
Value Added of Affiliates	4.3	0.001
Affiliate Employees	73,000	-

*Based on a historic-cost basis, data for 2008; all data for majority-owned nonbank affiliates

Trade

U.S. imports from the Czech Republic totaled $2.6 billion in 2008, triple the amount imported at the start of this decade. Imports consist of high-end goods like parts and components for nuclear reactors and electronic machinery. U.S. imports make-up only 10.2% of the country's Extra-EU trade, down from 21.0% in 2001, as the Czech Republic diversifies it's export base. Czech imports from the U.S. were relatively small, totaling $1.7 billion in 2008.

Top Ten U.S. Imports from Czech Republic, 2008 (in $ millions)

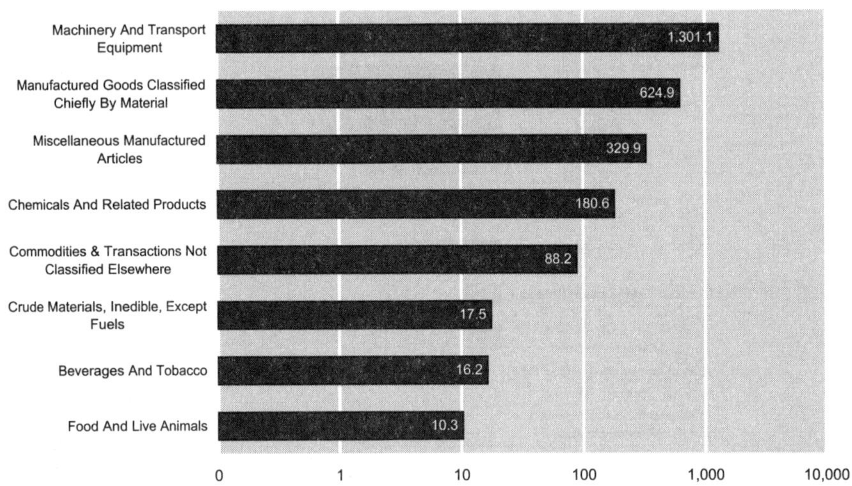

Source: Bureau of Economic Analysis, International Monetary Fund; Office of Trade and Industry Information

Denmark & the United States

Investment and Trade Figures

Investment

Bilateral direct investment between the U.S. and Denmark favored Denmark in 2008 with the U.S. investing nearly double that of which Denmark invested in the United States. Affiliate sales in the U.S. market hit $14.7 billion in 2007 while U.S. affiliate sales in Denmark were $16.6 billion. The affiliate employment balance favors Denmark, with U.S. affiliates in Denmark employing a little less than double that amount of Danish affiliates in the U.S.

Denmark - U.S. Global Linkages, 2007

(Billions of $)

	U.S. in Denmark	Denmark in U.S.
Foreign Direct Investment* (2008)	10.4	5.0
Total Assets of Affiliates	36.9	28.5
Foreign Affiliate Sales	16.6	14.7
Value Added of Affiliates	6.0	3.8
Affiliate Employees	37,800	24,400

*Based on a historic-cost basis, data for 2008; all data for majority-owned nonbank affiliates

Trade

Exports from Denmark to the U.S. totaled $6.2 billion in 2008, or 5.3% of the global total. Excluding intra-EU trade, the share of exports to the U.S. rises to 17.2%. Danish imports from the U.S. totaled $3.4 billion the same year, 3.0% of the global total and 10.5% excluding intra-EU trade. Machinery and transportation equipment, chemicals, and misc. manufactured articles dominate U.S. imports from the country.

Top Ten U.S. Imports from Denmark, 2008 (in $ millions)

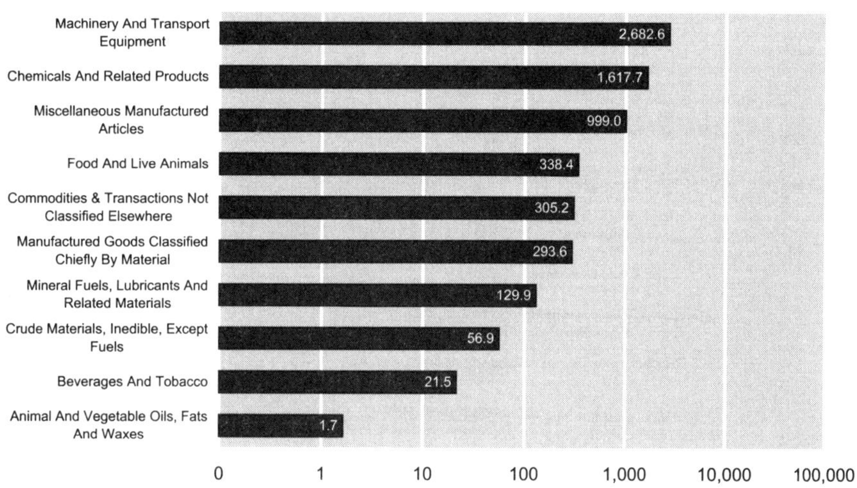

Source: Bureau of Economic Analysis, International Monetary Fund; Office of Trade and Industry Information

Estonia & the United States

Investment and Trade Figures

Investment

America's direct investment base in Estonia is the smallest out of all the EU12 countries. U.S. affiliates employed 2,500 people in 2007, placing Estonia toward the middle of the EU12 in terms of employment. U.S. investment in the country is expected to increase as the Baltic states emerge as a key gateway to Russia and beyond.

Estonia - U.S. Global Linkages, 2007

(Billions of $)

	U.S. in Estonia	Estonia in U.S.
Foreign Direct Investment* (2008)	0.02	-
Total Assets of Affiliates	0.3	0.0
Foreign Affiliate Sales	0.4	0.0
Value Added of Affiliates	0.1	0.0
Affiliate Employees	2,500	0

*Based on a historic-cost basis, data for 2008; all data for majority-owned nonbank affiliates

Trade

U.S. imports from Estonia totaled $600 million in 2008, nearly ten times greater than imports at the start of the decade. Mineral fuels, lubricants and related materials make-up half of U.S. imports from Estonia. Estonia imports very little from the U.S.; only 1.1% of total imports and 5.2% excluding intra-EU imports come from the United States.

Top Ten U.S. Imports from Estonia, 2008 (in $ millions)

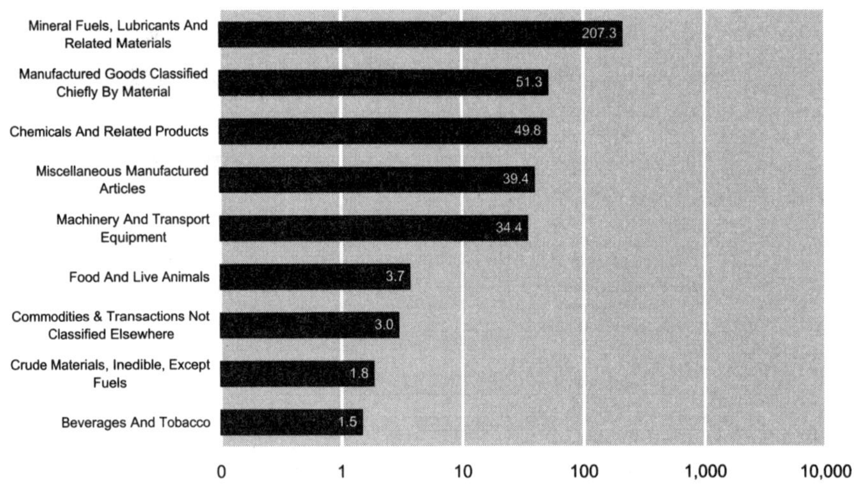

Source: Bureau of Economic Analysis, International Monetary Fund; Office of Trade and Industry Information

Finland & the United States

Investment and Trade Figures

Investment

The investment balance favors the United States, with Finnish investment in the U.S. totaling $12.5 billion in 2008 versus just $2.3 billion of U.S. investment in Finland. The affiliate employment balance slightly favors the U.S. by 3,000 jobs.

Finland - U.S. Global Linkages, 2007 (Billions of $)	U.S. in Finland	Finland in U.S.
Foreign Direct Investment* (2008)	2.3	12.5
Total Assets of Affiliates	21.4	-
Foreign Affiliate Sales	13.2	-
Value Added of Affiliates	3.1	3.3
Affiliate Employees	23,600	26,600

*Based on a historic-cost basis, data for 2008; all data for majority-owned nonbank affiliates

Trade

The U.S. received $6.2 billion, or 6.4% of the total goods exported to the world in 2008, but the share going to the U.S. rises to 14.4% of the global total after excluding intra-EU trade. Imports of U.S. goods constituted $1.9 billion, or 2.0% of the total amount imported from the world the same year and 5.3% when intra-EU imports are removed from the global total, down from a high of 22% in 1998.

Top Ten U.S. Imports from Finland, 2008 (in $ millions)

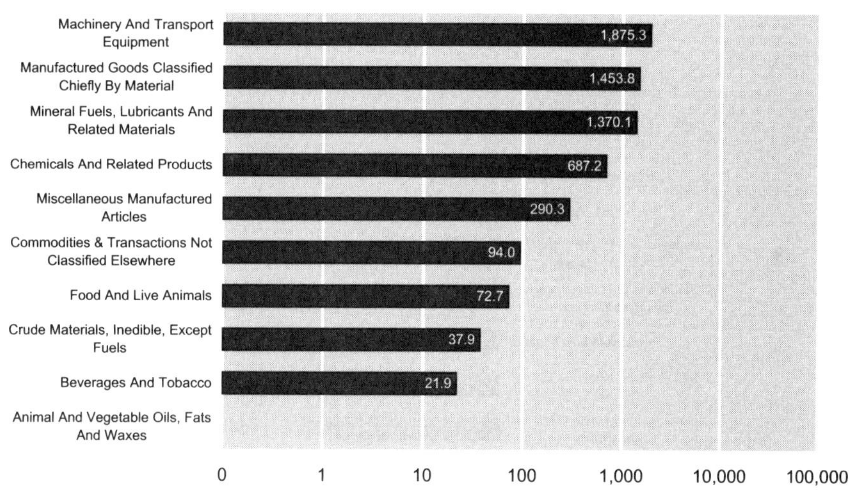

Source: Bureau of Economic Analysis, International Monetary Fund; Office of Trade and Industry Information

France & the United States

Investment and Trade Figures

Investment

The direct investment balance favors the U.S., with U.S. investment in France ($75.0 billion) just 46% of total French direct investment in the U.S. in 2008 ($163.4 billion). The U.S. is a significant market for French firms, with U.S. affiliates of French firms recording nearly $218 billion in sales during 2007. The employment balance now favors France. U.S. and French affiliates combined employed over 1 million workers in 2007.

France - U.S. Global Linkages, 2007 (Billions of $)	U.S. in France	France in U.S.
Foreign Direct Investment* (2008)	75.0	163.4
Total Assets of Affiliates	324.0	829.3
Foreign Affiliate Sales	214.4	217.6
Value Added of Affiliates	56.2	56.3
Affiliate Employees	616,100	500,100

*Based on a historic-cost basis, data for 2008; all data for majority-owned nonbank affiliates

Trade

The U.S. accounted for 5.8% of total exports from France in 2008, but a share of 15.2% of total exports when intra-EU trade is excluded. Products exported to the U.S. ran the gamut, from heavy machinery and transportation equipment to chemicals and agricultural products. Regarding imports, the U.S. supplied 4.3% of total imports by France in 2008, although the share rises to 13.0% after accounting for intra-EU trade, down from 25.0% in 1999.

Top Ten U.S. Imports from France, 2008 (in $ millions)

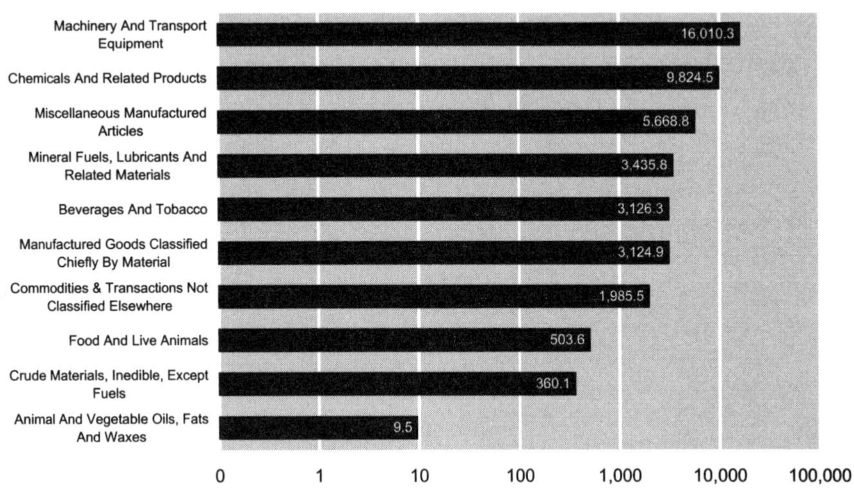

Source: Bureau of Economic Analysis, International Monetary Fund; Office of Trade and Industry Information

Germany & the United States

Investment and Trade Figures

Investment

The investment balance favors the U.S., with U.S. direct investment in Germany totaling $110.8 billion in 2007 versus $211.5 billion of German direct investment in the U.S. Germany's asset base in the U.S. exceeded America's total asset base in Germany by nearly 20% in 2007, although the value added by American affiliates operating in Germany ($86.6 billion in 2007) exceeded that of German affiliates in the United States. The employment balance favored the U.S. in 2007. U.S. and German affiliates combined employed over 1.5 million workers.

Germany - U.S. Global Linkages, 2007
(Billions of $)

	U.S. in Germany	Germany in U.S.
Foreign Direct Investment* (2008)	110.8	211.5
Total Assets of Affiliates	552.1	655.1
Foreign Affiliate Sales	313.9	382.8
Value Added of Affiliates	86.6	76.8
Affiliate Employees	610,600	639,200

*Based on a historic-cost basis, data for 2008; all data for majority-owned nonbank affiliates

Trade

Germany is the largest European exporter to the U.S., with exports to the U.S. totaling $104 billion in 2008. The U.S. accounted for just over 7.1% of total German exports, but 19.0% when intra-EU trade flows are excluded. Imports from the U.S. into Germany totaled $50.4 billion—that equates to 4.2% of total German imports or 11.5% excluding intra-EU trade. Nearly three-fourths of U.S. imports from Germany consist of chemicals and machinery and transportation equipment.

Top Ten U.S. Imports from Germany, 2008 (in $ millions)

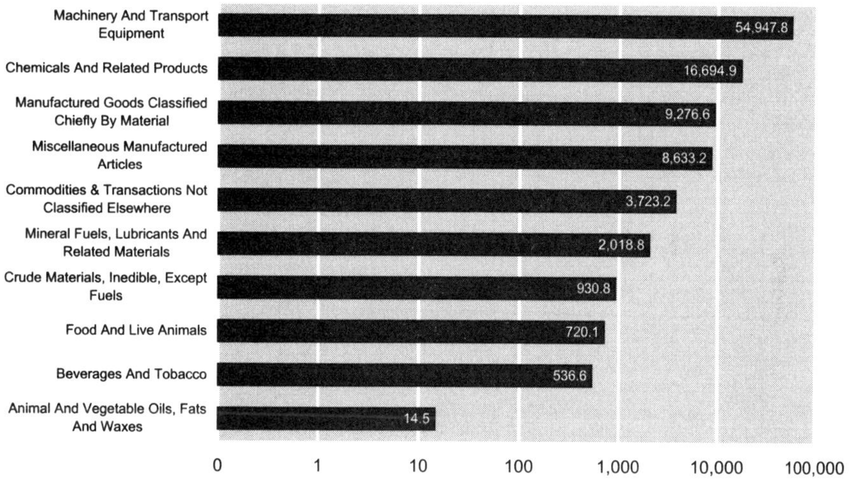

Source: Bureau of Economic Analysis, International Monetary Fund; Office of Trade and Industry Information

Greece & the United States

Investment and Trade Figures

Investment

The investment balance clearly favors Greece with America's direct investment position totaling $2.1 billion in 2008. No data is available regarding the investment position of Greece in the U.S. U.S. affiliate sales of just $8.2 billion in 2007 ranked among the lowest in the EU.

Greece - U.S. Global Linkages, 2007

(Billions of $)

	U.S. in Greece	Greece in U.S.
Foreign Direct Investment* (2008)	2.1	-
Total Assets of Affiliates	10.7	-
Foreign Affiliate Sales	8.2	-
Value Added of Affiliates	3.5	-
Affiliate Employees	16,600	-

*Based on a historic-cost basis, data for 2008; all data for majority-owned nonbank affiliates

Trade

Greek exports to the U.S. totaled more than $1 billion for the first time in 2008, while imports from the U.S. amounted to $2.3 billion. The U.S. accounted for 5.0% of total exports but nearly 11% excluding intra-EU exports. Greek imports from the U.S. were 3.0% of total imports from the world in 2008 and 7.0% excluding intra-EU imports.

Top Ten U.S. Imports from Greece, 2008 (in $ millions)

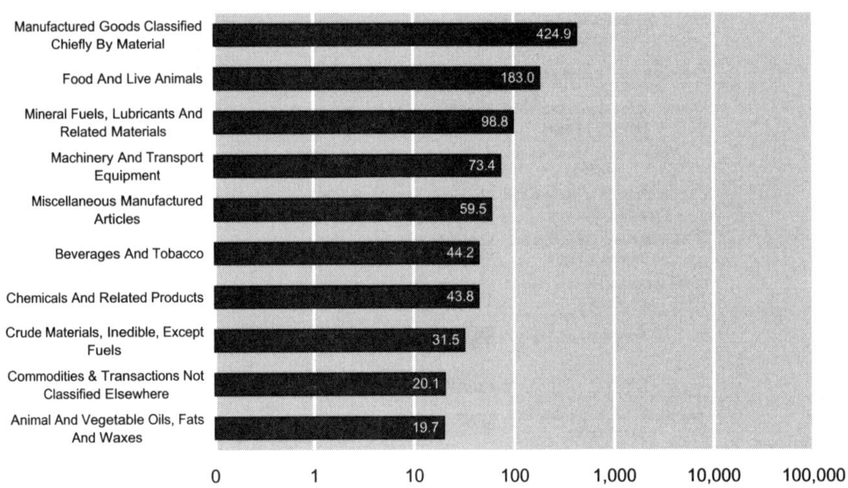

Source: Bureau of Economic Analysis, International Monetary Fund; Office of Trade and Industry Information

Hungary & the United States

Investment and Trade Figures

Investment

America's investment base in Hungary is among the largest in central Europe, with U.S. foreign direct investment totaling $5.1 billion on a historic cost basis in 2008. Value added by U.S.-owned affiliates totaled $5.0 billion. Affiliate employment in Hungary (64,000 workers) ranked third among EU12 countries. Hungarian affiliates in the U.S. invested a substantial amount in the U.S. in 2008, growing their investments in the U.S. 12% each year since 2003.

Hungary - U.S. Global Linkages, 2007

(Billions of $)

	U.S. in Hungary	Hungary in U.S.
Foreign Direct Investment* (2008)	5.1	62.5
Total Assets of Affiliates	38.6	-
Foreign Affiliate Sales	21.2	-
Value Added of Affiliates	5.0	0.03
Affiliate Employees	64,000	3,200

*Based on a historic-cost basis, data for 2008; all data for majority-owned nonbank affiliates

Trade

U.S. imports from Hungary totaled $2.5 billion in 2008, up from $620 million in 1997. The bulk of imports consists of parts and components, including those used in nuclear reactors. Vehicle and electronic shipments have increased along with greater affiliate production in the country. Hungary bought $1.5 billion worth of U.S. goods in 2008, 4% of the country's extra-EU imports.

Top Ten U.S. Imports from Hungary, 2008 (in $ millions)

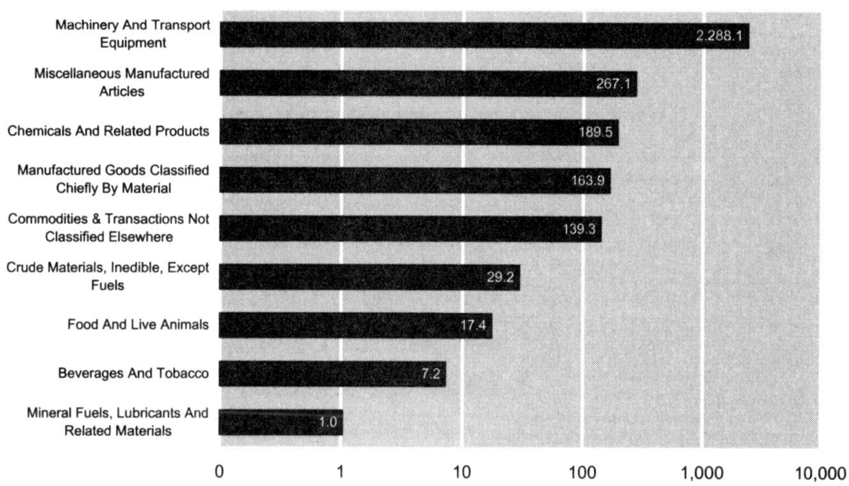

Source: Bureau of Economic Analysis, International Monetary Fund; Office of Trade and Industry Information

Ireland & the United States

Investment and Trade Figures

Investment

The investment balance favors Ireland, with U.S. investment in Ireland totaling some $146.2 billion in 2008 versus $34.1 billion of Ireland's investment in the U.S. Value added by U.S. affiliates totaled $53.8 billion in 2007. The affiliate employment balance favors Ireland by roughly 25,000 jobs. In particular, U.S. firms continue to build out their presence in Ireland's information technology industry while cutting back investment in the financial industry.

Ireland - U.S. Global Linkages, 2007

(Billions of $)

	U.S. in Ireland	Ireland in U.S.
Foreign Direct Investment* (2008)	146.2	34.1
Total Assets of Affiliates	559.3	-
Foreign Affiliate Sales	222.5	-
Value Added of Affiliates	53.8	6.8
Affiliate Employees	92,900	67,500

*Based on a historic-cost basis, data for 2008; all data for majority-owned nonbank affiliates

Trade

The U.S. is a key export destination for Ireland, with exports to the U.S. totaling $23.1 billion in 2008. The U.S. accounted for 18.6% of total exports from Ireland; when intra-EU exports are excluded from the total, the share of exports to the U.S. jumps to 50.0%. Seventy percent of U.S. imports from Ireland consist of chemicals and related products. The U.S. is also a key supplier to Ireland, with the U.S. accounting for 11.6% of total imports into Ireland in 2008 and 36.4% after excluding intra-EU trade.

Top Ten U.S. Imports from Ireland, 2008 (in $ millions)

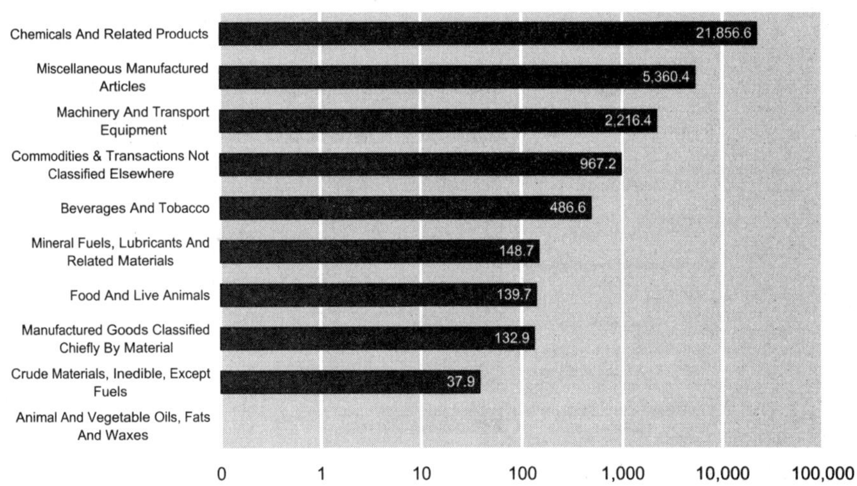

Source: Bureau of Economic Analysis, International Monetary Fund; Office of Trade and Industry Information

Italy & the United States

Investment and Trade Figures

Investment

The investment balance favors Italy—U.S. direct investment in Italy totaled $28.7 billion in 2008, versus the $17.6 billion invested by Italian firms in the U.S. U.S. investment was mostly concentrated in manufacturing, wholesale trade, information, and finance. Value added by U.S. affiliates in Italy was nearly four times as much as that produced by Italian affiliates in the U.S. With U.S. foreign affiliates employing some 243,000 workers in 2007, the employment balance clearly favors Italy.

Italy - U.S. Global Linkages, 2007

(Billions of $)

	U.S. in Italy	Italy in U.S.
Foreign Direct Investment* (2008)	28.7	17.6
Total Assets of Affiliates	147.9	64.9
Foreign Affiliate Sales	127.7	34.4
Value Added of Affiliates	32.5	8.9
Affiliate Employees	243,100	114,700

*Based on a historic-cost basis, data for 2008; all data for majority-owned nonbank affiliates

Trade

The U.S. accounted for 6.3% of total exports from Italy in 2008, but a share of 16% of total exports after excluding intra-EU trade, down from 26.0% at the start of the decade. Machinery, transportation goods, and manufactured goods were the top exports to the U.S. Regarding imports, the U.S. supplied 3.1% of total imports by Italy in 2008, although the share rises to 6.6% after accounting for intra-EU imports.

Top Ten U.S. Imports from Italy, 2008 (in $ millions)

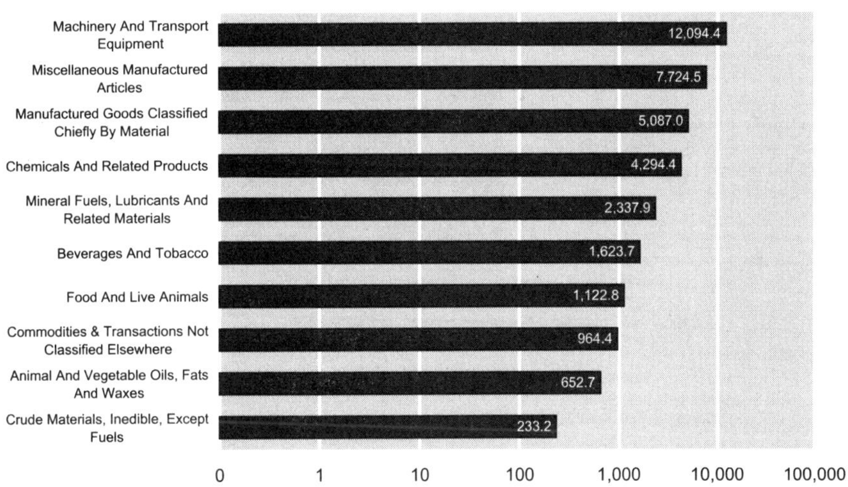

Source: Bureau of Economic Analysis, International Monetary Fund; Office of Trade and Industry Information

Latvia & the United States

Investment and Trade Figures

Investment

Latvia has attracted the least amount of foreign direct investment from the United States. Investment linkages are shallow but expected to gradually expand over the next decade. U.S. affiliates supported only 1,100 jobs, the lowest among EU12 countries, but more than double the jobs supported in Latvia in 2000.

Latvia - U.S. Global Linkages, 2007
(Billions of $)

	U.S. in Latvia	Latvia in U.S.
Foreign Direct Investment* (2008)	0.1	-
Total Assets of Affiliates	0.7	-
Foreign Affiliate Sales	0.3	-
Value Added of Affiliates	0.2	-
Affiliate Employees	1,100	-

*Based on a historic-cost basis, data for 2008; all data for majority-owned nonbank affiliates

Trade

U.S. imports from Latvia have increased steadily over the past decade, with imports consisting mainly of primary commodities like mineral fuels, chemicals, iron and steel. The U.S. imported $140 million worth of goods from Latvia in 2008. The U.S. is a small supplier to Latvia, with Latvian imports of U.S. goods totaling just $150 million in 2008, nearly 4% of Latvia's extra-EU imports.

Top Ten U.S. Imports from Latvia, 2008 (in $ millions)

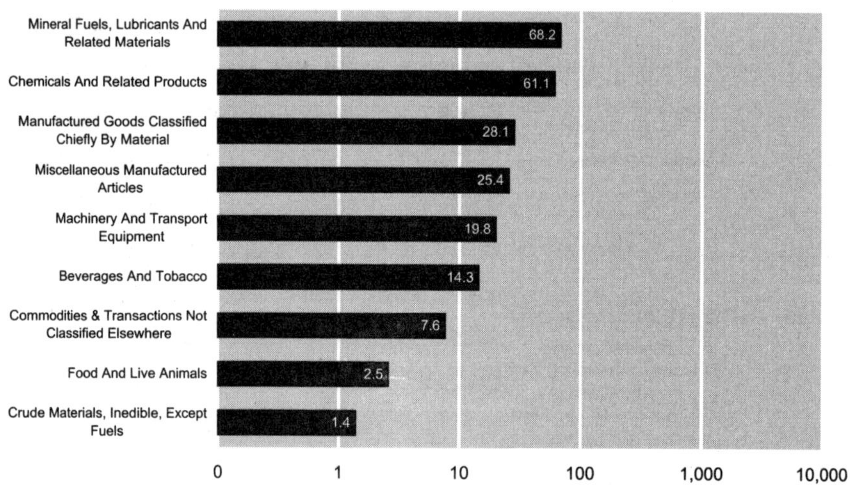

Source: Bureau of Economic Analysis, International Monetary Fund; Office of Trade and Industry Information

Lithuania & the United States

Investment and Trade Figures

Investment

Lithuania has yet to attract significant levels of U.S. foreign direct investment, however, as the Baltic states develop and become more integrated into the greater European market, U.S. investment flows are expected to increase.

Lithuania - U.S. Global Linkages, 2007
(Billions of $)

	U.S. in Lithuania	Lithuania in U.S.
Foreign Direct Investment* (2008)	0.1	-
Total Assets of Affiliates	0.3	-
Foreign Affiliate Sales	0.3	-
Value Added of Affiliates	0.1	-
Affiliate Employees	1,600	-

*Based on a historic-cost basis, data for 2008; all data for majority-owned nonbank affiliates

Trade

U.S. imports from Lithuania have grown over the past decade, rising from just $6 million in 1997 to a record $760 million in 2008. Rising shipments of mineral fuel led the import surge. Lithuanian imports from the U.S. have risen to $540 million in 2008, or 4.0% of the country's extra-EU imports.

Top Ten U.S. Imports from Lithuania, 2008 (in $ millions)

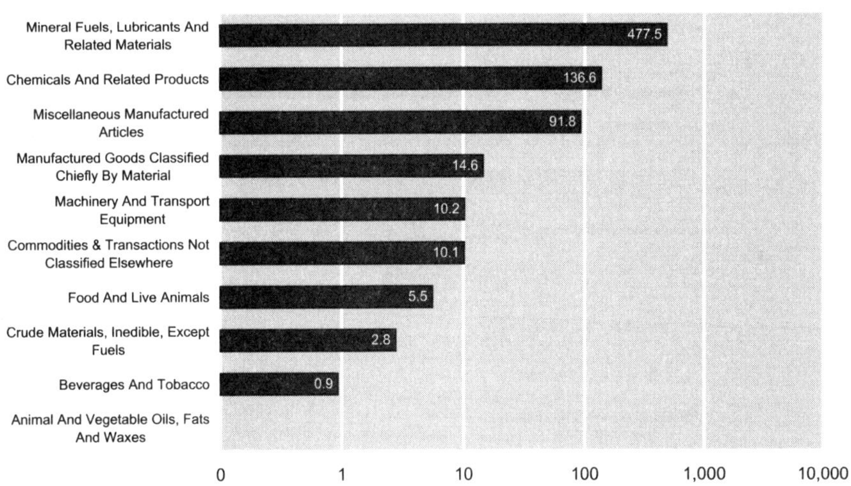

Source: Bureau of Economic Analysis, International Monetary Fund; Office of Trade and Industry Information

Luxembourg & the United States

Investment and Trade Figures

Investment

Investment between the U.S. and Luxembourg is skewed in favor of Luxembourg. The bulk of bilateral direct investment flows remain in financial services and related industries. U.S. affiliate sales in Luxembourg were triple that of affiliates in the U.S. The employee balance favors the U.S. 2 to 1.

Luxembourg - U.S. Global Linkages, 2007 (Billions of $)	U.S. in Luxembourg	Luxembourg in U.S.
Foreign Direct Investment* (2008)	163.2	113.2
Total Assets of Affiliates	863.6	11.9
Foreign Affiliate Sales	14.8	4.3
Value Added of Affiliates	1.2	1.7
Affiliate Employees	12,900	30,200

*Based on a historic-cost basis, data for 2008; all data for majority-owned nonbank affiliates

Trade

Trade volumes are rather small — exports to the U.S. totaled just $450 million in 2008, while imports from the U.S. were $790 million. The U.S. accounted for only 1.8% of total exports but nearly 15% excluding intra-EU exports. Imports from the U.S. accounted for 2.5% of the total in 2008 and 10% excluding intra-EU imports.

Top Ten U.S. Imports from Luxembourg, 2008 (in $ millions)

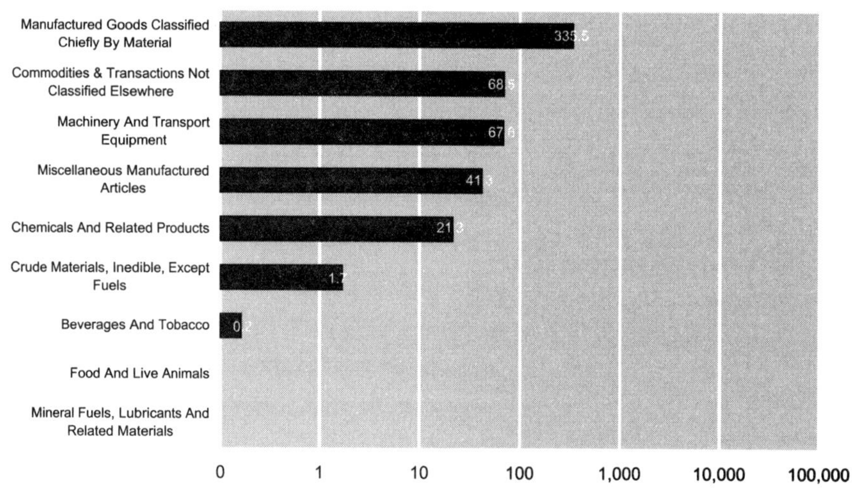

Source: Bureau of Economic Analysis, International Monetary Fund; Office of Trade and Industry Information

Malta & the United States

Investment and Trade Figures

Investment

Given its small size, Malta has not attracted much U.S. foreign direct investment. The country has received close to $400 million in U.S. investment each year for the past three years.

Malta - U.S. Global Linkages, 2007 (Billions of $)	U.S. in Malta	Malta in U.S.
Foreign Direct Investment* (2008)	0.4	-
Total Assets of Affiliates	2.2	-
Foreign Affiliate Sales	0.2	-
Value Added of Affiliates	0.1	-
Affiliate Employees	1,300	-

*Based on a historic-cost basis, data for 2008; all data for majority-owned nonbank affiliates

Trade

Trade between the two countries remains rather small. U.S. imports from Malta totaled $270 million in 2008 and were primarily concentrated in machinery, chemicals, and other manufactured items. Malta's imports from the U.S. totalled $100 million in 2008, 2.2% of total imports and 8% excluding intra-EU imports.

Top Ten U.S. Imports from Malta, 2008 (in $ millions)

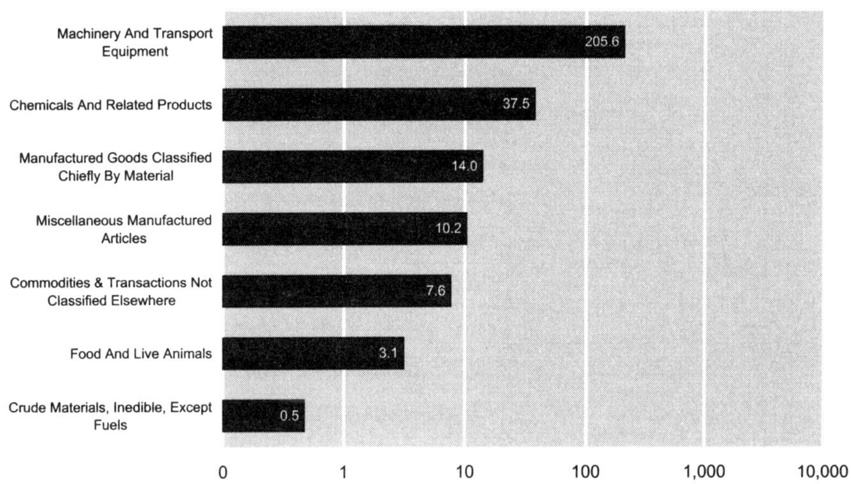

Source: Bureau of Economic Analysis, International Monetary Fund; Office of Trade and Industry Information

Netherlands & the United States

Investment and Trade Figures

Investment

Investment between the U.S. and the Netherlands is slightly skewed toward the latter, with America's investment stake in the Netherlands totaling $442.9 billion in 2008, versus $259.4 billion of Dutch direct investment in the U.S. The U.S. is a prime foreign destination for Dutch firms, who recorded $310.0 billion in affiliate sales in the U.S. during 2007. The employment balance favors the U.S. by more than 150,000 jobs, a smaller margin than previous years, though still a substantial gap.

Netherlands - U.S. Global Linkages, 2007 (Billions of $)	U.S. in Netherlands	Netherlands in U.S.
Foreign Direct Investment* (2008)	442.9	259.4
Total Assets of Affiliates	1,180.3	778.3
Foreign Affiliate Sales	188.7	310.0
Value Added of Affiliates	29.5	43.5
Affiliate Employees	223,800	386,500

*Based on a historic-cost basis, data for 2008; all data for majority-owned nonbank affiliates

Trade

The U.S. has accounted for 4% of total exports from the Netherlands, but a share of 17.8% of total exports when intra-EU trade is excluded, down from 23% in 2000. Top exports were diversified across several capital-intensive industries. Regarding imports, the U.S. supplied 7.5% of total imports by the Netherlands in 2008, although the share rises to 14.3% after accounting for intra-EU trade.

Top Ten U.S. Imports from Netherlands, 2008 (in $ millions)

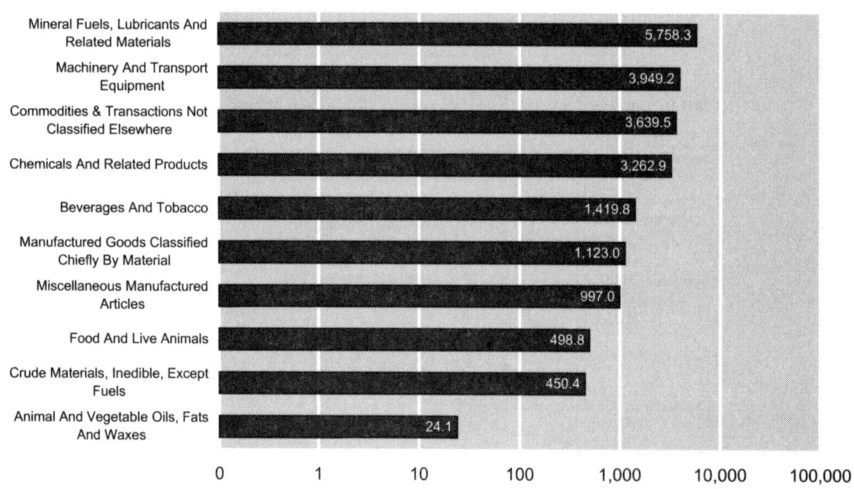

Source: Bureau of Economic Analysis, International Monetary Fund; Office of Trade and Industry Information

Norway & the United States

Investment and Trade Figures

Investment

The investment balance favors Norway, with U.S. direct investment totaling $10.9 billion in 2008 versus $6.8 billion of Norwegian direct investment in the U.S. The employment balance favors Norway, with U.S. foreign affiliates employing 32,900 Norwegian workers in 2007.

Norway - U.S. Global Linkages, 2007

(Billions of $)

	U.S. in Norway	Norway in U.S.
Foreign Direct Investment* (2008)	10.9	6.8
Total Assets of Affiliates	67.5	-
Foreign Affiliate Sales	41.5	-
Value Added of Affiliates	16.6	-0.3
Affiliate Employees	32,900	7,700

*Based on a historic-cost basis, data for 2008; all data for majority-owned nonbank affiliates

Trade

Norwegian exports to the U.S. totaled $7.5 billion in 2008, and were skewed toward mineral fuels (i.e. petroleum products). The U.S. accounted for just 4.5% of total Norwegian exports, but nearly 27% when Norway's trade with the EU flows are excluded. Imports from the U.S. into Norway totaled $4.8 billion—that equates to 5.4% of total Norwegian imports or 16.7% excluding Norway's trade with the EU.

Top Ten U.S. Imports from Norway, 2008 (in $ millions)

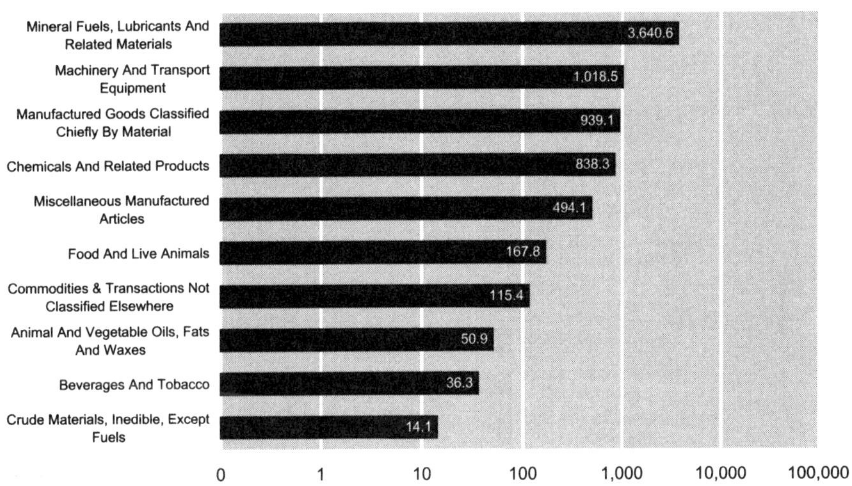

Source: Bureau of Economic Analysis, International Monetary Fund; Office of Trade and Industry Information

Poland & the United States

Investment and Trade Figures

Investment

As one of the largest markets in Central Europe, Poland has attracted significant sums of market-seeking U.S. foreign direct investment. At $29.1 billion, the U.S. asset base in Poland is larger than America's asset base in small developed nations like Finland or Greece. The U.S. affiliate work force of 120,700 workers is the largest among EU12 countries. Polish affiliates in the U.S. have yet to make significant investments in the country.

Poland - U.S. Global Linkages, 2007

(Billions of $)

	U.S. in Poland	Poland in U.S.
Foreign Direct Investment* (2008)	15.6	-
Total Assets of Affiliates	29.1	0.01
Foreign Affiliate Sales	28.5	0.01
Value Added of Affiliates	8.5	0.002
Affiliate Employees	120,700	-

*Based on a historic-cost basis, data for 2008; all data for majority-owned nonbank affiliates

Trade

U.S. imports from Poland have increased sharply over the past few years, clearing $2 billion in 2007 from just $700 million in 1997 and reaching $2.5 billion in 2008. Imports run the gamut - from heavy machinery, to electronic goods, to agricultural products. U.S. exports to Poland totaled nearly $3 billion in 2008, a share of 1.4% and rising to 5% excluding intra-EU trade.

Top Ten U.S. Imports from Poland, 2008 (in $ millions)

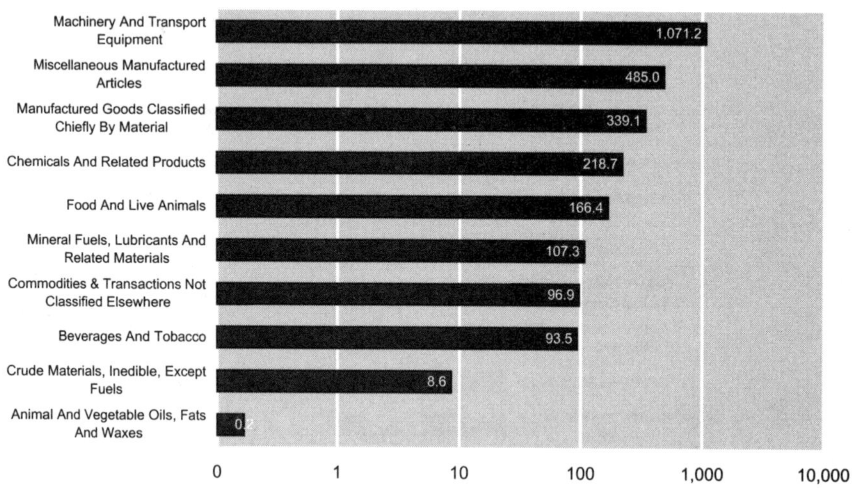

Source: Bureau of Economic Analysis, International Monetary Fund; Office of Trade and Industry Information

Portugal & the United States

Investment and Trade Figures

Investment

U.S. direct investment in Portugal totaled $3.4 billion in 2008, largely concentrated in wholesale trade, while U.S. affiliates employed 29,200 Portuguese workers.

Portugal - U.S. Global Linkages, 2007 (Billions of $)	U.S. in Portugal	Portugal in U.S.
Foreign Direct Investment* (2008)	3.4	0.0
Total Assets of Affiliates	41.0	-
Foreign Affiliate Sales	11.7	-
Value Added of Affiliates	4.5	-
Affiliate Employees	29,200	500

*Based on a historic-cost basis, data for 2008; all data for majority-owned nonbank affiliates

Trade

Portuguese exports to the U.S. fell slightly below $2 billion in 2008, while imports from the U.S. amounted to $1.5 billion. The U.S. accounted for 3.5% of total exports but a 12% share of Portugal's exports excluding intra-EU trade. Portuguese imports from the U.S. were 2% of total imports from the world in 2008 and 5.5% excluding intra-EU imports, down from an average of 13% in the 1990s.

Top Ten U.S. Imports from Portugal, 2008 (in $ millions)

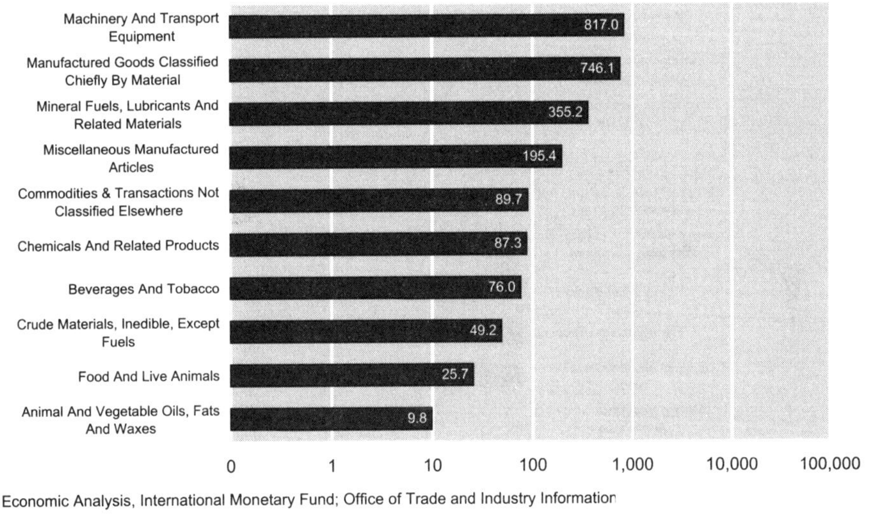

Source: Bureau of Economic Analysis, International Monetary Fund; Office of Trade and Industry Information

Romania & the United States

Investment and Trade Figures

Investment

America's asset base in Romania is rather small, with assets totaling just $3.9 billion in 2007. However, with Romania's inclusion into the EU, more U.S. firms are expected to increase their presence in Romania - albeit modestly - over the medium-term. U.S. affiliates employed 35,800 employees in 2007, placing Romania 5th among the EU12 countries in terms of jobs supported.

Romania - U.S. Global Linkages, 2007

(Billions of $)

	U.S. in Romania	Romania in U.S.
Foreign Direct Investment* (2008)	1.2	-
Total Assets of Affiliates	3.9	-
Foreign Affiliate Sales	4.7	-
Value Added of Affiliates	1.7	-
Affiliate Employees	35,800	-

*Based on a historic-cost basis, data for 2008; all data for majority-owned nonbank affiliates

Trade

U.S. imports from Romania totaled $840 million in 2008, a gradual rise from the levels of the late 1990s but off from a high of $1 billion in 2005. Imports included a variety of manufactured goods. The U.S. is a rather small supplier to Romania, with the U.S. accounting for just 1.5% of the nation's total imports and 4.5% excluding intra-EU trade.

Top Ten U.S. Imports from Romania, 2008 (in $ millions)

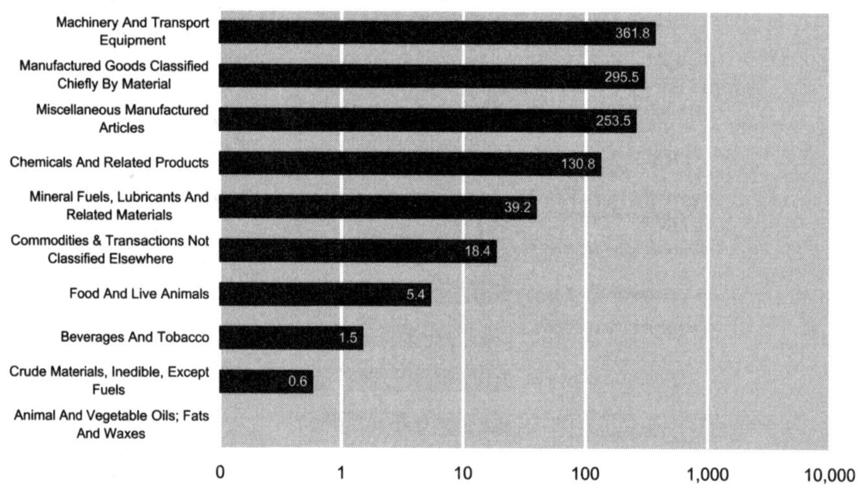

Source: Bureau of Economic Analysis, International Monetary Fund; Office of Trade and Industry Information

Slovakia & the United States

Investment and Trade Figures

Investment

America's asset base in Slovakia is small but expanding — total assets of U.S. affiliates in 2007 amounted to $635 million, while foreign affiliate sales reached $7.5 billion. Centered in the heart of eastern Europe, the nation is well positioned to capture U.S. investment in distribution, transportation, wholesale trade and other service-like activities. U.S. affiliates employed 35,900 workers in 2007, the fourth largest U.S. affiliate work force in eastern Europe.

Slovakia - U.S. Global Linkages, 2007
(Billions of $)

	U.S. in Slovakia	Slovakia in U.S.
Foreign Direct Investment* (2008)	0.6	-
Total Assets of Affiliates	6.7	-
Foreign Affiliate Sales	7.5	-
Value Added of Affiliates	2.2	-
Affiliate Employees	35,900	-

*Based on a historic-cost basis, data for 2008; all data for majority-owned nonbank affiliates

Trade

U.S. imports from Slovakia have surged, rising to over $1.4 billion in 2007 from levels under $200 million in the late 1990s. U.S. imports fell slightly in 2008 to $1.2 billion. Accounting for the surge has been rising motor vehicle imports from foreign affiliates producing in the country. Other imports include nuclear reactors, footwear and rubber. Imports have risen gradually as well hitting $460 million in 2008, 2.2% of total imports excluding intra-EU trade.

Top Ten U.S. Imports from Slovakia, 2008 (in $ millions)

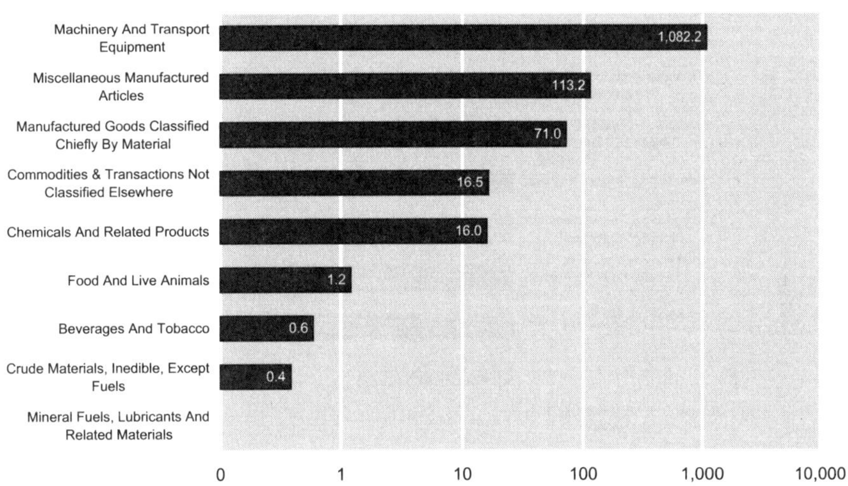

Source: Bureau of Economic Analysis, International Monetary Fund; Office of Trade and Industry Information

Slovenia & the United States

Investment and Trade Figures

Investment

Slovenia has experienced a gradual rise in U.S. foreign investment over the past few years. Total assets of affiliates amounted to $831 million in 2007. U.S. affiliates employed 4,600 workers in 2007, placing Slovenia in the middle of the EU12 countries in terms of employment. The country is expected to emerge as a bridge to the Balkan states over the next decade.

Slovenia - U.S. Global Linkages, 2007

(Billions of $)

	U.S. in Slovenia	Slovenia in U.S.
Foreign Direct Investment* (2008)	0.2	0.003
Total Assets of Affiliates	0.8	-
Foreign Affiliate Sales	1.2	-
Value Added of Affiliates	0.3	-
Affiliate Employees	4,600	500

*Based on a historic-cost basis, data for 2008; all data for majority-owned nonbank affiliates

Trade

U.S. imports from Slovenia have grown steadily since the late 1990s, however, falling slightly to $410 million in 2008. Imports included machinery, chemicals, furniture and glassware. Slovenia imported only 1.7% of the country's total imports from the U.S. or 5.7% excluding intra-EU trade in 2008.

Top Ten U.S. Imports from Slovenia, 2008 (in $ millions)

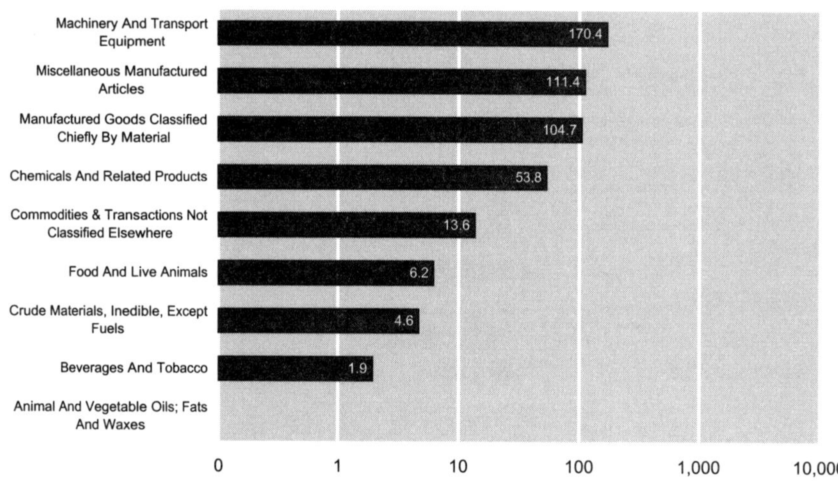

Source: Bureau of Economic Analysis, International Monetary Fund; Office of Trade and Industry Information

Spain & the United States

Investment and Trade Figures

Investment

The investment balance favored Spain in 2008, with U.S. investment in Spain ($69.6 billion) nearly double the size of total Spanish direct investment in the U.S. ($38.7 billion). The U.S., originally not a strategic priority to Spanish firms, received fives times more direct investment in 2008 from Spain than it did in 2005. The majority of 2008 investments were made in depository institutions. The employment balance is skewed in favor of Spain.

Spain - U.S. Global Linkages, 2007

(Billions of $)

	U.S. in Spain	Spain in U.S.
Foreign Direct Investment* (2008)	69.6	38.7
Total Assets of Affiliates	177.5	70.4
Foreign Affiliate Sales	95.3	13.4
Value Added of Affiliates	19.6	2.4
Affiliate Employees	197,100	41,000

*Based on a historic-cost basis, data for 2008; all data for majority-owned nonbank affiliates

Trade

The U.S. received $11.2 billion worth of goods, or 4.2% of total exports from Spain in 2008, but a share of 12.6% of total exports when intra-EU trade is excluded. Regarding imports, the U.S. supplied only 3.4% of total imports by Spain in 2008, although the share rises to 8% after accounting for intra-EU trade.

Top Ten U.S. Imports from Spain, 2008 (in $ millions)

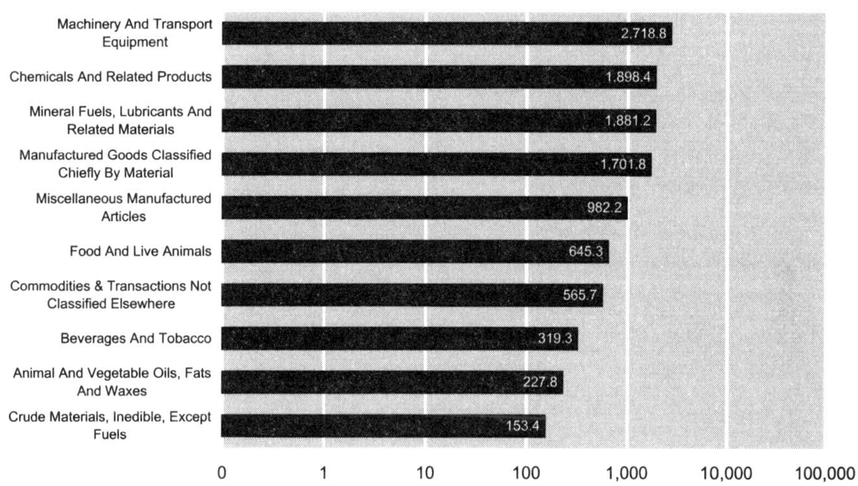

Source: Bureau of Economic Analysis, International Monetary Fund; Office of Trade and Industry Information

Sweden & the United States

Investment and Trade Figures

Investment

The investment balance slightly favors Sweden, with American direct investment in the Nordic country totaling $43.4 billion, while Swedish firms invested $35.0 billion in the U.S. in 2008. The employment balance is heavily in favor of the United States.

Sweden - U.S. Global Linkages, 2007

(Billions of $)

	U.S. in Sweden	Sweden in U.S.
Foreign Direct Investment* (2008)	43.4	35.0
Total Assets of Affiliates	119.0	-
Foreign Affiliate Sales	57.5	-
Value Added of Affiliates	13.8	12.2
Affiliate Employees	96,200	184,000

*Based on a historic-cost basis, data for 2008; all data for majority-owned nonbank affiliates

Trade

U.S. exports from Sweden totalled $12.1 billion in 2008, accounting for 6.6% of Sweden's global total and 16.2% of the total excluding intra-EU trade. Swedish imports of $5.3 billion from the U.S. accounting for 3.2% of Sweden's total imports in 2008, although the share rises to 10% excluding intra-EU imports.

Top Ten U.S. Imports from Sweden, 2008 (in $ millions)

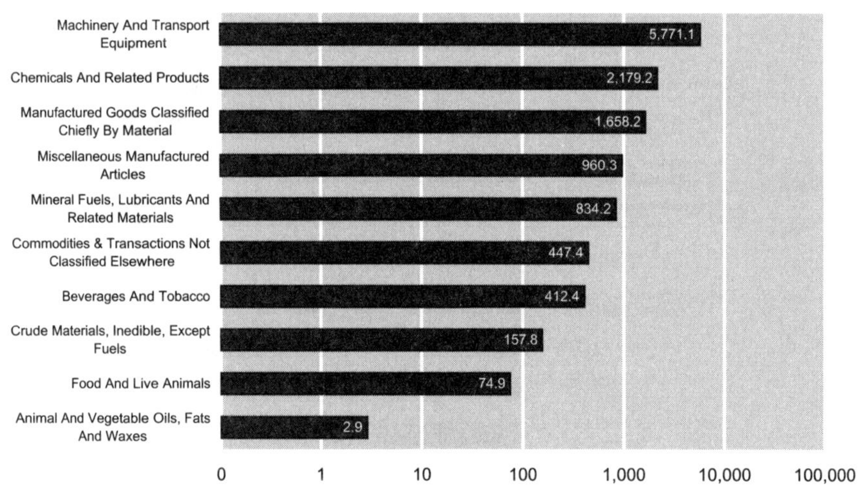

Source: Bureau of Economic Analysis, International Monetary Fund; Office of Trade and Industry Information

Switzerland & the United States

Investment and Trade Figures

Investment

The investment balance favors the U.S.— direct investment in Switzerland totaled $123.4 billion in 2008 versus $165.7 billion of Swiss direct investment in the U.S. Switzerland has one of the largest asset bases in the U.S. of any nation at $1.4 trillion (mainly in services like insurance and financial services). Even though the exact number of people employed by majority-owned bank and nonbank Swiss affiliates in the U.S. is not available due to data suppression to protect the identity of individual firms, we do know it is greater than 100,000, clearly favoring the United States, and was 416,100 in 2006.

Switzerland - U.S. Global Linkages, 2007 (Billions of $)	U.S. in Switzerland	Switzerland in U.S.
Foreign Direct Investment* (2008)	123.4	165.7
Total Assets of Affiliates	439.0	1,380.1
Foreign Affiliate Sales	238.9	-
Value Added of Affiliates	29.0	-
Affiliate Employees	83,000	100,000+

*Based on a historic-cost basis, data for 2008; all data for majority-owned nonbank affiliates

Trade

Swiss exports to the U.S. totaled $19.2 billion in 2008, representing 9.6% of all Swiss exports, and 24.3% when taken as a share of exports to regions outside the EU. In the same year, Switzerland imported American goods worth $10.6 billion, 5.8% of the global total, yet when imports from the EU were excluded, U.S. goods comprised 27.2% of Swiss imports.

Top Ten U.S. Imports from Switzerland, 2008 (in $ millions)

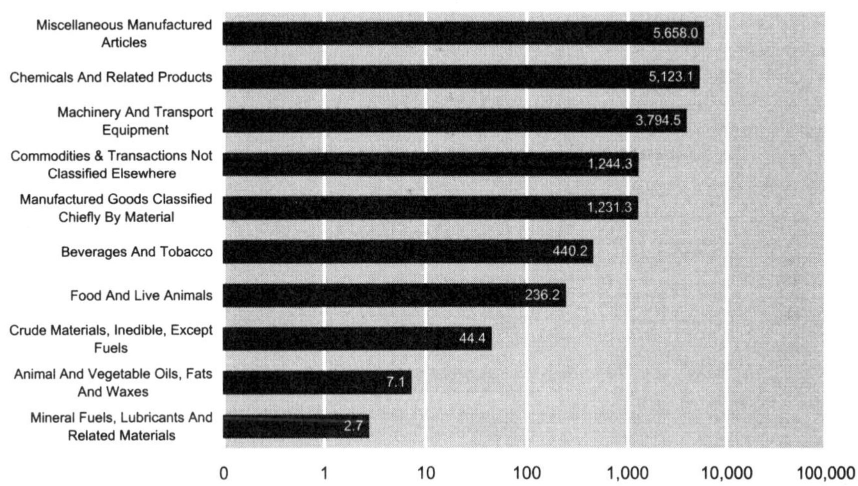

Source: Bureau of Economic Analysis, International Monetary Fund; Office of Trade and Industry Information

United Kingdom & the United States

Investment and Trade Figures

Investment

The U.S.-U.K. investment balance is fairly even, however the U.K. had a slightly larger presence in the U.S. in 2008. Sales of American and British affiliates totaled more than $1 trillion. U.S. affiliates employed more than 1 million workers in the U.K. while the exact number of U.S. workers employed by British affiliates is not available due to data suppression to protect the identify of individual firms, it is well over 100,000, and in fact was 908,800 in 2006.

United Kingdom - U.S. Global Linkages, 2007

(Billions of $)

	U.S. in United Kingdom	United Kingdom in U.S.
Foreign Direct Investment* (2008)	420.9	454.1
Total Assets of Affiliates	3,391.3	1,356.1
Foreign Affiliate Sales	625.4	446.9
Value Added of Affiliates	172.3	-
Affiliate Employees	1,191,900	100,000+

*Based on a historic-cost basis, data for 2008; all data for majority-owned nonbank affiliates

Trade

Bilateral trade flows are strong between the United Kingdom and the United States. Exports to the U.S. totaled $63.8 billion in 2008, 13.8% of total exports from United Kingdom and 31.7% when intra-EU exports are excluded from the global sum. Top exports to the U.S. include heavy machinery and chemical products. The U.S. was similiarly a key supplier to the United Kingdom in 2008, with $55.2 billion in imports from the U.S accounting for 8.7% of imports from the world and 18% excluding intra-EU trade.

Top Ten U.S. Imports from United Kingdom, 2008 (in $ millions)

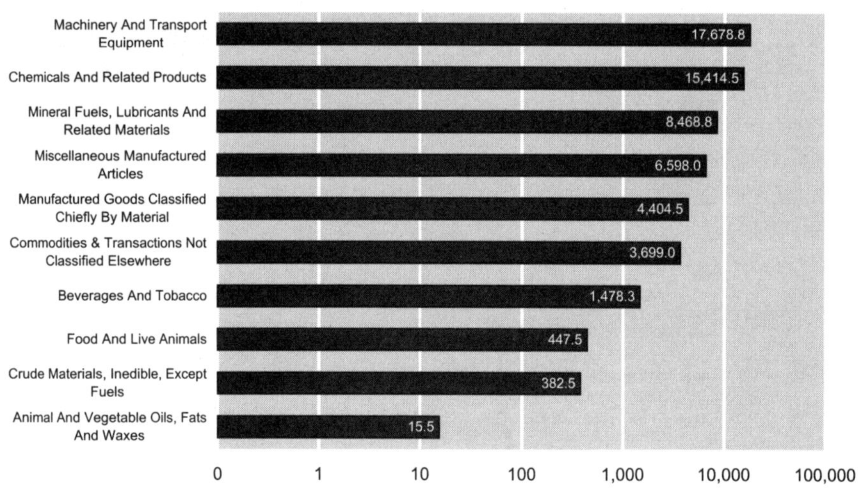

Source: Bureau of Economic Analysis, International Monetary Fund; Office of Trade and Industry Information

Chapter 5

What's Global is Local: Cities and Micro-Regions in the Transatlantic Economy

The vital stake Americans and Europeans have developed in the health of their respective economies, and in vibrant transatlantic commerce, is underscored most vividly in American and European cities and local regions. Inter-continental flows of particular kinds of goods, services, capital, people and ideas can be critical for a specific region or industry, even if domestic linkages overall are more important in the economy of the U.S. or European countries.

The political, economic and media errors that result from ignorance of these factors are shortchanging American and European consumers, producers, workers and their families. For example, even though most local stories seem to be about jobs being shifted "offshore," the fact is that most cities and regions in Europe and the U.S. also depend on "onshored" jobs—mainly from across the Atlantic.

In the wake of the economic and financial crisis and high unemployment rates across much of North America and Europe, local communities are struggling with concerns about job insecurity. Many worry that globalization means the replacement of high-wage, skilled manufacturing jobs with lower-wage services jobs. These concerns are real and certainly legitimate. But our own research supports that of the OECD and many economists, which indicates that for most regions and in most sectors such changes are more closely linked to productivity gains from technological advances and industry-level restructuring than to competition from low-wage economies.[1] Nonetheless, the volatile economic fortunes of local communities in the Great Recession have underscored the need for cities and regions to be resilient and adaptive.

Cities and microregions are increasingly becoming key drivers of economic growth and gateways to the global marketplace.[2] As the world's economy becomes more networked and "global," the "local" becomes more important. Globalization is simultaneously a tremendous force for geographic dispersion, because it can accelerate the diffusion of location and ownership of production across and among continents; and a powerful force for geographic concentration, because it can reward highly productive firms and workers who can capitalize on the knowledge, relationships and specialties that are often bunched spatially in key microregions or clusters.[3]

The world is getting "flatter" for routine types of activities, but for knowledge-intensive sectors and specialized industries it appears to be increasingly uneven, and therefore less

---

[1] See OECD, *Globalisation and Regional Economies: Can OECD Regions Compete in Global Industries?* (Paris, OECD, 2007), p. 13; *Global Location Trends: Annual Report 2009* (IBM, October 2009); OCO Insight, *A New Investment Paradigm*, 2008/2009, http://www.areadevelopment.com/article_pdf/id18985_NewInvestmentParadigm2009 final.pdf.

[2] See Allen J. Scott, *Regions and the World Economy: The Coming Shape of Global Production, Competition, and Political Order* (Oxford: Oxford University Press, 1998).

[3] OECD, Ibid.; E.E. Leamer, "A flat world, a level playing field, a small world after all, or none of the above? A review of Thomas L. Friedman's the world is flat," *Journal of Economic Literature* (2007) XLV:83–126.

equal. Rather than the world becoming flatter, for these types of activities the world actually appears to be becoming "spikier." As many rather mundane factors become less important across regions in the global economy, those features that distinguish regions from one another become more important. In short, a company's locational footprint, and a metropolitan region's distinctive characteristics, are becoming more important, not less, for economic success in the global economy.[4] Ann Markusen has called this the paradox of "sticky places within slippery space." [5] Michael Porter explains it in this way:

> Anything that can be efficiently sourced from a distance has essentially been nullified as a competitive advantage in advanced economies. Information and relationships that can be accessed through fax and email are available to everyone. Although global sourcing mitigates disadvantages, it does not create advantages . . . paradoxically, the most enduring competitive advantages in a global economy seem to be local.[6]

For these reasons, we are skeptical of extravagant claims of the "death of distance," i.e. the idea that national borders—or national choices—no longer matter. An integrated "flat" world market would mean free flows of goods, people and capital, and convergence in interest rates. That is far from the world we know today. "Distance always matters," notes Martin Wolf, "indeed, the policies and capacities of states remain central to any understanding of how economic globalization works." National boundaries have a powerful effect on economic activity: Toronto trades ten times as much with Vancouver as it does with Seattle.[7]

The slippery space of the global economy can lubricate and channels flows of goods, services, capital, people and ideas to specific geographical areas. Firms engaged in related activities may seek to be bunched so as to take advantage of each other's presence and to access local support facilities, specialized factor inputs, particular demand patterns, or shared service centers.[8]

---

[4] Leamer, Ibid.; Thomas Friedman, *The World is Flat: A Brief History of the Twenty-First Century* (New York: Farrar, Straus and Giroux, 2005), p. 11; Philip McCann, "Globalization and economic geography: the world is curved, not flat," *Cambridge Journal of Regions, Economy and Society*, 1 (3) : 357-370 (2008); Christian Ketels, *Clusters, Cluster Policy, and Swedish Competitiveness in the Global Economy*. Report No. 30 to Sweden's Globalisation Council (Stockholm: The Globalisation Council, 2009); Anthony J. Venables, "Shifts in economic geography and their causes," Paper prepared for the 2006 Jackson Hole Symposium, http://www.kansascityfed.org/PUBLICAT/SYMPOS/2006/pdf/venables.paper.0821.pdf.

[5] Ann Markusen, "Sticky places in slippery space: A typology of industrial districts," *Economic Geography*, 72,3 (1996); Alan Rugman and Karl Moore, "The Myths of Globalization," *Ivey Business Journal*, September/October 2001, Vol. 66, No. 1.

[6] Michael Porter, "Location, Competition, and Economic Development: Local Clusters in a Global Economy," *Economic Development Quarterly*, 14:15-34 (2000). Cited in *World Knowledge Economy Index 2008*, http://www.cforic.org/downloads.php.

[7] Frances Cairncross, *The Death of Distance* (Boston: Harvard Business School Press, 1997); Jeffrey Frankel, "Globalization of the Economy," in Joseph S. Nye and John D. Donahue, eds., *Governance in a Globalizing World* (Cambridge, MA: Visions of Governance for the 21st Century), p. 46; Robert O. Keohane and Joseph S. Nye, in Nye and Donahue, Ibid, p. 15; Martin Wolf, *Why Globalization Works* (New Haven: Yale University Press, 2004), pp. 16, 112; Michael D. Bordo, Barry Eichengreen and Douglas A. Irwin, "Is Globalization Today Really Different From Globalization a Hundred Years Ago?" in Susan M. Collins and Robert Z. Lawrence, eds., *Brookings Trade Forum 1999* (Washington, DC: Brookings, 1999); World Bank, *World Development Report 2009: Reshaping Economic Geography* (Washington, D.C.: 2009).

[8] Michael Porter has demonstrated how local productivity advantages resulting from agglomeration—such as access to specialized inputs, employees, information, and institutions—can encourage firms to cluster and rein-

In short, just as globalization has nullified traditional forms of competitive advantage within companies, it has heightened the importance of competitive advantages lying outside companies—that is, in the business environment in which they are located. Companies don't just compete with the internal capabilities of their rivals, but also with the respective business environment strengths and weaknesses those rivals can tap into.[9] A key strategic challenge for many companies today is to ensure that specific corporate activities are placed in locations that are consistent with a company's overall market position.

Cluster strength not only is a significant indicator of competitiveness, it is also an important determinant of prosperity differences among European regions and across the Atlantic. Quantitative studies across many countries and regions offer clear evidence of a positive relationship between employment in strong clusters and economic performance. Data from Europe and North America indicate that differences in the strength of cluster specialization explain on average around one third of the difference in GDP per capita levels across the transatlantic space.[10]

More detailed U.S. data also show that differences in specialization are associated with differences in relative wages across locations within specific industries. This industry-level wage effect is on average twice as important as the composition of a regional economy across industries in explaining differences in average GDP per capita levels across U.S. regions. Data also suggests that companies in strong clusters receive more foreign direct investment, achieve higher levels of productivity, and reach higher levels of innovation. Evidence is also emerging that clusters are particularly strong when it comes to fostering entrepreneurship and the commercial use of knowledge, not just the creation of knowledge. More importantly, new studies also indicate that survival rates and firm growth are higher in strong clusters as well. Based on these findings, Ketels argues that cluster policies could be more effective than traditional entrepreneurship policies that have tended to create new companies but failed to trigger their growth into larger businesses.[11]

The cluster of science- and technology-based companies around Cambridge, England—one of the world's densest concentrations of such businesses—offers a good example of both

---

force these clusters over time, as new firms become attracted by the same advantages of concentration. See Porter, op. cit.; Also D. Rees and T. McLean, "Trends in Location Choice," in A. Jolly, ed., *European Business Handbook 1997* (London: Kogan Page and Confederation of British Industry, 1997); John Dunning, "Location and the Multinational Enterprise: A Neglected Factor?" in *Journal of International Business Studies*, 29,1 (1998).

[9] Porter, op. cit.; OECD, op. cit., p. 3; Ketels, op. cit.; Peter Marsh, "How to play the home advantage," *Financial Times*, November 27, 2008.

[10] European Commission, *Innovation Clusters in Europe: A Statistical Analysis and Overview of Current Policy Support*, PRO INNO Europe Paper No. 5, Brussels: December 2007; Michael E. Porter, "The Economic Performance of Regions," *Regional Studies*, Vol. 37 (2003), No. 6/7.

[11] Ketels, op. cit.; Gustavo Bobonis and Howard Shatz, "Agglomeration, Adjustment, and the Role of State Level Policies in the Location of Foreign Direct Investment in the United States,"*Review of Economics and Statistics*, Vol. 89 (2007), 30–43; Vigdis Boasson and Alan MacPherson, "The role of geographic location in the financial and innovation performance of publicly traded pharmaceutical companies: empirical evidence from the United States, *Environment and Planning A*, Vol. 33 (2001), 1431–1444; Stuart Rosenthal and William Strange, "Agglomeration and Hours Worked," *Review of Economics and Statistics*, Vol. 90 (2008), 105–188; Luigi Guiso and Fabiano Schivardi, *What determines entrepreneurial clusters?* EUI Working Papers, ECO 2007/48 (Florence: July 2007); Edward Glaeser and Wiliam Kerr, "Local Industrial Conditions and Entrepreneurship: How much of the Spatial Distribution can we explain?" NBER Working Paper 14407 (Cambridge: October 2008); D. Audretsch and D. Dohse, "Location: A Neglected Determinant of Firm Growth. *Review of World Economics*, 143(1), 79–107 (2007); Karl Wennberg and Göran Lindqvist, "The effect of clusters on the survival and performance of new firms," *Small Business Economics*, June 2008.

the importance of city-regions in spurring growth and the critical role of transatlantic investment. In 2008 the leading 1,000 companies in the city registered combined sales of £4.3 billion, enjoyed profits of £337 million and employed 30,000 people.[12] Many of the most promising companies are owned by U.S. companies, who are attracted by the UK's strength in small tech-based companies in general and the Cambridge cluster's entrepreneurial climate and record of innovation in particular, and who have injected sizable R&D funding into the region.

Metropolitan areas are increasingly where wealth creation and origination of products and services happens. Already, 75% of global added-value is produced in cities and their inhabitants generate 9 out of 10 innovations.[13] Cities, themselves virtually complete economies in some instances, are increasingly becoming focal points of global economic activity. A closer look at their performance can help us gauge trends at the level of countries or continents.

All of these factors indicate that a microregion's competitiveness in the new global economy is likely to have as much to do with location *competence* as location *cost*. In the slippery space of the global economy, companies looking to invest could be looking beyond low costs to the ability of localities to offer a value-added environment. Increasingly, the most critical question potential investors are asking is not "How cheap are you?" but rather "How connected are you?" Dynamic "learning regions" attuned to knowledge-driven best practice and based on interrelated business networks are more likely to attract footloose firms.[14]

If a microregion wants to sustain its competitiveness, its key goal must be to become a sticky place in the slippery space of the global economy. As core operations of companies become both more mobile and more knowledge-intensive, the competitive position of a microregion will depend increasingly on its ability to convince corporations that it offers the full range of capabilities that best enable them to exploit their assets and partnerships. Local governments from Alabama to Catalonia play important roles as agents or network-makers as they seek to convince foreign executives to invest in their communities.[15]

U.S. and European Cities and Regions in the Global Knowledge Economy

While advances in telecommunications and information technologies have made it possible for companies and individuals to source work far more widely, the geographic concentration of related resources and industries, in particular of knowledge-intensive activities, remains one of the most striking features of any nation or region, especially in the economies of Europe and the United States.

A good deal of media reporting and political debate focuses on "footloose firms" relocating their production facilities to low-cost locales in developing countries. This is certainly one consideration when it comes to corporate investment decisions. But a single-minded focus

---

[12] Cambridge University Institute for Manufacturing; Peter Marsh, "A World to scale," *Financial Times*, January 21, 2010.

[13] Ernst & Young, *European Investment Report 2009*, http://www.eyeim.com/pdf/EIM%202008%20Report%20final.pdf.

[14] John Dunning, *Regions, Globalization, and the Knowledge-Based Economy* (Oxford: Oxford University Press, 2002), pp. 21, 29-30.

[15] See M. Salomon, "Local Governments as Foreign Policy Actors and Global Cities Network-Makers: The Cases of Barcelona and Porto Alegre," http://www.lboro.ac.uk/gawc/rb/rb305.html.

on cost alone ignores what is often a more significant calculus in the minds of corporate executives: in an increasingly competitive world economy, a company's "knowledge edge" may be even more important than its labor costs. Not only might an extra slice of knowledge translate into an extra slice of profit, a company's "knowledge advantage" could ultimately be the most critical element in its success. And in today's world, a company's "knowledge edge" may come as easily from across the ocean as from across town or across the nation. In short, "onshored" knowledge—and the competitive networks and jobs it creates—may be as significant for any particular company—and thus the region in which it is located—as domestically-sourced investments.

The higher intensity of competition due to globalization has forced companies to focus even more on productivity, especially innovation and knowledge. Companies need to leverage the opportunities of the global economy to become both more efficient and more innovative.[16] The drive for efficiency has led companies to turn to external partners for activities no longer provided within the company—the phenomenon known as "outsourcing." The drive for innovation has led companies to turn to external partners as sources of ideas. This can mean forging new networks in specific locations. Whether the motivation is efficiency or innovation, or some combination of the two, the result is that companies are increasingly on the look for external partners. And at least some of these partnerships turn out to be most effective and innovative if they are based on geographic proximity.

Regional economies across the transatlantic space have evolved away from manufacturing production toward knowledge-intensive service activities. Yet even as multinational companies have dispersed their production to take advantage of low-cost production, they have also tended to concentrate their activities when it comes to both medium- and high-technology industries. The OECD reports that localized knowledge spillovers (due to inter-firm linkages, a versatile labour pool, strong innovation- related infrastructures, etc.) can be a tangible source of productivity gain for firms and can constitute a persuasive argument against relocation or in favor of investment. For example, even as the Detroit region experiences ongoing restructuring and manufacturing job losses, the accumulated research capacities in the region continue to draw in R&D-related investment.

The concentration of innovation-related assets is also striking. The ten leading regions in Europe in terms of GDP per capita account for more than one-third of all patents. Moreover, there is a very strong link between certain characteristics of regional economies and innovation. For example, the level of patenting activity is strongly correlated with GDP per capita, with students in higher education, and with employment in high-technology industries. There is also evidence of specialization across leading regions with respect to the types of patent and sectors of activity. The Eindhoven region in the southern Netherlands, for example, has attained a strong position in innovation in the semiconductor and materials engineering fields, and Stockholm, Sweden has done the same in the field of ICT innovation.[17]

The OECD has conducted extensive research into global competitiveness, and concludes that economic competitiveness should be analyzed in terms of stocks and investments in knowledge, with a firm focus on regions. And most knowledge-intensive investment activi-

[16] Ketels, op. cit.; Suzanne Berger, *How we compete: What Companies Around the World are Doing to Make it in Today's Global Economy* (Doubleday: New York, NY: 2005).

[17] See OECD, op. cit., p. 11-13.

ties remain heavily concentrated in microregions within the advanced industrialized countries, particularly in Europe and the United States.[18]

The OECD concludes that "in terms of long run growth discussions, the critical issue for the emerging economic geography of the twenty-first century is the location and spatial distribution of knowledge-assets." [19] Geographical proximity is becoming more important for knowledge-related activities, which are increasingly located in high agglomeration city-regions, while low-skill, routine, and low value-added activities are becoming spatially dispersed across the global economy.[20]

We have looked at various measures examining U.S. and European cities and microregions in the global knowledge economy. The results offer different wake-up calls for metropolitan regions on the different sides of the Atlantic. In general, European metro areas lag significantly behind their U.S. counterparts as competitive world knowledge regions, as well as in per capita R&D expenditures and labor productivity. U.S. cities, on the other hand, appear to be relatively less "connected" to other major world metropoles in terms of advanced producer services. This could perhaps reflect their continuing focus on the large domestic U.S. market; but it could also mean that in general many U.S. metropolitan areas are not making the kinds of international connections likely to be needed if they are to attract investment and be attractive "sticky places" in the slippery space of the global economy. In short, both European and U.S. cities must continually raise their game if they are to maintain their competitive positions in the 21st century.

The Most Competitive World Knowledge Regions

According to the 2008 World Knowledge Competitiveness Index, the U.S. metropolitan region of San Jose, California, the home of Silicon Valley, tops the rankings, due to its enormous investment in knowledge-intensive business development, investment in education and business R&D, high productivity and earnings. Boston, which thrives on high levels of educational and financial capital, ranks #2. Hartford, Connecticut rose to #3 worldwide, with strong R&D spending and private equity investment, which translate into a top global productivity score. The neighboring region of Bridgeport, Connecticut ranks #4, with San Francisco ranking #5. These top five regions between them underline the significant concentration of knowledge competitiveness in northern California and Southern New England. Stockholm ranks #6, the top European city-region, based on impressive rankings in business R&D spending, biotechnology and chemical sector employment, and higher education spending. The top twenty knowledge regions include 13 U.S. regions, 5 European regions, and 2 Japanese regions. Regions in Denmark, Finland, Sweden and the Netherlands all registered improvements, but London dropped 46 places to 102nd. And while European and Asian regions overall showed improvements, North American regions registered declines, including New York, Austin, Atlanta and Washington, DC.[21]

---

[18] See Vincenzo Spiezia, "Measuring Regional Economies," OECD Statistics Brief, October 2003, No. 6; John H. Dunning, *Regions*, op. cit.

[19] OECD, op. cit.

[20] Leamer, op. cit.; McCann, op. cit; http://www.oecd.org/dataoecd/49/34/40665323.pdf.

[21] The Index uses 19 knowledge economy benchmarks, including employment levels in the knowledge economy, patent registrations, R&D investment by the private and public sector, education expenditure, information and communication technology, infrastructure, and access to private equity. The full report is available at http://www.cforic.org/downloads.php.

World Knowledge Competitiveness Index 2008

Rank		Knowledge Competitiveness Index 2008	Rank 2005	Change in Rank 2005-08
1	San Jose-Sunnyvale-Santa Clara, US	248.3	1	0
2	Boston-Cambridge-Quincy, US	175.3	2	0
3	Hartford, US	175.1	4	1
4	Bridgeport-Stamford-Norwalk, US	174.7		
5	San Francisco-Oakland-Fremont, US	160.8	3	-2
6	Stockholm, Sweden	151.8	8	2
7	Seattle-Tacoma-Bellevue, US	151.3	5	-2
8	Providence-Fall River-Warwick, US	147.1		
9	Tokyo, Japan	147.0	22	13
10	San Diego-Carlsbad-San Marcos, US	146.1	7	-3
11	Los Angeles-Long Beach-Santa Ana, US	144.4	10	-1
12	Shiga, Japan	140.9	57	45
13	Grand Rapids, US	140.0	6	-7
14	Iceland	139.8		
15	Detroit-Warren-Livonia, US	138.1	15	0
16	West, Sweden	137.9	37	21
17	Oxnard-Thousand Oaks-Ventura, US	137.1		
18	Sacramento–Arden-Arcade–Roseville, US	133.6	11	-7
19	West, Netherlands	132.4	77	58
20	Pohjois-Suomi, Finland	132.1		
21	Minneapolis-St. Paul-Bloomington, US	131.7	13	-8
22	Portland-Vancouver-Beaverton, US	129.7	18	-4
23	Etela-Suomi, Finland	129.1	20	-3
24	Kanagawa, Japan	128.6	81	57
25	Durham, US	127.7		
26	Colorado Springs, US	124.4		
27	Singapore	123.1	78	51
28	Switzerland	122.5	44	16
29	Île de France, France	121.8	29	0
30	Toyama, Japan	120.5	80	50
31	Osaka, Japan	119.6	72	41
32	Riverside-San Bernardino-Ontario, US	119.3	16	-16
33	Philadelphia-Camden-Wilmington, US	117.7	17	-16
34	Luxembourg	116.9	58	24
35	New York-Northern New Jersey-Long Island, US	116.8	12	-23
36	Denmark	116.7	51	15
37	Tochigi, Japan	116.1	73	36
38	South, Sweden	115.2	46	8
39	Greensboro-High Point, US	113.5	40	1
40	Lansi-Suomi, Finland	112.5		
41	Washington-Arlington-Alexandria, US	112.4	23	-18
42	Austin-Round Rock, US	112.3	19	-23
43	Kyoto, Japan	111.9	96	53
44	Milwaukee-Waukesha-West Allis, US	111.2	24	-20
45	Denver-Aurora, US	110.7	14	-31
46	Chicago-Naperville-Joliet, US	109.4	28	-18
47	Brussels, Belgium	109.4	45	-2
48	Israel	109.3	86	38
49	Baltimore-Towson, US	108.9	27	-22
50	Rochester, US	108.8	9	-41
51	Shizuoka, Japan	106.8	71	20
52	Dallas-Fort Worth-Arlington, US	106.6	21	-31
53	Taiwan	106.5	99	46
54	Eastern, UK	106.1	62	8
55	Baden-Württemberg, Germany	106.0	54	-1
56	Aichi, Japan	105.6	75	19
57	Ostra Mellansverige, Sweden	105.3		
58	Phoenix-Mesa-Scottsdale, US	103.3	38	-20
59	Buffalo-Niagara Falls, US	102.8	25	-34

World Knowledge Competitiveness Index 2008 (continued)

Rank		Knowledge Competitiveness Index 2008	Rank 2005	Change in Rank 2005-08
60	Virginia Beach-Norfolk-Newport News, US	102.5	48	-12
61	East Netherlands	102.1		
62	Cleveland-Elyria-Mentor, US	101.9	39	-23
63	Bayern, Germany	101.8	65	2
64	Indianapolis, US	101.7	32	-32
65	North, Netherlands	101.6	89	24
66	Raleigh-Cary, US	100.7	31	-35
67	Charlotte-Gastonia-Concord, US	100.7	41	-26
68	South, Netherlands	100.0	50	-18
69	Ulsan, Korea	100.0	113	44
70	Houston-Sugar Land-Baytown, US	99.9	26	-44
71	Richmond, US	99.9	33	-38
72	Pittsburgh, US	99.3	43	-29
73	Vlaams Gewest, Belgium	99.1	79	6
74	South East, UK	98.9	55	-19
75	Norway	98.6	52	-23
76	Ontario, Canada	98.5	66	-10
77	Hessen, Germany	97.9	67	-10
78	Columbus, US	96.0	30	-48
79	East, Austria	94.7	70	-9
80	Salt Lake City, US	94.3	34	-46
81	Akron, US	93.0		
82	Hamburg, Germany	92.4	76	-6
83	Quebec, Canada	92.2	85	2
84	Southern and Eastern, Ireland	91.2		
85	Alberta, Canada	91.0	98	13
86	Kansas City, US	90.0	42	-44
87	Centre-est, France	89.7	82	-5
88	San Antonio, US	89.4	47	-41
89	Cincinnati-Middletown, US	89.2	36	-53
90	Memphis, US	88.9	61	-29
91	St. Louis, US	88.8	49	-42
92	Nashville-Davidson--Murfreesboro, US	87.6	59	-33
93	Bremen, Germany	86.4	95	2
94	Louisville, US	86.1	53	-41
95	Atlanta-Sandy Springs-Marietta, US	85.9	35	-60
96	Lombardia, Italy	85.7	84	-12
97	West, Austria	85.2	90	-7
98	Tampa-St. Petersburg-Clearwater, US	85.1	64	-34
99	Victoria, Australia	82.9	88	-11
100	North West, Italy	82.6	101	1

Patent Registration: The Importance of Transatlantic Cooperation

Patent data show a significant degree of internationalization of research activities. On average, over 15% of the patents filed by an OECD country in 2004-06 under the Patent Cooperation Treaty (PCT) concerned inventions made abroad. International co-authorship has also been growing fast. In 2007, 21.9% of scientific articles involved international co-authorship, a figure three times higher than in 1985.[22]

Countries like Japan, the United States and the Netherlands, ranking among the top ten OECD countries in PCT patent applications per million inhabitants, seem to co-invent

[22] *OECD Science, Technology and Industry Scoreboard 2009* (Paris: OECD, December 2009).

mostly within their borders. In 2005, in these three countries and Korea, more than 70% of co-inventions were domestic. Other countries like Turkey, the Slovak Republic and Canada, seem more oriented toward international rather than national co-operation.

There are some interesting examples of strong transatlantic cooperation in terms of patent co-invention between regions. Istanbul, Turkey, the OECD region with the highest percentage of foreign co-patenting, shared 94% of its foreign co-inventions with North America, and only slightly more than 5% with regions in Europe. Another striking example is California, which in 2005 shared 64% of its foreign co-inventions with Europe and only 16% with other non-U.S. regions in North America. The Southeast of England and the Southern and Eastern region of Ireland each share about 50% of their foreign co-inventions with regions in North America, and only about 40% with regions in Europe. Lisbon, Portugal and the western Netherlands share about 40 percent of their foreign co-inventions with regions in North America.[23]

Investment in Research and Development (R&D)

The U.S. government plays a major role in stimulating R&D in the United States, and these funds find their way to a number of key locations across the country. The U.S. capital region of Washington, DC, extending northeastward to the Baltimore-Towson region,

Regions with the highest number of foreign co-inventors by partner continent (TL2), 2005

	Europe	North America	Japan and Korea	Australia
Zapadne Slov.-SK	13	1	0	0
Oslo Og Aker.-NO	47	4	0	0
Alsace-FR	502	40	10	0
Wien-AT	123	18	1	2
Central Hung.-HU	56	7	3	0
Ostschweiz-CH	675	92	34	3
Attiki-GR	15	4	1	0
Lombardia-IT	124	47	0	1
Stockholm-SE	182	62	4	5
Baden-Wuertt.-DE	1080	350	73	11
Etela-Suomi-FI	153	46	14	2
Praha-CZ	19	8	0	0
Mazowieckie-PL	7	3	0	0
Vlaams Gewest-BE	419	179	14	3
Navarra-ES	17	8	0	0
California-US	606	152	141	54
West-Ned.-NL	242	132	12	1
Lisboa-PT	11	8	0	0
Kanto-JP	272	276	21	1
South East-UK	221	293	23	14
Sout. & Eas.-IR	39	56	1	5
Distrito Fed.-ME	6	10	0	1
Capital Reg.-KR	59	114	22	1
Ontario-CA	137	482	12	2
N. S. Wales.-AU	47	77	7	99
Istanbul-TR	1	15	0	0

Data for Iceland, Denmark, and New Zealand are not available at the regional level.

[23] See OECD, *Regions at a Glance 2009* (Paris: OECD, 2009), p. 30.

Regions with highest number of foreign co-inventors by partner continent

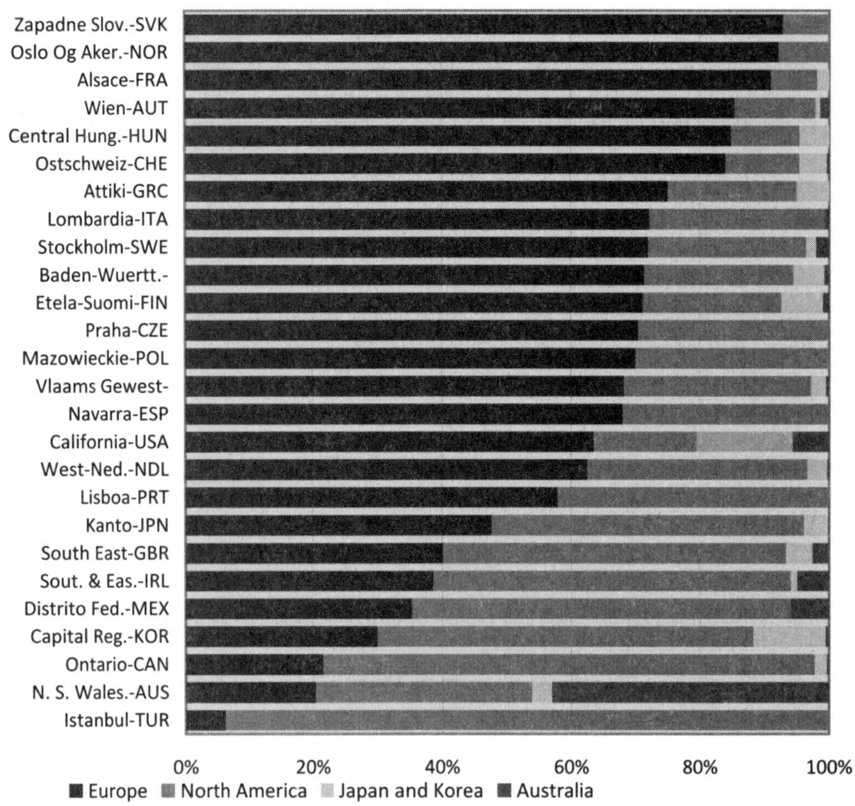

Patent Registrations per 1 Million Inhabitants—Top Twenty Regions 2008

Rank	Top 20 Regions	Index 2008	Change in Rank 2005-08
1	Tokyo, Japan	708.7	0
2	Osaka, Japan	346.9	1
3	San Jose-Sunnyvale-Santa Clara, US	252.3	1
4	San Diego-Carlsbad-San Marcos, US	252.3	4
5	Los Angeles-Long Beach-Santa Ana, US	252.3	2
6	San Francisco-Oakland-Fremont, US	252.3	0
7	Riverside-San Bernardino-Ontario, US	252.3	-2
8	Oxnard-Thousand Oaks-Ventura, US	252.3	
9	Sacramento--Arden-Arcade--Roseville, US	252.3	0
10	Boston-Cambridge-Quincy, US	250.4	1
11	Minneapolis-St. Paul-Bloomington, US	243.1	-1
12	Portland-Vancouver-Beaverton, US	217.0	2
13	Colorado Springs, US	208.5	
14	Denver-Aurora, US	208.5	-1
15	Bridgeport-Stamford-Norwalk, US	206.0	
16	Hartford, US	206.0	7
17	South Netherlands	205.3	32
18	Kyoto, Japan	196.2	12
19	Baden-Württemberg, Germany	187.4	25
20	Shanghai, China	186.0	-18

Per Capita Research and Development Expenditure by Government—Top Twenty Regions 2008 (Expenditure per capita in US$ - PPP adjusted)

Rank	Top 20 Regions	R&D Expenditure Index	Change in Rank 2005-08
1	Washington-Arlington-Alexandria, US	815.9	0
2	Baltimore-Towson, US	744.8	0
3	Beijing, China	534.8	11
4	Richmond, US	441.8	-1
5	Virginia Beach-Norfolk-Newport News, US	438.9	-1
6	Boston-Cambridge-Quincy, US	398.3	-1
7	Providence-Fall River-Warwick, US	314.5	
8	Hartford, US	313.1	-2
9	Bridgeport-Stamford-Norwalk, US	313.1	
10	San Francisco-Oakland-Fremont, US	257.3	-1
11	San Diego-Carlsbad-San Marcos, US	257.3	1
12	Oxnard-Thousand Oaks-Ventura, US	257.3	
13	Riverside-San Bernardino-Ontario, US	257.3	-3
14	San Jose-Sunnyvale-Santa Clara, US	257.3	-6
15	Los Angeles-Long Beach-Santa Ana, US	257.3	-4
16	Sacramento--Arden-Arcade--Roseville, US	257.3	-3
17	Seattle-Tacoma-Bellevue, US	196.0	-10
18	Denver-Aurora, US	185.8	-2
19	Colorado Springs, US	185.8	
20	Phoenix-Mesa-Scottsdale, US	171.5	-5
22	Lazio, Italy	158.2	-5
23	Prague, Czech Republic	157.4	-5
27	Berlin, Germany	139.6	-8
28	Bremen, Germany	122.7	-5
29	Iceland	112.6	
44	Île de France, France	103.7	-17
58	Bratislavsk, Slovak Republic	87.3	30
59	Hamburg, Germany	86.9	-19
62	Central, Italy	83.3	42
65	Etela-Suomi, Finland	79.6	-40
75	Comunidad de Madrid, Spain	72.9	-27
77	Budapest, Hungary	67.0	-28
78	Stockholm, Sweden	64.8	-9
80	Baden-Württemberg, Germany	62.4	-23
82	South East, UK	59.9	-7
83	East Netherlands	57.9	
84	Luxembourg	54.1	0
85	West, Netherlands	52.2	-20
86	Eastern, UK	51.0	-9
87	Norway	50.6	-17

Source: OECD

ranks as the top region in the world in terms of per capita R&D expenditure by government. The Virginia metropolitan region of Richmond, extending to Virginia Beach-Norfolk-Newport News, home to a good deal of U.S. military activity, also ranked at the top. New England cities such as Boston, Providence, Hartford and Bridgeport also ranked within the top ten, followed by a string of California metropolitan regions, from San Francisco to Los Angeles and San Diego. Beijing, China was the only non-U.S. city even breaking into the top 20, with European cities all far behind in terms of government-channeled R&D expenditures.

In terms of per capita R&D expenditure by business, U.S. cities also dominate the rankings, with only the Swedish regions of Göteberg and Stockholm and four Japanese regions breaking into the top 20. Sweden's strong business R&D investments are also apparent in

Per Capita Research and Development Expenditure by Business—Top Twenty Regions 2008 (Expenditure per capita in US$ - PPP adjusted)

Rank	Top 20 Regions	R&D Expenditure Index	Change in Rank 2003-08
1	Hartford, US	299.9	2
1	Bridgeport-Stamford-Norwalk, US	299.9	
3	Boston-Cambridge-Quincy, US	298.2	2
4	Grand Rapids, US	271.5	3
4	Detroit-Warren-Livonia, US	271.5	1
6	Seattle-Tacoma-Bellevue, US	267.7	-5
7	West, Sweden	264.5	-3
8	Providence-Fall River-Warwick, US	238.3	
9	San Diego-Carlsbad-San Marcos, US	236.6	3
9	San Jose-Sunnyvale-Santa Clara, US	236.6	-2
9	Los Angeles-Long Beach-Santa Ana, US	236.6	0
9	San Francisco-Oakland-Fremont, US	236.6	-2
9	Oxnard-Thousand Oaks-Ventura, US	236.6	
9	Riverside-San Bernardino-Ontario, US	236.6	-5
9	Sacramento--Arden-Arcade--Roseville, US	236.6	-2
16	Shiga, Japan	227.0	0
17	Stockholm, Sweden	216.3	-15
18	Shizuoka, Japan	212.4	2
19	Aichi, Japan	210.9	0
20	Kanagawa, Japan	185.4	6

Source: OECD

Per Capita Research and Development Expenditure by Business—Top Twenty European Regions 2008

Rank	Top 20 European Regions	R&D Expenditure Index	Change in Rank 2005-08
1	West, Sweden	264.5	-3
2	Stockholm, Sweden	216.3	-15
3	Eastern, UK	178.0	4
4	Île de France, France	170.0	-11
5	Baden-Württemberg, Germany	169.8	-8
6	Pohjois-Suomi, Finland	161.8	
7	Luxembourg	155.3	-17
8	South, Sweden	149.4	-13
9	Etela-Suomi, Finland	143.0	-18
10	Bayern, Germany	136.2	-10
11	Switzerland	135.5	1
12	Hessen, Germany	127.4	-7
13	South East, UK	120.7	-7
14	Lansi-Suomi, Finland	118.5	-44
15	Ostra Mellansverige, Sweden	117.0	
16	South Netherlands	115.3	-18
17	Denmark	96.3	-8
18	Hamburg, Germany	92.8	11
19	Bremen, Germany	92.5	6
20	East, Austria	91.9	-19

Source: OECD

the strong showing of Sweden's regions within Europe's top 20 regions in this category, accompanied by five German regions.

Labor productivity, or output per employee, is another area where U.S. city-regions show a clear advantage, with only Luxembourg and Brussels, Belgium breaking into the top 20. Although European regions had been catching up with their American counterparts in the 1970s and 1980s, this process stalled in the 1990s and U.S. metro regions remain ahead of the game.

Index of Labor Productivity (Output per Employee)—Top Twenty Regions 2008

Rank	Top 20 Regions	Index 2008	Change in Rank 2005-08
1	Hartford, US	185.2	2
2	San Jose-Sunnyvale-Santa Clara, US	159.5	3
3	Bridgeport-Stamford-Norwalk, US	159.4	
4	New York-Northern New Jersey-Long Island, US	147.4	6
5	Buffalo-Niagara Falls, US	142.8	8
6	Washington-Arlington-Alexandria, US	142.2	10
7	Boston-Cambridge-Quincy, US	141.0	5
8	Rochester, US	140.2	3
9	San Francisco-Oakland-Fremont, US	139.7	-3
10	Virginia Beach-Norfolk-Newport News, US	138.0	35
11	Providence-Fall River-Warwick, US	136.6	
12	Los Angeles-Long Beach-Santa Ana, US	136.1	3
13	Seattle-Tacoma-Bellevue, US	136.0	4
14	San Diego-Carlsbad-San Marcos, US	134.4	10
15	Luxembourg	132.6	-13
16	Brussels, Belgium	132.5	-15
17	Greensboro-High Point, US	131.6	44
18	Charlotte-Gastonia-Concord, US	131.1	4
19	Durham, US	129.1	
20	Philadelphia-Camden-Wilmington, US	129.0	10

Index of Labor Productivity (Output per Employee)—Top Twenty European Regions 2008

Rank	Top 20 European Regions	Index 2008	Change in Rank 2003-08
1	Luxembourg	132.6	-6
2	Brussels, Belgium	132.5	-14
3	Île de France, France	129.0	-10
4	North, Netherlands	119.5	60*
5	West, Netherlands	119.0	34*
6	Southern and Eastern, Ireland	117.1	
7	Hamburg, Germany	113.1	-24
8	Norway	111.6	-24
9	South Netherlands	111.5	36*
10	London, UK	109.1	1
11	Vlaams Gewest, Belgium	108.0	7
12	Stockholm, Sweden	105.3	-21
13	East Netherlands	103.4	
14	Lombardia, Italy	101.8	-40
15	Lazio, Italy	99.8	-25
16	North West, Italy	98.6	-36
17	East, Austria	97.2	-33
18	Hessen, Germany	97.0	-26
19	Etela-Suomi, Finland	95.3	-34
20	Bayern, Germany	94.2	-11

Source: OECD

U.S. and European Cities in the Global Information and Services Economy

Globalization and revolutionary advances in informational technology have changed the roles of cities and microregions in the international economy. At one level, such communities occupy a particular space at a specific place. Their physical location is an important determinant of their competitive position in the economy. At another level, however, such communities occupy a particular space within a network of interconnected places. Their competitive position can depend not only on their physical location, but the degree to

20 Most Connected Cities in Advanced Producer Services, 2000 and 2008

	2000			2008	
1	London	100.00	1	New York	100.00
2	New York	97.10	2	London	98.64
3	Hong Kong	73.08	3	Hong Kong	81.33
4	Tokyo	70.64	4	Paris	77.91
5	Paris	69.72	5	Singapore	74.15
6	Singapore	66.61	6	Tokyo	72.58
7	Chicago	61.18	7	Sydney	71.76
8	Milan	60.44	8	Shanghai	70.05
9	Madrid	59.23	9	Beijing	68.77
10	Los Angeles	58.75	10	Milan	67.67
11	Sydney	58.06	11	Madrid	66.42
12	Frankfurt	57.53	12	Moscow	64.24
13	Amsterdam	57.10	13	Seoul	63.54
14	Toronto	56.92	14	Brussels	63.53
15	Brussels	56.51	15	Toronto	62.29
16	Sao Paulo	54.26	16	Buenos Aires	61.21
17	San Francisco	50.43	17	Mumbai	60.24
18	Zurich	48.42	18	Kuala Lumpur	58.87
19	Taipei	48.22	19	Taipei	56.77
20	Jakarta	47.92	20	Sao Paulo	56.49
22	Buenos Aires	46.81	22	Zurich	55.83
23	Mumbai	46.81	25	Amsterdam	54.60
27	Shanghai	43.95	27	Jakarta	54.03
28	Kuala Lumpur	43.53	30	Frankfurt	52.31
29	Beijing	43.43	31	Chicago	52.20
30	Seoul	42.32	44	Los Angeles	41.77
37	Moscow	40.76	49	San Fransisco	40.01

Note: Individual city connectivity scores are shown as a proportion of the most connected city, i.e. New York in 2008 =100.00). From B. Derudder, P.J. Taylor, P. Ni, A. De Vos, M. Hoyler, H. Hanssens, D. Bassens, J. Huang, F. Witlox and X. Yang, "Pathways of growth and decline: connectivity changes in the world city network, 2000-2008," http://www.lboro.ac.uk/gawc/rb/rb310.html. The data collection exercise was carried out in the first half of 2008 and so represents a key benchmark of the state of the world city network just before the crash of the global financial system.

which they are integral nodes in a broader web of flows of information and ideas. Saskia Sassen and Manuel Castells have identified global cities as critical nodes through which such "spaces of flows" are created and sustained.[24]

In short, the traditional national "space of places" has been supplemented by a new global "space of flows" —and cities are the critical nodes where both spaces come together. The information revolution has not only enabled a tremendous dispersion of economic activities, it has generated a need for new concentrations in services management and organization, and these functions have largely been captured by particular cities and micro-regions. In this sense the global economy may be viewed as an archipelago of interlinked city-regions that are not only linked to their traditional "hinterland" within their own region or country, but also to an increasingly important "hinterworld" of interconnected cities and regions that can be important to a particular city's prosperity.[25]

---

[24] Saskia Sassen, *The Global City* (Princeton, NJ: Princeton University Press, 1991); Manuel Castells, *The Rise of Network Society* (Oxford: Blackwell, 1996); Manuel Castells, *Communication Power* (Oxford: Oxford University Press, 2009); P.J. Taylor, "World City Networks: Measurement, Social Organization, Global Governance, and Structural Change," http://www.lboro.ac.uk/gawc/rb/rb333.html.

[25] D. Held, A. McGrew, D. Goldblatt, and J. Perraton, *Global Transformations* (Cambridge: Polity, 1999; L. Halbert and K. Pain, "PAR-LON - Doing Business in Knowledge-Based Services in Paris and London: A Tale of One City?" http://www.lboro.ac.uk/gawc/rb/rb307.html.

The Globalization and World Cities research group devised a network model to measure the global connectivity of 307 cities across the world, and present an overview of the 20 cities with the greatest global network connectivity (GNC) in 2000 and 2008. They rank cities in terms of how interconnected they are globally in terms of "advanced producer services" —office networks of leading firms in complex, high-value decision-making functions and transactions in such areas as finance, management consultancy, accountancy, advertising and law. According to this measure, New York and London rank as the most connected global cities in advanced producer services. Although New York and London change positions, they remain at the top.[26] Hong Kong, Paris, Singapore and Tokyo follow.

Below the top six, and reflecting the rise of Asian metropoles as key nodes of the global knowledge economy, cities such as Chicago, Los Angeles and Amsterdam have slipped to such cities as Shanghai, Beijing and Seoul. In fact, it is striking that only the two North American cities of New York and Toronto were considered to be among the top 20 "most connected" cities in 2008, as opposed to 9 Asian cities. While cities such as Los Angeles, San Francisco, Miami, Chicago, St. Louis, Cologne and Düsseldorf remain well-connected,

I ♥ NY. But do I ♥ NY-LON? And what about NY-LON-KONG?[1]

> *"... London and New York are very special cities and in this sense they represent the two poles of a transatlantic metropolis."*
>
> —*Peter Hall*

As the past decade began, *Newsweek* magazine featured on its front cover a young woman wearing a T-Shirt with the slogan "I ♥ NY-LON" rather than the familiar slogan of "I ♥ New York," and accompanied by the headline: "A tale of one city: living, working and playing in New York and London." This was followed by a short-lived British television drama, entitled NY-LON, which chronicled the troubled romance between a chap from London and a New York City girl.

The NY-LON phenomenon has been perhaps the most visible and dramatic example of the symbiotic relationship between globalization and city-regions in the transatlantic economy. The image of a New York—London dyad underscores the fact that in many respects both cities have been the twin poles of globalization, and as such have been reconfiguring themselves to become more intensely connected both to each other and to much of the rest of the world.

It has been a tale of money, ambition, and yes, troubled romance. Linked in such areas as film, theater, television, pop music, publishing, communication technologies, research and development, business services and the life sciences, the two cities have come together more than ever before. An extensive network of personal contacts between New Yorkers and Londoners facilitates an intense flow of people, goods, services and ideas. Once centers of manufacturing, each has been able to shift its economic focus to the services sector. Their histories as major ports have rendered each open to international trade and investment. They are also cities of immigrants. New

[26] Halbert and Pain, Ibid.; Taylor, op. cit.

York, of course, has long been thought of as a city of immigrants, but so now is London. In 2006, according to the London Labour Force Survey, 31% of the city's residents had been born outside Britain; that compared with 34% of New Yorkers who hailed from outside the U.S. that year.

Each city's economic success is increasingly dependent on business operations by foreign-owned companies. A study commissioned by the Partnership for New York City determined that FDI (most of it from Europe) was responsible for about 10% of the total economic output of New York City, and for creating one in twenty jobs in the New York City economy. Nearly half of all FDI within New York state has flowed into the finance and insurance sectors. FDI (most of it from the United States) is even more important to London, accounting for more than 25% of the London economy. Total annual investment from foreign businesses in London topped $66 billion in 2005—more than total foreign investment in all of China and India combined. London remains the #1 European destination for U.S. FDI and the biggest magnet for global FDI into Europe; more than 7% of all FDI companies coming into Europe set up business in London. Over 6,700 U.S. companies currently operate in London, and one in ten businesses investing in London come from the tri-state area surrounding New York City.

Both are also trading cities. Each has benefited from the past decade's worldwide growth in trade, and each has been a major contributor to its country's growth in services exports. New York is the leading U.S. metro exporter to the UK, France, Germany and Switzerland. London's total exports of goods and services rose from £38bn in 2002 to £59bn in 2007, over 80% (£49 billion) of which was accounted for by services. That represents over a third of the UK's services exports. Moreover, each city's prime trading markets are Europe and North America. Rapidly developing markets are offering traders new opportunities, but the economic base for both is still the Atlantic Basin, and the first rule of business—and politics—is don't forget your base.

Connected by fiber-optic cable and more than 300 flights a week, the two cities forged a financial network that has been able to lubricate the global economy. As the transatlantic and global services economy took off, the two cities positioned themselves as synergistic nodes for firms competing in global markets. And as both cities developed their global reach, they each expanded beyond their traditional domestic *hinterlands* to encompass new global *hinterworlds* supplying back-office functions and new innovations.

As the twin epicenters of the financial crisis, both cities were hit hard. By some estimates New York City's gross municipal product fell by $10 billion in 2008. Financial institutions in both cities were complacent about risk and equally complicit in their speculative excesses. Changes in the political and regulatory climate in both countries makes future prospects uncertain; legislation could include special levies on bankers' bonuses, high taxes on high earners, restrictions on firms that have taken government bail-out money, and tougher regulations on the size and operations of banks.

Signs are mixed. Despite the downturn, in 2009 London was voted the #1 European city for business for the 20th year running, and a survey of corporate executives ranked New York #1 globally in terms of anticipated new foreign direct investment for 2010. But a poll of Bloomberg subscribers in October found that London had dropped behind Singapore into third place as the city most likely to be the best financial hub two years from now. And a December 2009 survey of executives by Eversheds, a law firm, found that Shanghai could overtake London within the next ten years.

And so, as both cities struggle to recapture their economic vitality, the world of global competition and cooperation marches on. *Time* magazine upped the ante on *Newsweek* by extending its NY-LON dyad into NY-LON-KONG, a 21st-century triad that includes Hong Kong as Asia's emerging financial center, tied closely to New York and London but positioned to ease China's integration into the modern global economy. Clever. But Vincent Cheng, Chairman of the Hongkong and Shanghai Banking Corporation, quickly captured both the hopes and the anxieties associated with China's rising power by turning *Time*'s slogan around and suggesting a more portentous candidate for English Word of the Next Decade: HONG-NY-LON.

[1] Drawn from S. McGuire & M. Chan, "The NY-LON life", *Newsweek*, November 13, 2000, pp. 40 -47; Michael Elliott, "A Tale Of Three Cities," *Time*, January 17, 2008, http://www.time.com/ time/magazine/article/0,9171,1704398,00.html; http://is.gd/21wyN; http://www.london.gov.uk/mayor/economic_unit/docs/CapImpact_damian_walne.pdf; http://www.lboro.ac.uk/gawc/rb/rb328.html; Peter Hall, "Londra, metropolis riluttante", *Urbanistica*, May-August 2003, pp. 21-31; *Foreign Direct Investment: Bringing the Benefits of Globalization Back Home* (New York: Partnership for New York City, June 2008), available at http://www.nycp.org/publications/2008_0627_FDI.pdf; R.G. Smith, "Networking the City," http://www.lboro.ac.uk/gawc/rb/rb169.html; "Foul-weather friends: How London risks losing its global appeal," *The Economist*, Dec 17, 2009, http://www.economist.com/businessfinance/displaystory.cfm?story_id=15124793; Vincent Cheng, "NY-LON-KONG — Hong Kong as Asia's Financial Centre," May 27, 2008, *http://www.hsbc.com.hk/1/2/about/speeches/08may27e;* http://www.areadevelopment.com/article_pdf/id18985_NewInvestmentParadigm2009final.pdf.

cities outside the transatlantic space, such as Shanghai, Beijing, Moscow, Seoul, and Tel Aviv, are quickening the pace of integration.

U.S. Metropolitan Regions: Exports to Europe

Although in overall terms the U.S. now trades more with Asia, Europe retains critical importance as an export market for a vast number of American cities and metropolitan regions. The city of Philadelphia, for instance, exports more to the UK alone than to all of Asia. The UK is also the most important export market in the world for the Washington, DC metropolitan region. And the second-largest global export market for goods from the New York metropolitan area? Switzerland.

These strong export ties are echoed in communities across the nation. A considerable number of U.S. metropolitan areas export more to the EU than to other world regions such as Asia or Latin America or to economic blocs such as APEC, NAFTA, ASEAN or OPEC.

Metro Areas for which EU was No. 1 Export Destination Region in 2007

1 Aguadilla-Isabela-San Sebastian, PR
2 Bloomington, IN
3 Fort Walton Beach-Crestview-Destin, FL
4 Gainesville, FL
5 Greenville, NC
6 Greenville, SC
7 Hartford-West Hartford-East Hartford, CT
8 Hattiesburg, MS
9 Lawton, OK
10 Little Rock-North Little Rock, AR
11 Norwich-New London, CT
12 Richmond, VA
13 Salt Lake City, UT
14 San Juan-Caguas-Guaynabo, PR
15 Savannah, GA
16 Worcester, MA

Metro Areas for which EU was No. 1 Export Destination Region in First Half of 2008

1 Bloomington, IN
2 Dayton, OH
3 Fort Walton Beach-Crestview-Destin, FL
4 Gainesville, FL
5 Greenville, SC
6 Hartford-West Hartford-East Hartford, CT
7 Madera, CA
8 Naples-Marco Island, FL
9 Norwich-New London, CT
10 Port St. Lucie-Fort Pierce, FL
11 Providence-New Bedford-Fall River, RI-MA
12 Salt Lake City, UT
13 San German-Cabo Rojo, PR
14 San Juan-Caguas-Guaynabo, PR
15 Savannah, GA
16 Worcester, MA

Cities ranging from Bloomington, Indiana and Savannah, Georgia to Lawton, Oklahoma, Little Rock, Arkansas or Richmond, Virginia export more to the EU than to any other world region or economic entity.

A number of U.S. metropolitan areas send more than half their total exports to Europe. The strong export link of some cities is due in large part to a dominant local company, such as Georgia-Pacific in Hattiesburg, Mississippi or Rio Tinto/Kennecott Utah Copper in Salt Lake City, Utah. Others owe their high European export concentration to strong European investment in their own communities. European companies that invest in U.S. cities and towns tend to export their products back to Europe, creating both investment- and trade-generated local jobs. Still other metro areas have a diversified economy that generate products in high demand in Europe. Whatever the reason, many local American communities have developed a strong stake in a healthy and growing European economy.

Top Metro Exporters to the European Union by Percent of Total, 2007

	Region	% of Total Exports
1	San Juan-Caguas-Guaynabo, PR	63.712%
2	Salt Lake City, UT	58.207%
3	Bloomington, IN	57.777%
4	Worcester, MA	57.628%
5	Norwich-New London, CT	53.664%
6	Hattiesburg, MS	51.158%
7	Aguadilla-Isabela-San Sebastian, PR	50.888%
8	Hartford-West Hartford-East Hartford, CT	49.281%
9	Greenville, SC	49.260%
10	Savannah, GA	46.773%
11	Little Rock-North Little Rock, AR	45.761%
12	Madera, CA	44.594%
13	Naples-Marco Island, FL	43.686%
14	Gainesville, FL	43.364%
15	Richmond, VA	43.277%
16	Prescott, AZ	42.150%
17	Providence-New Bedford-Fall River, RI-MA	42.029%
18	Muskegon-Norton Shores, MI	41.645%
19	Modesto, CA	41.535%
20	Columbia, SC	41.121%

Top Metro Exporters to the European Union by Percent of Total, First Half of 2008

	Region	% of Total Exports
1	Salt Lake City, UT	69.698%
2	San Juan-Caguas-Guaynabo, PR	66.779%
3	Norwich-New London, CT	59.500%
4	Providence-New Bedford-Fall River, RI-MA	58.148%
5	Worcester, MA	57.670%
6	Greenville, SC	57.296%
7	Bloomington, IN	53.869%
8	Hartford-West Hartford-East Hartford, CT	50.487%
9	Prescott, AZ	47.434%
10	Madera, CA	45.939%
11	Naples-Marco Island, FL	45.595%
12	Gainesville, FL	44.932%
13	Muskegon-Norton Shores, MI	44.214%
14	Aguadilla-Isabela-San Sebastian, PR	44.211%
15	Ames, IA	42.459%
16	Dayton, OH	41.620%
17	Hattiesburg, MS	41.524%
18	Fort Walton Beach-Crestview-Destin, FL	41.019%
19	Iowa City, IA	40.992%
20	Savannah, GA	39.914%

Top Metro Exporters to the European Union by Value, 2007

Rank	Region	Export Value, US$
1	New York-Northern New Jersey-Long Island, NY-NJ-PA	22,251,393,772
2	Seattle-Tacoma-Bellevue, WA	11,337,618,140
3	Houston-Sugar Land-Baytown, TX	9,717,179,602
4	Los Angeles-Long Beach-Santa Ana, CA	9,401,401,238
5	San Juan-Caguas-Guaynabo, PR	9,328,709,989
6	Boston-Cambridge-Quincy, MA-NH	7,804,982,996
7	Philadelphia-Camden-Wilmington, PA-NJ-DE-MD	6,422,965,324
8	Chicago-Naperville-Joliet, IL-IN-WI	6,065,427,079
9	San Jose-Sunnyvale-Santa Clara, CA	5,441,164,495
10	Cincinnati-Middletown, OH-KY-IN	5,001,192,326
11	Minneapolis-St. Paul-Bloomington, MN-WI	4,804,072,757
12	Detroit-Warren-Livonia, MI	4,601,023,719
13	Greenville, SC	4,490,251,589
14	Dallas-Fort Worth-Arlington, TX	4,025,679,273
15	San Francisco-Oakland-Fremont, CA	3,789,220,633
16	Hartford-West Hartford-East Hartford, CT	3,486,640,333
17	Indianapolis-Carmel, IN	3,267,024,189
18	Salt Lake City, UT	3,238,063,357
19	Phoenix-Mesa-Scottsdale, AZ	3,203,808,740
20	Atlanta-Sandy Springs-Marietta, GA	3,000,754,773

Many U.S. metropolitan regions are significant exporters to Europe, and the top 20 metro region exporters to Europe are evenly divided among East Coast, West Coast, and Midwestern cities. The New York city area leads all metropolitan regions in merchandise exports to Europe, registering over $22 billion in exports to Europe in 2007—twice as much as the West Coast metro area of Seattle, Washington, which ranked as the #2 U.S. metro exporter to Europe with over $11.3 billion in exports. Houston, Texas was third with $9.7 billion, followed by Los Angeles with $9.4 billion, Boston with $7.8 billion, Philadelphia with $6.4 billion, Chicago ($6.1 billion), San Jose-Sunnyvale-Santa Clara, California ($5.4 billion) and Cincinnati, Ohio ($5 billion).

Top Metro Exporters to the European Union by Value, First Half of 2008

Rank	Region	Export Value, US$
1	New York-Northern New Jersey-Long Island, NY-NJ-PA	13,230,221,928
2	Seattle-Tacoma-Bellevue, WA	6,221,139,015
3	San Juan-Caguas-Guaynabo, PR	5,823,349,126
4	Houston-Sugar Land-Baytown, TX	5,760,950,730
5	Los Angeles-Long Beach-Santa Ana, CA	5,406,199,388
6	Boston-Cambridge-Quincy, MA-NH	4,379,838,929
7	Philadelphia-Camden-Wilmington, PA-NJ-DE-MD	4,165,661,444
8	Chicago-Naperville-Joliet, IL-IN-WI	3,341,014,680
9	San Jose-Sunnyvale-Santa Clara, CA	2,904,488,576
10	Salt Lake City, UT	2,788,173,049
11	Greenville, SC	2,732,891,813
12	Cincinnati-Middletown, OH-KY-IN	2,699,036,369
13	Minneapolis-St. Paul-Bloomington, MN-WI	2,508,248,278
14	Detroit-Warren-Livonia, MI	2,078,313,478
15	Dallas-Fort Worth-Arlington, TX	1,982,437,371
16	San Francisco-Oakland-Fremont, CA	1,935,616,485
17	Hartford-West Hartford-East Hartford, CT	1,882,526,542
18	Providence-New Bedford-Fall River, RI-MA	1,819,427,028
19	Atlanta-Sandy Springs-Marietta, GA	1,699,909,367
20	Miami-Fort Lauderdale-Miami Beach, FL	1,663,912,476

Top Metro Exporters to France by Value, First Half of 2008

Rank	Region	Export Value, US$
1	New York-Northern New Jersey-Long Island, NY-NJ-PA	1,427,429,993
2	Seattle-Tacoma-Bellevue, WA	967,527,481
3	Los Angeles-Long Beach-Santa Ana, CA	634,848,595
4	Houston-Sugar Land-Baytown, TX	
5	Boston-Cambridge-Quincy, MA-NH	380,820,054
6	Detroit-Warren-Livonia, MI	298,460,138
7	San Juan-Caguas-Guaynabo, PR	289,010,494
8	Cincinnati-Middletown, OH-KY-IN	(W)
9	Hartford-West Hartford-East Hartford, CT	(W)
10	Indianapolis-Carmel, IN	(W)

Top Metro Exporters to Germany by Value, First Half of 2008

Rank	Region	Export Value, US$
1	New York-Northern New Jersey-Long Island, NY-NJ-PA	2,117,724,472
2	Boston-Cambridge-Quincy, MA-NH	1,035,477,660
3	San Jose-Sunnyvale-Santa Clara, CA	971,114,652
4	Los Angeles-Long Beach-Santa Ana, CA	878,645,720
5	Chicago-Naperville-Joliet, IL-IN-WI	797,071,498
6	Seattle-Tacoma-Bellevue, WA	670,279,978
7	Hartford-West Hartford-East Hartford, CT	591,762,639
8	Greenville-Mauldin-Easley, SC	(W)
9	San Juan-Caguas-Guaynabo, PR	(W)
10	Tuscaloosa, AL	(W)

Top Metro Exporters to United Kingdom by Value, First Half of 2008

Rank	Region	Export Value, US$
1	New York-Northern New Jersey-Long Island, NY-NJ-PA	3,347,696,260
2	Philadelphia-Camden-Wilmington, PA-NJ-DE-MD	2,202,721,173
3	Los Angeles-Long Beach-Santa Ana, CA	1,529,810,308
4	Houston-Sugar Land-Baytown, TX	818,020,846
5	Seattle-Tacoma-Bellevue, WA	816,711,959
6	Boston-Cambridge-Quincy, MA-NH	753,957,540
7	Washington-Arlington-Alexandria, DC-VA-MD-WV	698,256,694
8	Cincinnati-Middletown, OH-KY-IN	666,419,931
9	Providence-New Bedford-Fall River, RI-MA	(W)
10	Salt Lake City, UT	(W)

(W) : Data withheld to avoid disclosing figures for individual companies.

While such exports can be significant, for cities such as Los Angeles trade with Europe is less significant than trade with Asia-Pacific nations, reflecting the basic difference between trade-dominated U.S. commerce across the Pacific and investment-dominated U.S. commerce across the Atlantic. Given that overall transatlantic investment is more significant than transatlantic trade, it is particularly interesting to note which metro regions' exports to Europe are particularly high as a percentage of overall trade. Taking this approach, Salt Lake City Utah ranks number one, with Europe accounting on average for 61.7% of its overall global exports in 2007 and the first half of 2008. Worchester, Massachusetts (57.6%) was next, followed in order by Bloomington, Indiana (56.3%); Norwich-New London, Connecticut (55.6%); Greenville, South Carolina (51.9%); Hartford, Connecticut (49.7%); Hattiesburg, Mississippi (47.9%); Providence, Rhode Island (47.4%); Madera, California (45%); Naples, Florida (44.4%); and Prescott, Arizona (43.9%).

Certain U.S. metropolitan regions also have strong export links to particular European countries. Top metro regions exporting to France in 2008 were, in order, New York, Seattle, Los Angeles, Houston, Boston, Detroit, Cincinnati, Hartford and Indianapolis. Top metro exporters to Germany were New York, Boston, San Jose-Sunnyvale-Santa Clara, Los Angeles, Chicago, Seattle, Hartford, Greenville, South Carolina, and Tuscaloosa, Alabama. Top metro exporters to the United Kingdom were New York, Philadelphia, Los Angeles, Houston, Seattle, Boston, Washington DC, Cincinnati, Providence, and Salt Lake City.

While the New York City region is the top U.S. metro exporter to France, Germany and the UK, and while Seattle, Boston and Los Angeles are also top exporters to all three countries, Houston ranks as the #4 exporter to France but does not rank among the top ten exporters to Germany or the UK. San Jose, California is the #3 exporter to Germany, Chicago ranks #5, and Hartford, Connecticut ranks #7, but none ranks among the top ten exporters to France or the UK. And the Washington, DC metro area is a top exporter to the UK but does not figure among the most important exporters to Germany or France.

In terms of ranking exports as a share of Gross Metropolitan Product (GMP), Decatur, Illinois is in the top spot, followed by Laredo, Texas; Peoria, Illinois; El Centro, California; and Hot Springs, Arkansas. Each of these metros had export values measuring more than 50% of their GMP. Exports are an important growth driver and job creator in many smaller metropolitan areas such as these. Reliable infrastructure is critical to these localities, as are easy linkages to the transportation, information and capital networks that fuel the global economy.[27]

[27] http://www.usmayors.org/pressreleases/uploads/report-200906-metroeconomies.pdf.

Special Focus
Transatlantic Motors: Selected Case Studies

How are microregions of the U.S. connected to Europe, and how are European microregions connected to the United States? How is the economic vitality of a city like Cincinnati sustained by its ties to Europe? How is the competitiveness of a region like Catalonia sustained by its links to the United States? Comprehensive data is unavailable at local levels that could help us answer such questions fully, but in this section we cast light on the still poorly understood flows and interdependencies that exist among city-regions across the Atlantic by illustrating how four European and four U.S. city-regions have become motors of the transatlantic economy.

Lyon and Rhône-Alpes, France

The Rhône-Alpes region in southeastern France, with a population of slightly more than 6 million bordering Switzerland and Italy, has historically been one of France's strongest economic performers and a magnet for capital from the U.S. and other countries. Rhône-Alpes has the 5th largest GDP of any region in Europe, is the second largest economy in France, and in 2007 and 2008 had the second largest number of jobs created by foreign investment in France,[28] trailing only the Paris region of Ile-de-France. As a region, Rhône-Alpes actually produces more wealth annually than some EU countries, including Greece, Ireland, Finland, and Portugal. The major metropolitan areas in Rhône-Alpes are Grenoble and France's second largest city Lyon. They boast numerous institutions of higher education, an outstanding quality of life, proximity to major tourist attractions and favorable real estate prices.

Rhône-Alpes authorities are seeking to complement the core of chemical and pharmaceutical companies in their region with nano- and biotech and alternative energy firms.[29] In 2005 the French government began establishing and funding regional "competitiveness clusters," providing investors with incentives to locate their companies close to appropriate clusters and to tap networks of like-minded businesses, research institutions and laboratories.[30] Rhône-Alpes hosts 10 such clusters, with the most promising and beneficial opportunities for foreign participation coming from Lyon Biopole (advanced vaccines and diagnostics), Axelera (chemicals and environment) and Imaginove (video games and interactive media), all located around Lyon. City officials took further actions to entice foreign investors to the city by granting tax exemptions for innovative start-up companies, engaging in revitalization of former industrial quarters and focusing on developing a livable and walkable large business center. Grenoble is similarly devoting significant resources to the GIANT Project, which aims to transform a large patch of the city into an MIT-like environment, dominated by research institutions and first-class recreation and business facilities.[31]

---

[28] Invest in France Agency, "The Contribution of Foreign Direct Investment to Employment in France," 2008 Report, p.20.

[29] Ross Tieman, "Rhone-Alpes Region: Aim is to be a leader of the knowledge economy," *Financial Times*, December 16, 2009.

[30] http://www.invest-in-france.org/international/en/French-Clusters.html; accessed January 5, 2010.

[31] http://www.leti.fr/en/Join-us/Welcome-to-CEA-Leti/Leti-s-environment; accessed January 5, 2010.

Much of Rhône-Alpes' economic success of has been driven by U.S. companies, which employ the most workers in foreign-capitalized enterprises in Lyon and continue to create a substantial number of new jobs. The United States owns 26.5% of all the foreign-owned companies in the Rhône-Alpes region, making it the largest foreign capital investor in the region. Nearly 400 U.S. companies have chosen the region for their operations. U.S. corporate investment in Rhône-Alpes' software and IT sector, in particular, has been responsible for more than half the jobs generated annually. Prominent U.S.-based companies participate in the Biopole and Imaginove clusters in the Lyon metropolitan area, with several of them opening new facilities or continuing expansion plans even during the recent hardest months of the economic crisis.

In addition, the United States has been the fourth largest export market for Rhône-Alpes in recent years.[32] U.S. exports to the Rhône-Alpes region amount to $2 billion per year and consist primarily of pharmaceuticals, electrical and electronic components, mechanical equipment, chemicals, rubber and plastics, and automotive parts. U.S. imports from the Rhône-Alpes region amount to $3 billion per year and consist primarily of mechanical equipment, fuel and combustibles, chemicals, and electrical and electronic components. Rhône-Alpes has incubators in Atlanta and Philadelphia, and has developed an Economic Development Partnership with Colorado.

The ongoing global crisis has not spared Rhône-Alpes, and significant decreases in activities have been recorded in the wholesale, car and transport and manufacturing sectors. Foreign investment and trade have also dropped noticeably. Moreover, despite the advantages of the world-renowned Lyon Biopole, Imaginove and Axelera, as well as national and regional efforts to promote a competitive "knowledge economy," not enough direct investment projects have occurred in the cluster-related sectors. In fact, most U.S.-generated foreign investment jobs in Rhône-Alpes since 1994 have been concentrated in production and manufacturing, and the largest share of exports to the U.S. has typically been in mechanical equipment and machines.[33] So the region faces challenges, but it is unlikely to be successful without maintaining its critical economic links to the United States.

Barcelona and Catalonia, Spain

Situated in the northeast corner of Spain, Catalonia has a diversified and globally-integrated economy that has evolved from its traditional industrial base to a value-added service economy. The region is driven by its capital Barcelona, named the fourth-best city for business in Europe in 2009,[34] the fifth-leading city in Europe in terms of attracting foreign direct investment,[35] and #1 in terms of cities improving themselves and #1 in terms of

---

[32] Lyon key figures 2008.pdf; Pub-25-7616.pdf; Direction Regionale du Commerce Exterieur Rhône Alpes, "Les échanges extérieurs de la région Rhône-Alpes en 2008," February 20, 2009; François Alland and Jacques Ardoin, "Relation économique entre la région Rhône-Alpes et les Etats-Unis," Direction Regionale du Commerce Exterieur Rhone Alpes, May 15, 2007; http://france.usembassy.gov/root/pdfs/rhonealpesprofile.pdf.

[33] Ross Tieman, "Rhone-Alpes Region: Aim is to be a leader of the knowledge economy," *Financial Times*, December 16, 2009; Invest in France – American Investments in France Map 1994 - 2007; Rae_criseavril09.pdf.

[34] http://www.europeancitiesmonitor.eu/wp-content/uploads/2009/10/ECM_2009_Final.pdf; accessed January 8, 2010.

[35] According to *Cushman & Wakefield's 2008 annual survey*, Barcelona ranked fifth among 33 top European cities in attracting foreign direct investment, following London, Paris, Frankfurt and Brussels. Moreover, in 1990, the first year in which Cushman & Wakefield conducted its annual study, Barcelona was in the eleventh position, while the four first places were occupied by the same four first cities.

quality of life for employees. Catalonia typically attracts over 15% of total productive foreign direct investment in Spain[36] and is home to over 3,000 foreign-controlled enterprises. Catalonia performs well in both mature and emerging industries, and has had success enticing foreign companies with high-skilled labor availability, excellent infrastructure and logistics, and favorable policies and regional tax breaks. Since 2003 new FDI projects have been concentrated mostly in information and communication technologies (ICT) and software, business services and consumer products,[37] marking a definite emphasis on developing a strong knowledge economy. Similar to their colleagues in many leading regions in Europe, Catalan officials have supported the expansion of clusters in emerging industries such as biotechnology and renewable energy sources. As of 2009, 42 such clusters existed, employing more than 235,000 workers.[38] 24% of all Spanish biotech companies are located in Barcelona, and Catalonia leads all Spanish regions in new patents.[39]

The economic links between Catalonia and the United States have been exceptionally strong for many years. Nearly 400 U.S. companies were based in Catalonia in 2008, third behind those from Germany and France.[40] Catalonia hosts over 60% of all U.S.-owned enterprises in Spain, highlighting the economic significance of the region for American business interests and the ability of the local administration to maintain an environment attractive to U.S. investment. FDI from the U.S. of over €200 million in 2008 accounted for 9.7% of the total for the region[41] and over 45% of the total U.S. FDI in Spain.[42] Catalan imports from the United States rose by roughly 52% between 2000 to 2008.[43] During the same period, the region drastically increased its trade turnover with the world, but the United States has maintained a 3% share in both its exports and imports.[44]

The economic crisis has hit Catalonia along with other Spanish regions; 3.5% of Catalonia's GDP has been spent on support for ailing sectors within the limits set by the European Union.[45] The global crisis has severely cut into the region's trade activity and preliminary numbers for 2009 indicate that exports to the United States have fallen below €1 billion, a ten-year low and 30% below 2008 numbers, while U.S. imports have retreated to 2005 levels.[46] While the challenging times have forced significant involvement of public resources to spur job creation and economic activity in the region,[47] they also present an opportunity for

---

[36] Ied2008_angles_corrected.pdf; 2007 and 2008 were exceptions to the trend due to several very large deals concentrated in Madrid.

[37] Foreign Investment in the Barcelona Area and Catalonia, Barcelona City Council and Invest in Catalonia Agency, November 2009, p.27.

[38] Foreign Investment in the Barcelona Area and Catalonia, Barcelona City Council and Invest in Catalonia Agency, November 2009, p.52.

[39] Ibid., p.54.

[40] Foreign Investment in the Barcelona Area and Catalonia, Barcelona City Council and Invest in Catalonia Agency, November 2009, p.25.

[41] Ied2008_angles_corrected.pdf, p.13.

[42] Ibid., p.14.

[43] http://datacomex.comercio.es/principal_comex_es.aspx; query submitted January 10, 2010.

[44] Ibid.

[45] http://www.europesworld.org/NewEnglish/Home_old/Article/tabid/191/ArticleType/ArticleView/ArticleID/21467/Default.aspx; accessed January 8, 2010.

[46] http://datacomex.comercio.es/principal_comex_es.aspx; query submitted January 10, 2010.

[47] http://w3.bcn.es/V01/Serveis/Noticies/V01NoticiesLlistatNoticiesCtl/0,2138,242671375_242692218_3_1093360134,00.html?accio=detall&home=; accessed January 10, 2010.

policymakers to focus on a few internationally competitive emerging sectors and position Catalonia for long-term success. In a recent survey American companies have pointed out that the connections between academic institutions and the business community could be improved, given that some leading education facilities are located in Catalonia (e.g. ESADE, one of the top business schools in the world) and foreign enterprises' need for entrepreneurial, business-savvy and globally-active employees. Furthermore, expanded access to venture capital could be critical in the short-term, as many U.S. enterprises will be increasingly looking into the promising fields of nanotechnology, renewable energy and biotech.[48]

Stuttgart and Baden-Württemberg, Germany

The German *Land* of Baden-Württemberg has a deep economic relationship with the United States. According to the *Deutsche Bundesbank*, in 2007 219 companies with U.S. ownership shares were active in Baden-Württemberg, employing a total of approximately 59,000 people, with a combined annual turnover of €18.5 billion. After the Netherlands and Switzerland, the U.S. is the third largest investor in this part of Germany. In 2007, the total amount of U.S. FDI in Baden-Württemberg amounted to €14.2 billion. The five largest U.S. corporations in Baden-Württemberg in order are IBM Germany (Stuttgart) with 21,500 employees, Hewlett-Packard (Böblingen) with 8,200 employees, Alcatel-Lucent (Stuttgart) with 5,800 employees, John Deere (Mannheim) with 5,600 employees and Agilent (Böblingen) with 1,400 employees. Baden-Württemberg is using its automobile base to increasingly diversify into other high value added manufacturing sectors.

The U.S. is by far the most important market for outward direct investments from Baden-Württemberg. In 2007 869 companies from Baden-Württemberg had shares with U.S. companies and employed 157,000 workers in the United States.

In 2008, the U.S. was the number one trading partner for Baden-Württemberg. Baden-Württemberg imports from the U.S. amounted to €11.46 billion. Products from the U.S. are dominated by chemical products, IT equipment and automotive parts. In 2008, Baden-Württemberg's exports to the U.S. amounted to €13.2 billion, 38% of which came from the automotive sector.

In 2008, over 626,172 U.S. tourists visited the region. This makes Americans the third largest group of foreigners to visit the area after the Swiss and the Dutch. According to the U.S. Embassy, 57,000 U.S. citizens live in Baden-Württemberg. This includes 13,500 U.S. soldiers, 8,000 civilians working for the military and 20,000 family members. Baden-Württemberg is home of two major U.S. commands: USEUCOM and the recently established AFRICOM, both located in Stuttgart. U.S. Army Europe (USAREUR) is located in Heidelberg but is relocating to Wiesbaden in the German state of Hesse. The estimated economic impact of the U.S. military on the local economy in Baden-Württemberg for 2007 was $828.6 million.

R&D partnerships are also critical. Baden-Württemberg shares about 20% of its foreign co-inventions with regions in North America. Examples of research partnership include that between the Research Institute for Motor Vehicles of Stuttgart University and the

---

[48] Foreign Investment in the Barcelona Area and Catalonia, Barcelona City Council and Invest in Catalonia Agency, November 2009, p.72; M. Angels Planas, *Foreign Investment in Catalonia, 2008* (Invest in Catalonia, November 2009).

Center for Automotive Research (CAR) at Ohio State University concerning global challenges to the automotive sector; an International Center for Advanced Communication Technologies (InterACT), sponsored jointly by the Interactive Systems Laboratories of the Technical University of Karlsruhe and Carnegie Mellon University. In 2008, the Fraunhofer Institute for Solar Energy Systems ISE and the Massachusetts Institute of Technology (MIT) agreed to establish a research center for renewable energy in the immediate vicinity of the MIT campus. In addition, Baden-Württemberg maintains exchange agreements with five U.S. states and state university systems (California, Massachusetts, North Carolina, Oregon and Connecticut). The Baden-Württemberg Exchange Programs originated from a legislative partnership formed between the State of Connecticut and Baden-Württemberg in 1989. The agreement invited all students enrolled in four-year colleges and universities in Connecticut to study at any institution of higher learning in Baden-Württemberg. The exchange agreements offer tuition-free places in the U.S. to 760 students from Baden-Württemberg universities. An additional 200 students go to the U.S. tuition-free through bilateral agreements between universities. Of the 3,200 U.S. students in Germany, nearly 800 attend a Baden-Württemberg university. Thirty cities in Baden-Württemberg maintain sister city relationships with U.S. communities.

Stockholm and Göteborg, Sweden

Sweden was the most innovative country in the world in 2009, according to the Innovation Capacity Index, a recent ranking of 131 countries.[49] Foreign-owned companies are attracted to Sweden's innovative climate and employ more than 600,000 people, or about one quarter of all employees in the private sector. Much of the investment is funneled to Swedish high-tech and R&D strongholds in manufacturing, engineering, ICT, life sciences and other sectors.[50] Sweden offer a prominent example of the competitive advantage offered by clusters of firms in single geographic regions; 34% of Sweden's jobs is accounted for by industries that strongly co-locate. The Swedish economy is dominated by four moderately-sized regions that account for close to 75% of the country's labor force. The two top regions, Stockholm and Göteborg, are each strongly tied to the United States.

Roughly every fifth employee in the Göteborg region works in a foreign owned company. U.S. companies employ most of these people, registering close to 30,000 jobs in 2008, an increase of about 5,000 since 2006 and almost triple that of companies from second-ranked UK.[51] U.S. companies are attracted by the region's climate for innovation; the Göteborg region is one of the world's most knowledge competitive regions. The World Knowledge Competitiveness Index 2008 ranks the Göteborg region 16th among the 145 most competitive knowledge regions in the world. It is the European region registering the highest per capita expenditure on research and development by business, and seventh highest in world.[52] It was also declared Europe's top "entrepreneurial city" in 2007.[53]

---

[49] According to the Index, "Sweden is impressive not only in combining open and transparent government, universal social protections, and high levels of competitiveness and productivity and making it one of the most innovative economies in the world but equally so in the extent to which the country's excellent policy framework has turned the private sector into the main engine of innovation." www.innovationfordevelopmentreport.org.

[50] http://www.areadevelopment.com/article_pdf/id18985_NewInvestmentParadigm2009final.pdf.

[51] *Foreign Owned Companies in the Göteberg Region.*

[52] World Knowledge and Competitiveness Index 2008.

[53] In the European Cities Entrepreneurship Ranking 2007 (ECER 2007, www.altidiem.com).

Stockholm is Scandinavia's economic center, with the largest gross regional product (GRP). It is also the metropolitan area with the highest growth in GRP over the last five years. Like Göteborg, Stockholm is one of the world's most innovative regions. It consistently ranks at the top of the European Innovation Scoreboard, which takes account of such factors as innovation drivers, knowledge creation, innovations and entrepreneurship, applications and intellectual property. In relation to its workforce, Stockholm is the fourth most patent-intensive region in the EU. If only high-tech patents are taken into consideration, Stockholm ranks third. Around 34% of all patent applications and 35% of all venture capital investments in Sweden are made in Stockholm County. Most of these are in IT and electronics, but industry, chemicals and biotechnology account for the largest investments. Foreign direct investments in Stockholm doubled between June 2007 and June 2009, despite the global recession.[54]

More than a fifth of Stockholm County's 10,000 export companies export to the United States. Over the last ten years, the number of foreign subsidiaries owned by companies in Stockholm County has almost tripled. Swedish companies based in Stockholm County have 1,120 affiliates in North America. U.S. companies, in turn, are the largest foreign employer in Stockholm County, accounting for close to 35,000 jobs in 2007.[55]

Hartford, Connecticut

Hartford, the capital city of the U.S. state of Connecticut, is among the oldest cities in the United States and is a showcase for the transatlantic economy. It metropolitan population of 1.2 million makes it the largest in Connecticut. It ranks as the #1 region in the world in terms of labor productivity, as the #1 region in the world in terms of per capita R&D expenditure by business and the #8 region in the world in terms of per capita R&D expenditure by government. According to the World Knowledge Competitive Index, Hartford is the 3rd most competitive knowledge region in the world. It also ranks as the 16th top region in the world in terms of patent registrations. It ranks just behind Boston in terms of concentration of institutions of higher learning in New England. Hartford is the 38th leading U.S. metropolitan area in total economic production and generates more economic activity than 12 U.S. states. Its Gross Metropolitan Product in 2008 was $74.857 billion.[56]

Hartford has developed exceptionally strong stakes in vibrant transatlantic commerce and a healthy European economy. Of the $7.075 billion in merchandise goods Hartford exported outside the United States in 2007, $3.487—49.3%, roughly half—went to the European Union. In the first half of 2008 the percentage rose slightly to 50.5%. Hartford exports more to the EU than to the nations of APEC and more than three times than to NAFTA partners Canada and Mexico. Hartford's top global trade partner is Germany.

Transportation equipment accounts for over half of Hartford's exports. The major corporations are Pratt & Whitney and Hamilton Sundstrand, both of which manufacture airplane components and are subsidiaries of the manufacturing conglomerate United Technologies (UTC), the 18th largest U.S. manufacturer in 2009,[57] headquartered in Hartford. Both

---

[54] http://www.stockholmbusinessregion.se/templates/page____41847.aspx?epslanguage=EN.

[55] Statistics Sweden Business Register.

[56] http://www.usmayors.org/pressreleases/uploads/report-200906-metroeconomies.pdf.

[57] *Industry Week.*

Hamilton Sundstrand and Pratt & Whitney are suppliers to both Boeing and Airbus, which accounts for the region's strong trade ties to the EU. Hamilton Sundstrand, headquartered in Windsor Locks, in a complex that employs 4,100, is responsible for supplying 13 major systems/components for the new Airbus A380, which is expected to generate more than $3 billion in revenue for Hamilton Sundstrand.[58] The company also built the power distribution center for Airbus Military's A400M transport aircraft, which made its maiden flight in November 2009 in Seville.[59] Pratt and Whitney, headquartered in East Hartford, one of the top three jet engine companies in the world, supplies the engines for the Airbus A380 as part of a joint venture with GE Aviation. Germany's leading engine manufacturer, MTU Aero Engines, also has an affiliate located near East Hartford. Its design center in Rocky Hill develops components, modules and repair techniques.

Hartford is also a leading center for financial services. Nicknamed the "Insurance Capital of the World" , Hartford houses many of the world's insurance company headquarters, and insurance remains the region's major industry. German and Dutch companies have become critical to the Hartford economy. Following the Lehman collapse at the height of the financial crisis in October 2008, Germany's Allianz SE made a $2.5 billion investment in The Hartford, acquiring 24% of the company. The investment hasn't done so well. The Hartford was saved again with TARP money, but nonetheless, Allianz still holds the stake and the investment came at a crucial time for the firm.[60] HSB Group, including the Hartford Steam Boiler Inspection and Insurance Company, founded in 1866 and formerly a subsidiary of AIG, was bought in April 2009 by Munich Re for $739 million.[61] Dutch banking giant ING Financial Advisors and ING Retirement Plans are also headquartered in the Hartford area (Windsor). At the beginning of 2009, ING employed 1,969 employees in the Hartford area, including 1,800 in Windsor, the most of any ING location in the U.S. ING built a $100 million facility in Windsor in 2006.[62]

Ahlstrom, a Finnish company that is a global leader in the development, manufacture and marketing of high performance fiber-based materials," also has its North American headquarters and a plant in Windsor Locks. North America accounts for 24.6% of the company's world sales.

Cincinnati, Ohio

About 220 European companies are present with investments in the Cincinnati metropolitan area. Top European investors are from the German states of Bavaria, including Munich, Cincinnati's sister city; Baden-Württemberg, particularly Stuttgart; and North Rhine-Westphalia. Cincinnati, like Charlotte, North Carolina, has found it to be in its interest to

---

[58] The company also stands to gain from a successful bid by Northrop Grumman/EADS for the U.S. Air Force refueling tanker, which is currently the subject of a controversial contract fight between EADS and Boeing. should the Air Force award the contract to Boeing, however, the company is also likely to manufacture parts for a Boeing version of the refueling tanker. See http://www.hamiltonsundstrand.com/vgn-ext-templating-hs/v/index.jsp?vgnextoid=e8e77729081581l0VgnVCM100000c45a529fRCRD.

[59] http://www.cnbc.com/id/34430896.

[60] http://www.hartfordinfo.org/issues/documents/economicdevelopment/htfd_courant_100708.asp.

[61] http://www.hartfordinfo.org/issues/documents/downtowndevelopment/htfd_courant_040209.asp.

[62] http://www.hartfordinfo.org/issues/documents/economicdevelopment/htfd_courant_011409_1.asp; http://www.hartfordinfo.org/issues/documents/Region/htfd_courant_110706.asp.

partner with German development agencies and PR companies to promote a region rather than simply a brand or a particular product. Roughly 80% of European FDI in the Cincinnati metropolitan area, which straddles three states, is in Ohio; 15-17% in Kentucky; and 3-5% in Indiana. The UK's BAE Systems employs about 1,600 people at its West Chester, Ohio facilities, which manufacture primarily for the U.S. military, specializing in troop protection materials, including armored all-terrain vehicles, armor kits, and ballistic glass.[63] In April 2008 the German insurance giant Munich Re acquired the Amelia, Ohio-based Midland Company for $1.3 billion, and employs 1,000 local workers at Midland's American Modern Home Insurance Group unit, which generates about 95 percent of Midland's revenues.[64] ZF Steering Systems, the U.S. affiliate of German steering system manufacturer ZF Lenksysteme GmbH, opened a $39.5 million manufacturing plant in Florence, KY in 2006, employing about 365 people, and in November 2009 announced a $96 million expansion that will add 299 jobs over the next three years.[65]

European firms have been attracted to Cincinnati's strong presence in consumer products, symbolized by such companies as Kroger, Macy's, and Procter and Gamble.

Los Angeles County[66]

Angelenos think of their city as a Pacific Powerhouse. In terms of trade, that is certainly true. Nine of the city's top ten partners in two-way trade are Pacific nations. Germany, at #7, is the lone standout among Europeans.[67] But in terms of investments coming into the region and local jobs generated by foreign-owned companies, Los Angeles County has developed considerable stakes in healthy transatlantic commerce.

The five-county Southern California region is by some measures the largest trading region in the United States. But it is largely an import hub, receiving goods and services imported largely from China, Japan and other Asian sources, and ranking only 7th in the country in terms of exports. China remained firmly in first place as the Los Angeles Customs District top trading partner in 2008 with a two-way trade value of $186.6 billion (using "general imports," reflecting the total cargo unloaded).[68] Japan was a distant number two, with a total value of $59.3 billion, followed by South Korea with a 2008 two-way trade value of $22.2 billion.

[63] http://www.baesystems.com/Newsroom/NewsReleases/autoGen_108412155057.html; http://cincinnati.bizjournals.com/cincinnati/stories/2009/09/28/story2.html.

[64] http://cincinnati.bizjournals.com/cincinnati/stories/2007/10/15/daily28.html.

[65] http://www.northernkentuckyusa.com/uploads/ZF%20Steering%20Profile%20&%20Map.pdf; http://cincinnati.bizjournals.com/cincinnati/stories/2009/11/09/story1.html.

[66] This data is based on *Foreign Direct Investment In Los Angeles County*, 2008-2009 Report & Survey (May 2009), and *International Trade Trends & Impacts: The Southern California Region*, 2008 Results and 2009 Outlook (May 2009), two research studies conducted by the Los Angeles County Economic Development Corporation (LAEDC) in cooperation with the Word Trade Center Association of Los Angeles-Long Beach (WTCA LA-LB) and with several Consulates General and Trade Commissions in California: http://www.laedc.org/reports/FDI-2009.pdf.

[67] Five European nations made the top 20 trading partners roster for Los Angeles. Germany set the pace, with a 2008 value of $9.0 billion. The Los Angeles Customs District actually ran a positive trade balance with some European countries, including the Netherlands (+$0.8 billion in 2008), France (+$0.3 billion) and the UK (+$0.04 billion).

[68] Based on "general imports," reflecting the total cargo unloaded.

Although Southern California has a strong export manufacturing sector which services markets around the world, the region has emerged as the single largest transshipment point between the most active global exporting region, East Asia, and the world's number one source of demand, the United States. Export-oriented manufacturing is an essential component of the regional economy, but an equally important contribution to the Los Angeles transshipment/distribution sectors and, therefore, to the region's jobs and general economic welfare, is made by transient exports produced outside the region —elsewhere in the United States and abroad—and en route to destinations outside Southern California.[69] Like most of the rest of the country, Los Angeles was hit hard by the recession, and the turmoil extended to trade. The number of loaded import containers handled at the ports of Los Angeles and Long Beach dropped 9.7% in 2008, the second year of decline.

Los Angeles' most robust transatlantic connections, however, are in investment, not trade. Of the 4,521 foreign-owned and -affiliated business establishments in Los Angeles County in 2008, almost half (48.5%) had a parent company based in Europe. Asian parent companies ranked second, with a 43.1% share. Only 7.4% had a parent company in Canada or Mexico, and a negligible number were owned by companies from Latin America. Measured by establishments, the top five sources of foreign direct investment by country are Japan, the UK, France, Germany and Canada. The "second five" group of countries includes three from Europe—Switzerland, Italy, and the Netherlands, and two from Asia—Taiwan and Australia.

A total of 136,000 direct employees work in foreign-owned and -affiliated establishments in L.A. County. They earn about $7.6 billion annually. In terms of both employment and wages in Los Angeles County, Europe is the largest contributor of foreign direct investment with 63,500 employees and $3.7 billion in wages. Asia-Oceania is the second largest source with 62,000 employees and $3.3 billion in wages in the County.[70]

Indirect FDI employees account for another 223,000 jobs, so that total FDI employees account for 359,000 jobs—9.9% of all private-sector workers in Los Angeles County, or one in ten employees countywide. The average wage for employees of foreign-owned and -affiliated businesses ($56,000) exceeds the County average wage for employees of all businesses ($47,700).

Foreign-owned businesses choose to invest in Los Angeles County for a variety of reasons, including the size of the regional consumer market, international market access (e.g., local airports, ocean ports); the size of regional business base; the weather; and proximity to industry clusters. They are concerned by labor costs, obtaining skilled employees, health care costs, business taxes and housing affordability.

U.K.-owned and -affiliated companies account for 20,300 jobs and $1.2 billion in wages in Los Angeles County. Manufacturing is the largest major industry sector in terms of both employment and wages (5,900 employees and $403 million respectively). Transportation and warehousing (3,200 employees and $164 million in wages) is the second largest followed by wholesale trade (2,600 employees and $133 million in wages), and finance and insurance (1,500 employees and $107 million in wages).

[69] http://www.usc.edu/dept/LAS/SC2/lowenth_1.html.

[70] Measuring employment by country, the top six FDI source countries are: Japan 49,600 workers; United Kingdom 20,300 workers; France 16,700 workers; Germany 9,700 workers; Switzerland 7,000 workers; Canada 7,000 workers.

Employment and Wages of Foreign-owned Establishments in Los Angeles County by Regions of the World, 2007

Region	Employment	Wages ($bill)	% of Total Employment	% of Total Wages
Europe	63,500	$3.717	46.7%	48.7%
Asia - Oceania	62,000	$3.318	45.6%	43.5%
Latin America & Caribbean	8,800	$0.472	6.5%	6.2%
Middle East - Africa	1,000	$0.065	0.7%	0.9%
North America	900	$0.054	0.7%	0.7%
Total	36,000	$7.626	100.0%	100.0%

Sources : Dun & Bradstreet; foreign consulates and trade commissions; Los Angeles Economic Development Commission

French-owned and -affiliated companies in Los Angeles County are responsible for 16,700 jobs and $1 billion in wages. Manufacturing is the largest major industry sector in terms of employment (4,900 employees). Information; arts, entertainment, and recreation; and finance and insurance are the next largest industries with 4,300 and 3,000 employees respectively. Information is the largest major industry sector in terms of wages ($380 million) followed by manufacturing ($347 million), finance and insurance ($89 million), and arts, entertainment, and recreation ($70 million).

German-owned and -affiliated establishments generate 9,700 jobs and $546 million in wages in Los Angeles County. Manufacturing is the top industry in terms of both employment and wages with 4,100 workers and $289 million in wages. Retail trade is next with 2,900 workers and $92 million in wages.

Swiss-owned and -affiliated companies account for 7,000 jobs and $446 million in wages in Los Angeles County. Manufacturing generates the most employment (1,900 jobs) followed by management of companies and enterprises (1,600 jobs) and finance and insurance (1,100 jobs). Management of companies and enterprises accounts for the largest payroll ($137 million) followed by manufacturing ($108 million) and finance and insurance ($100 million).

Italian-owned and affiliated companies account for 2,000 jobs and $72 million in wages in Los Angeles County. Retail trade is the top industry with 1,400 jobs and $43 million in wages. Dutch-owned and -affiliated establishments in Los Angeles County account for 3,100 jobs and $177 million in wages. The sector with the largest number of employees and wages is manufacturing with 1,000 jobs and $59 million in wages.

Madera County, California

The transatlantic economy is not only based on services and manufacturing, nor is it only about investment flows rather than trade. Madera, California is a good example of the importance of transatlantic agricultural trade. Madera County exports agricultural products to 60 different countries around the world. It ranks 13th among California counties in overall agriculture production and 23rd among the 4,000 counties in the United States.

The Madera region is closely linked to Europe: in 2007 and the first half of 2008, almost half (45.3%) of Madera County's global exports went to Europe. This was one-third more than Madera County exported to NAFTA partners Canada and Mexico (29.7%) and almost three times more than Madera County exported to all of Asia (15.7%).

Why does Madera have such exceptional ties to Europe? Three words—almonds, pistachios, wine.

Madera County is the 5th largest almond producing county in California, producing over $212 million worth of almonds in 2008. 63% of almonds produced in California are exported, and almonds are California's top agricultural export to the EU, with $940 million in total exports to the EU in 2007, including $260 million to Spain, $210 million to Germany, and $82 million to Italy. The EU is the largest export market for California almonds, accounting for 50% of exports in 2007. Almonds were Madera County's 3rd largest agricultural product in 2008, behind grapes and milk, with a large percentage going to the EU.

Madera County is the 2nd largest pistachio producing county in California, producing $178,831,000 worth of pistachios in 2008. 45% of pistachios produced in California are exported, and pistachios are California's 3rd highest agricultural export to the EU, with $225 million in total exports to the EU in 2007, including $62 million to the Netherlands, $33 million to Belgium and $24 million to France. The EU is the largest export market for California pistachios, accounting for 62% of exports in 2007. Pistachios were Madera County's 4th largest agricultural product in 2008.

Madera also has an active wine industry, and wine is California's 2nd largest agricultural export. The EU is the largest export market for California wine, accounting for 52% ($424 million) of in total exports to the EU in 2007, with 30% ($247 million) going to the U.K. alone Madera County is the 7th largest wine grape producing county in California. The wine industry also generates spillover effects; the top manufacturing firms in the area are all related to the wine industry. This includes Saint-Gobain Containers, Inc., the French bottle producing firm and leading producer of bottles for the U.S. wine industry. As of March 2009, Saint-Gobain was the area's 2nd largest manufacturing employer, with 370 employees.[71]

[71] http://www.madera-county.com/agcommissioner/cropreports/pdfs/crops2008.pdf; http://www.cdfa.ca.gov/ Statistics/; http://www.maderachamber.com/content/view/42/92/; http://www.maderachamber.com/content/view/105/92/; http://www.sgcontainers.com/index.nsf/vwNV4/89996F84CD8193D18525747F004A874C?OpenDocument.

Notes on Data and Sources

Employment, Investment, and Trade Linkages for the 50 U.S. States and Europe

Data for investment as well as investment related jobs and foreign affiliate sales are from the U.S. Commerce Department's Bureau of Economic Analysis. Investment data measure gross property, plant, and equipment of affiliates. Europe includes France, Germany, Netherlands, Switzerland, and the United Kingdom. Data on European investment flows around the world are from the European Commission's Eurostat database. Europe includes the EU27. Trade data are from the International Trade Administration's Office of Trade and Industry Information at the U.S. Commerce Department and the Foreign Trade Division of the U.S. Census Bureau. Europe includes the EU-27 as well as: Albania, Andorra, Armenia, Azerbaijan, Belarus, Bosnia and Herzegovina, Croatia, Faroe Islands, Georgia, Gibraltar, Iceland, Kazakhstan, Kosovo, Kyrgyzstan, Liechtenstein, Macedonia, Moldova, Monaco, Montenegro, Norway, Russian Federation, San Marino, Serbia, Svalbard and Jan Mayen Island, Switzerland, Tajikistan, Turkey, Turkmenistan, Ukraine, Uzbekistan, and Vatican City. The top ten exports to Europe bar chart employs a logarithmic scale to facilitate cross state comparisons.

Investment and Trade for the EU 27, Norway and Switzerland and the U.S.

Investment and foreign affiliate data are from the Bureau of Economic Analysis. Trade data are from the IMF Trade Statistics. Data for the top ten U.S. imports bar charts are from the Office of Trade and Industry Information of the International Trade Administration. They employ logarithmic scales to facilitate cross-country comparisons.

About the Authors

Daniel S. Hamilton and **Joseph P. Quinlan** have authored and edited a series of award-winning books and articles on the modern transatlantic economy, including *Globalization and Europe: Prospering in the New Whirled Order* (2008); *Germany and Globalization* (2008); *France and Globalization* (2008); *The Transatlantic Economy 2009*; *Sleeping Giant: Awakening the Transatlantic Services Economy* (2007); *Protecting Our Prosperity: Ensuring Both National Security and the Benefits of Foreign Investment in the United States* (2006); *Deep Integration: How Transatlantic Markets are Leading Globalization* (2005); and *Partners in Prosperity: The Changing Geography of the Transatlantic Economy* (2004). Together they received the 2007 Transatlantic Leadership Award from the European-American Chamber of Commerce and the 2006 Transatlantic Business Award from the American Chamber of Commerce to the European Union.

Daniel S. Hamilton is the Richard von Weizsäcker Professor and Director of the Center for Transatlantic Relations at the Paul H. Nitze School of Advanced International Studies, Johns Hopkins University. He also serves as Executive Director of the American Consortium on EU Studies (ACES), designated by the European Commission as the EU Center of Excellence Washington, DC. He has served as Deputy Assistant Secretary for European Affairs and Associate Director of the Policy Planning Staff at the U.S. Department of State. His latest publication is *Shoulder to Shoulder: Forging a Strategic U.S.-EU Partnership* (2010).

Joseph P. Quinlan is a Senior Fellow at the Center for Transatlantic Relations, with extensive experience in the U.S. corporate sector. He is a leading expert on the transatlantic economy and well-known global economist/strategist on Wall Street. He specializes in global capital flows, international trade and multinational strategies. He lectures at New York University, and his publications have appeared in such venues as *Foreign Affairs*, the *Financial Times* and the *Wall Street Journal*.